THE DEATH OF THE GROWN-UP

THE DEATH OF THE GROWN-UP

HOW AMERICA'S

ARRESTED DEVELOPMENT

IS BRINGING DOWN

WESTERN CIVILIZATION

DIANA WEST

ST. MARTIN'S PRESS ✹ NEW YORK

Some portions of this book have previously appeared in *The Washington Times, The Weekly Standard,* and *The New Criterion.*

Library of Congress Cataloging-in-Publication Data

West, Diana, 1961–
    The death of the grown-up : how America's arrested development is bringing down western civilization / Diana West.—1st ed.
        p.   cm.
    Includes bibliographical references.
ISBN-13: 978-0-312-34048-3
ISBN-10: 0-312-34048-6
        1. Youthfulness—Social aspects—United States.   2. Adulthood—United States.
    3. Popular culture—United States.   4. United States—Social conditions—1945–
    5. United States—Moral conditions.   6. United States—Civilization—1945–   I. Title.

HN59.W36   2007
305.240973'09045—dc22

                                                                                    2007014402

First Edition: August 2007

10   9   8   7   6   5   4   3   2   1

TO DAD, WHO SAW IT ALL,

AND TO JIM, WHO SAW ME THROUGH

CONTENTS

ACKNOWLEDGMENTS

None of this would have been written without three people: my dedicated agent, Craig Wiley, and two editors at St. Martin's—Elizabeth Beier, who refused to let go of the idea, and Michael Flamini, whose enthusiasm and support made it possible for the idea to become a book. I would also like to thank Andrew Bostom for his essential expertise.

PREFACE

In the late 1960s—1969, to be precise—my parents decided to take our family of four away from Los Angeles to live in Ireland for a year. This was no "sabbatical" year out; my father was a writer, not an academic. We had no Irish roots drawing us back to the Old Sod. It was a wholly, happily, arbitrary decision. With the advance for a novel my dad ultimately didn't write (I'll get to that below), my parents once again failed to buy an apartment building—my mother's recurring, if insincere, lament on financial stability—so they could move abroad for a while. This would extend the book money, the parental rationale went, because we could live more cheaply than at home in some plainly impoverished, but richly atmospheric Western European country, a few of which still existed in those days. Even then, though, living like an American anywhere in Western Europe was never going to add up to an austerity package. But what fun.

The way I remember it—I was going on eight—my parents were sitting up on their bed one Sunday night, leafing through travel brochures on Portugal, while my brother and I were watching *The Wonderful World of Disney* from a spot on the floor at the foot of the bed. The Disney movie of the week was titled something like *The Secrets of Boyne Castle,* and the sparkling lushness of the movie's Emerald Isle locations, castle and all, was spellbinding. "We should go there," said Jed, turning my parents' attention to the screen.

We did. After renting our house in Laurel Canyon—and our cat, as my own daughters have disbelievingly pointed out—after crossing the country by train in five days (Jed and I barely made it back on board in time after a station stop in Albuquerque), after crossing the Atlantic on an ocean liner in seven days (the SS *Nieu Amsterdam,* an art deco gem), we arrived in Cobh, County Cork, on the southern coast of Ireland. Did I mention my dad didn't like to fly? Anyway, it was a momentous crossing. Between the time we sailed out of lower Manhattan and the time we docked in Ireland, big doings had convulsed his publishing house. His novel was to have been about a Berkeley professor and Spanish Civil War veteran who had had an Orwell-like epiphany regarding the evils of the communist Left, which he saw reconstituted around him in the antiwar campus protest movement. This, apparently, had not pleased the little commissars on the editorial staff—some number of whom had been in or of the campus protest movement—and they threatened to resign en masse if my dad's book stayed on the list. Not the most liberal reaction, at least in the classical sense of the word, but so it went. To make a short story shorter, my dad ended up writing another book that year.

There was another rupture to come as a result of that same passage to Ireland, one I didn't fully comprehend until recently. On returning to the States toward the end of 1970, it became clear that our year away from American culture had been transformative—at least for me. At first, the change seemed superficial. Back in the fourth grade in Hollywood, California, after a few funny looks from other kids, I quickly stopped standing up when the teacher addressed me as I had been expected to do in the third grade in County Wicklow, Ireland; the chirpy Anglo-Irish delivery I had picked up in Eire faded out about as fast. But there was something else about the experience that turned out to be formative in a lasting way. That year in Brittas Bay, a seaside hamlet forty miles south of Dublin, we had a radio tuned to the BBC, but no television, no record player. There were, of course, no such things as CDs, iPods, or the Internet. We rode horses year round—my brother hunted; I was too young—and, in high summer, swam in the very icy Irish Sea. In the evenings, before a genuine coal fire, we read and played gin rummy. We all drew pictures of each other. I learned to write with pen and ink at my two-room schoolhouse. The most significant twentieth century interjection into this nineteenth-century idyll—besides cars and indoor plumbing (and not everyone in our community had that by a long shot)—must have been the small stash of cassette tapes that my dad had brought from home.

He had made these tapes, idiosyncratically enough, by hanging a microphone in front of the television at home to record portions of old movies that aired, sometimes at very odd hours, in those pre-DVD days. The songs of *Seven Brides for Seven Brothers* (1954), for example, by Johnny Mercer and Gene de Paul, formed a big part of our Irish soundtrack, which I now see had the curious effect of sending me off to school on misty mornings partly blowing, partly humming "Bless Your Beautiful Hide" under my breath. Or maybe it would be "The Road to Zanzibar," by Johnny Burke and Jimmy Van Heusen, as crooned by Bing Crosby in, well, *The Road to Zanzibar* (1941), starring Crosby, Dorothy Lamour, and Bob Hope. You get the idea. Another part of the family scene were extended audio clips—non sequiturs to me, who hadn't actually seen the movies—from high-style dramas like *The General Died at Dawn* (1936), starring Gary Cooper, Madeleine Carroll, and Akim Tamiroff, with an exotically thrilling score by Werner Janssen.

There was nothing unusual about such "family entertainment" in a house where old movies commanded special attention, and not just because my dad was a screenwriter as well as a novelist. He had spent his formative years, all of them, under the gilded dome of the Loews Kings movie palace on Flatbush Avenue in Brooklyn, not just seeing *Dinner at Eight* as soon as it came out in 1933, but seeing it eight times. His father, a former vaudevillian, managed the Kings (still standing) through Hollywood's golden age, and there my father received a cinematic and musical education he passed on, in some large measure, to us, his kids. By 1969, this period of the 1930s and 1940s already seemed like a long time ago, although it is interesting to note that *The General Died at Dawn,* for example, was thirty-three years old in 1969, a little younger then than *Easy Rider* (1969) is now.

The point is, it was the year of Woodstock, and I, an American kid, wasn't listening to Joni Mitchell, The Who, Joe Cocker, or even David Cassidy. I wasn't watching *Rowan & Martin's Laugh-In,* or even *Bonanza.* When I left the States, I was a seven-year-old who bobbed and bounced to whatever came out of the little speaker holes in the the pink transistor radio my parents told me to take upstairs; when I came back home again and turned nine, I really didn't want to turn on the radio. I did eventually, but not until long after our Irish idyll had come to an end. Having been temporarily yanked from the mainstream, reentry as a teenager was perhaps inevitable, if only for social survival. But the mainstream was never my natural habitat. And it still isn't.

I mention all this simply to shed a little light on the unusual way I have come to regard popular culture from a distance. We're all creatures of our times, but due to some tricks of fate and family, I ended up something of an odd duck, seeing currents and making connections that aren't as apparent when you're in the swim of things. Because, above all, *The Death of the Grown-Up* is about seeing currents and making connections that are difficult to see and make in the rush of midstream. Once upon a time, in the not too distant past, childhood was a phase, adolescence did not exist, and adulthood was the fulfillment of youth's promise. No more. Why not? A profound civilizational shift has taken place, but, shockingly, it is one that few recognize. The *New Criterion*'s Roger Kimball may have summed up this collective myopia best: "Having changed ourselves, we no longer perceive our transformation." It is this transformation that the following pages illustrate and analyze, in the process suggesting what it is about our past we might better appreciate, not just to enhance our future, but more important, to help us survive. Chucking maturity for eternal youth may have created the culture of perpetual adolescence, but it should now become apparent that this isn't the same thing as achieving cultural longevity. The question is, what if it turns out that forever young is fatal?

THE DEATH OF THE GROWN-UP

1. RISE OF THE TEEN AGE

If a society is to preserve its stability and a degree of continuity, it must know how to keep its adolescents from imposing their tastes, attitudes, values, and fantasies on everyday life.

—ERIC HOFFER, 1973[1]

Once, there was a world without teenagers. Literally. "Teenager," the word itself, doesn't pop into the lexicon much before 1941. This speaks volumes about the last few millennia. In all those many centuries, nobody thought to mention "teenagers" because there was nothing, apparently, to think of mentioning.

In considering what I like to call "the death of the grown-up," it's important to keep a fix on this fact: that for all but this most recent episode of human history, there were children and there were adults. Children in their teen years aspired to adulthood; significantly, they didn't aspire to adolescence. Certainly, adults didn't aspire to remain teenagers.

That doesn't mean youth hasn't always been a source of adult interest: Just think in five hundred years what Shakespeare, Dickens, the Brontës, Mark Twain, Booth Tarkington, Eugene O'Neill, and Leonard Bernstein have done with teen material. But something has changed. Actually, a lot of things have changed. For one thing, turning thirteen, instead of bringing children closer to an adult world, now launches them into a teen universe. For another, due to the permanent hold our culture has placed on the maturation process, that's where they're likely to find most adults.

This generational intersection yields plenty of statistics. More adults, ages eighteen to forty-nine, watch the Cartoon Network than watch CNN.[2] Readers as old as twenty-five are buying "young adult" fiction written expressly for teens.[3] The average video gamester was eighteen in 1990; now he's going on thirty.[4] And no wonder: The National Academy of Sciences has, in 2002, redefined adolescence as the period extending from the onset of puberty, around twelve, to age thirty.[5] The MacArthur Foundation has gone farther still, funding a major research project that argues that the "transition to adulthood" doesn't end until age thirty-four.[6]

This long, drawn-out "transition" jibes perfectly with two British surveys showing that 27 percent of adult children striking out on their own return home to live at least once; and that 46 percent of adult couples regard their parents' houses as their "real" homes.[7] Over in Italy, nearly one in three thirty-somethings never leave that "real" home in the first place.[8] Neither have 25 percent of American men, ages eighteen to thirty.[9] Maybe this helps explain why about one-third of the fifty-six million Americans sitting down to watch *SpongeBob SquarePants* on Nickelodeon each month in 2002 were between the ages of eighteen and forty-nine.[10] (Nickelodeon's core demographic group is between the ages of six and eleven.) These are grown-ups who haven't left childhood. Then again, why should they? As movie producer and former Universal marketing executive Kathy Jones put it, "There isn't any clear demarcation of what's for parents and what's for kids. We like the same music, we dress similarly."[11]

How did this happen? When did this happen? And why? More than a little cultural detective work is required to answer these questions. It's one thing to sift through the decades looking for clues; it's quite another to evaluate them from a distance that is more than merely temporal. We have changed. Our conceptions of life have changed. Just as we may read with a detached noncomprehension how man lived under the divine right of monarchs, for example, it may be that difficult to relate to a time when the adolescent wasn't king.

About a hundred years ago, Booth Tarkington wrote *Seventeen,* probably the first novel about adolescence. Set in small-town America, the plot hinges on seventeen-year-old William Baxter's ability to borrow, on the sly, his father's dinner jacket, which the teenager wants to wear to impress the new girl in town. In other words, it's not a pierced tongue or a tattoo that wins the babe: it's a tuxedo. William dons the ceremonial guise of adulthood to stand out—favorably—from the other boys.

That was then. These days, of course, father and son dress more or less alike, from message-emblazoned T-shirts to chunky athletic shoes, both equally at ease in the baggy rumple of eternal summer camp. In the mature male, these trappings of adolescence have become more than a matter of comfort or style; they reveal a state of mind, a reflection of a personality that hasn't fully developed, and doesn't want to—or worse, doesn't know how.

By now, the ubiquity of the mind-set provides cover, making it unremarkable, indeed, the norm. But there is something jarring in the everyday, ordinary sight of adults, full-grown men and women both, outfitted in crop tops and flip-flops, spandex and fanny packs, T-shirts, hip-huggers, sweatpants, and running shoes. And what's with the captain of industry (Bill Gates), the movie mogul (Steven

Spielberg), the president (Bill Clinton), the financier (Warren Buffet), all being as likely to walk out the door in a baseball cap as the Beave? The leading man (Leonardo DiCaprio) even wears it backward. "Though he will leave the hotel later with a baseball cap turned backwards . . . he is not so much the boy anmore," *The Washington Post* observes of the thirty-year-old actor. No, not so much.[12]

If you've grown up with—or just grown with—the perpetual adolescent, you see nothing amiss in these familiar images. It is the mature look of men from Joe DiMaggio to FDR—the camel hair coats, the double-breasted suits, the fedoras—that seems only slightly less fantastic to the modern eye than lace-collared Elizabethan dandies. The image of man, particularly as it has been made indelible on the movie screen, has changed from when Cary Grant starred in *The Philadelphia Story,* or William Powell starred in anything. In an essay called "The Children Who Won't Grow Up," British sociology professor Frank Furedi sums up the difference.

> John Travolta nearly bust a gut being cute in *Look Who's Talking,* while Robin Williams demonstrated he was adorable as Peter Pan in *Hook.* Tom Hanks is always cute—a child trapped in a man's body in *Big,* and then *Forrest Gump,* the child-man that personifies the new virtues of infantilism.[13]

Such virtues require little effort besides dodging maturity. "I'm not old enough to be a 'mister,' " goes the middle-aged refrain, a reflexive denial of the difference between old and young. This plaintive little protest is no throwaway line. Rather, it's a motto, even a prayer, that attests to our civilization's near-religious devotion to perpetual adolescence.

Such devotion is quickly caricatured in the adulation of the craggy rock star, age sixty-three, still singing "(I Can't Get No) Satisfaction." But the desiccated oldster cavorting like the restless youngster is hardly the end of the phenomenon. In a world where distinctions between child and adult have eroded, giving rise to a universal mode of behavior more infantile than mature, Old Micks are no more prevalent than Baby Britneys—which is as good a name as any for the artless five- or six-year-olds taught to orgasmo-writhe (*à la poppette du jour*), belly bare and buttocks wrapped like sausages. At one time, so sexually charged a display by a child would have appalled the adults around her; now, Baby Britneys—and they are legion—delight their elders, winning from them praise, Halloween candy, even Girl Scout music badges.

What caused the change? Even now, the Baby Boom figures into any explanation of our cultural mentality. But before the first Boomers came of age, a tectonic shift in sensibilities was already taking place that the multitudes of adolescents in the making would later magnify, accelerate, and institutionalize.

To make a snapshot case, consider the respective images of two screen god-desses that took shape on either side of World War II: Jean Harlow, the arche-typal platinum blonde of the 1930s, and Marilyn Monroe, the definitive 1950s sexpot. While both women's lives ended prematurely, Harlow from illness, Mon-roe from suicide, it is Monroe who lives on as the "icon" everlasting, the symbol of an industry to which her contributions are surprisingly limited. The salient point is this: Prewar Harlow, who began her career at age nineteen (and died at age twenty-six), never played anything but womanly roles. Prostitute, stage star, executive secretary, or social climber, she always projected an adult sensibility. Postwar Monroe, on the other hand, made a career out of exuding a breathy, helpless sexuality that, in spite of her mature age (she died at thirty-five), was consistently and relentlessly childlike. There's a reason movie audiences were willing to redirect their screen idolatry from the younger femme fatale (emphasis on "femme") to the older sex kitten (emphasis on "kitten"). That is, the sequen-tial popularity of such actresses reflects more than a simple variation on a theme of blonde loveliness. Rather, it reflects a changing paradigm of womanhood it-self, a shift that signifies, to borrow a phrase from the late Senator Moynihan, the dumbing down of sexuality, a force at the crux of the infantilizing process—and the sexual revolution to come.

It came. Instead of sifting through the rubble of the old social structure—blasted to bits, of course, as new sexual behaviors and attitudes volcanically emerged—let's look at Baby Britney again. Some three decades after the sexual revolution, she rises from the ruins to symbolize the extent to which sexuality, particularly female sexuality, has been snatched from its traditional time and place in human development—as a rite of passage to adulthood, to marriage, to having children—and grafted onto girlhood, even toddlerhood, much to the re-gret of those among us who persist in costuming our wee ones on Halloween as cats, princesses, and cowgirls.

Why the regret? Because not everyone has gone along with the new order. A sizable segment of the population still resists the pressure to transfer the mile-stones of maturity—including, besides sexuality, a large chunk of financial and other freedoms—to the very young. These are people who instinctively acknowl-edge differences between adults and children, and who harbor, maybe secretly, a nostalgic appreciation for the old-fashioned maturation process. Even as age has been eliminated from the aging process, they have a hunch that society has stamped out more than gray hair, smile lines, and cellulite. What has also disap-peared is an appreciation for what goes along with maturity: forbearance and honor, patience and responsibility, perspective and wisdom, sobriety, decorum, and manners—and the wisdom to know what is "appropriate," and when.

This is not to say that gray lives and blue noses offer the only anchors against the hedonistic currents of the times. There is a wide and complex range of experience—emotional, aesthetic, physical, mental, and spiritual—for which only the maturing human being is even eligible. Of this, of course, the immortal bards were well aware; today's artists are numb to it. Etched onto our consciousnesses, in the universal shorthand of Hollywood and Madison Avenue, is the notion that life is either wild or boring; cool or uncool; unzipped or straitlaced; at least secretly licentious or just plain dead. And framing these stark and paltry choices for us is the same kind of black-and-white sermonizing that once preached milk-and-honey visions of heaven and fire-and-brimstone visions of hell. Instead of eternal salvation, of course, we now seek instant fulfillment; instead of damnation, we do anything it takes to avoid the deep, dark rut of middle-class convention. Or so we claim.

That's why, between the Very Beginning and Journey's End, an important aspect of Middle Age has gone missing—the prime of "making a life." The phrase is Lionel Trilling's, the esteemed critic and English professor, who, in the shank of the 1960s, saw that this work of making a life, "once salient in Western culture," as he put it, was effectively over. This act of conceiving of human existence, one's own or another's, as if it were a work of art that could be judged by established criteria, he wrote, "was what virtually all novels used to be about; how you were born, reared, and shaped, and then how you took over and managed for yourself as best you could. And cognate with the idea of making a life, a nicely proportioned one, with a beginning, a middle, and an end, was the idea of making a self, a good self."[14]

We still, of course, have the beginning, but the middle only stretches on in a graceless vector that stops, one day, at an endpoint. Such a life is not, in Trilling's words, nicely proportioned, but it is, as he shrewdly thought, propelled by a new cultural taboo against admitting personal limitation—one of the tribal beliefs that sets Baby Boomers apart from their parents. As Trilling could see, "If you set yourself to shaping a self, a life, you limit yourself to that self and that life." And "limitation," particularly to the perpetual adolescent, is bad.

> You close out other options, other possibilities which might have been yours. Such limitation, once acceptable, now goes against the cultural grain—it is almost as if the fluidity of the contemporary world demands an analogous limitlessness in our personal perspecive. Any doctrine, that of the family, religion, the school, that does not sustain this increasingly felt need for a multiplicity of options and instead offers an ideal of a shaped life, a formed life, has the sign on it of a retrograde and depriving authority, which, it is felt, must be resisted.[15]

Trilling was writing in what his wife Diana Trilling has chronicled as the personally painful aftermath of the 1968 student sacking of Columbia, his beloved alma mater, and where he had taught English for four decades. But if the raging turmoil around him destroyed the "shaped life" he admired, it inaugurated a new way of life defined by its very shapelessness: being without becoming; process without culmination; journey without end; indeed, the state of perpetual adolescence that is a way of life to this day.

Theories abound to explain why this happened, ranging from a high incidence of second marriages, which presumably inspires childish behavior, to a low incidence of deprivation, which presumably inspires childish behavior. "Permissive society" is always a choice culprit; ditto the warm and enveloping cushion of affluence. Anxiety about societal change is another possible rationale. "Nostalgia for childhood" is what Professor Furedi called it when he came across a knot of college students clustered around a television showing *Teletubbies*. His diagnosis? "Profound insecurity about the future."[16]

Of course, that's what they were saying half a century ago. If profound insecurity about the future really were the cause, profound insecurity about the future—sea monsters, starvation, wild savages—would have worried rock-of-ages Pilgrim Fathers into awkward-age Pilgrim Sons. Or the Black Death would have left Europe in a unified fetal position rather than on the brink of the Renaissance. Or, to look into the more recent past, the Great Depression would have driven jobless, hungry Americans into a mass-cultural second childhood. Instead, of course, the early twentieth-century flowering of popular arts in music and theater and film was uninterrupted by such insecurity—insecurity not only about the future, but also about that day's supper—culminating in jazz, swing, the American popular song, the American musical comedy, Hemingway, and the golden age of Hollywood, not to mention an astonishingly widespread appreciation of it all, and definitely not *Teletubbies*. In fact, it was during the period of peace, prosperity, and bright futures that followed World War II that the adult began to ape the adolescent. Something else triggered the evolutionary tailspin.

It's no coincidence that the cultural dive became most vividly noticeable about the same time the popular culture, particularly the new medium of television, settled into its rut of portraying age as "square," and youth as "hip." For something like fifty years, media culture, from Hollywood to journalism to music to Madison Avenue, has increasingly idealized youth even as it has increasingly lampooned adulthood, particularly fatherhood. But the culture culprit, too, is not a satisfactory answer. After all, there's plenty of "old" out there these days, from sixty-five-year-old Paul McCartney to eighty-two-year-old Paul Newman, that the media culture still celebrates as ever "hip" and never "square." Assorted

AARP-members—from seventy-year-old Jack Nicholson to seventy-nine-year-old Maya Angelou—still swim in the cultural mainstream.

Caveats against trusting anyone over thirty aside, senior citizenship doesn't invalidate the casual, anti-Establishment pose of an old Jack Nicholson, or the stick-it-to-The-Man edge of an elderly Maya Angelou. That's because media culture is as anti-authority as it is anti-adult. So long as there is that requisite whiff of subversion, that pro forma slap at the boogey bourgeoisie, even advanced age is irrelevant to cultural currency, which explains a lot about the backward ballcap of the middle-aged midlevel manager and the acid-washed hip-huggers of the car pool queen. These props of youth are also props of "edgy" attitude—a determined bid to embody "hip," not "square," and always "unconventional." A way to smack, at least, of smacking at the bourgeoisie even while maneuvering the Chevy Suburban into the mega-mall parking lot.

The better part of a century ago, George Orwell found himself chafing under similar, artificial constraints. In a review of *The Rock Pool,* a forgettable British novel of the 1930s, Orwell bemoaned this same blinkered philosophy presented by the author, Cyril Connolly. He seems to suggest, Orwell wrote, "there are only two alternatives" in life—degradation (good) or respectability (bad)—an either-or dilemma Orwell found "false and unnecessarily depressing."

Of course, the future author of *1984* didn't know the half of it, writing at a time when the more countercultural behaviors described in *The Rock Pool*—"drinking, cadging and lechering"—were still largely confined to, or at least accepted by, only an elite margin of society. Orwell rapped Connolly's admiration for his antiheroes—the main character ends up prizing his "present degradation" over "respectable life in England"—and interpreted it as a sign of the novelist's "spiritual inadequacy." Orwell went on,

> For it is clear that Mr. Connolly prefers [his antiheroes] to the polite and sheeplike Englishmen; he even compares them, in their ceaseless war against decency, to heroic savages struggling against Western civilization. But this, you see, only amounts to a distaste for normal life and common decency. . . . The fact to which we have got to cling, as to a lifebelt, is that it *is* possible to be a normal decent person and yet to be fully alive.[17]

Alas, the great man sounds a little desperate. Maybe he foresaw, in that characteristically prescient way of his, that society was preparing to amputate notions of "normal" and "decent" from anything connected to being "fully alive." The operation, as it turned out, was a big success. "Decency" has become a euphemism for narrowness and even bigotry, while "normal" is a sarcastically loaded term of opprobrium set off not by a scarlet letter exactly, but certainly by scarlet quotation marks. Being "fully alive" in today's culture has little to do with Orwell's "lifebelt," that life lived according to a traditional assortment of "normal" and "decent" experiences. Rather, it is more directly tied to a tally of one's *ab*normal or *in*decent life experiences—outright vices that include destructive drug use, dicey sexual couplings, or prankishly criminal behavior.

This is an adolescent attitude but it is at least semiuniversal among adults. But something funny happened on its way to the masses. Flouting convention— or simply appearing to—has become as conventional as it gets. When the JC Penney catalog, purveyor to the heartland, can mass-market an erstwhile symbol of social subversion—the black vinyl motorcycle jacket with metal studs and a matching Brando cap—to the family pooch, loyal retainer of home and hearth, it is time to acknowledge how very square "hip" has become. And how very old— literally and figuratively—"youthful rebellion" has become.

Until the second half of the last century, there existed a state of tension, hostility even, between the middle class and the avant garde—a pair of cultural combatants variously and overlappingly known as the bourgeoisie and the art world; the Establishment and the counterculture; the silent majority and the protest generation; squares and cool people; Us and Them. In 1965, Lionel Trilling coined the phrase "adversary culture" to describe the avant garde slice of life, breakaway movement, or class born of modernism, that had detached itself from the habits and thoughts of the larger mainstream culture to judge, condemn, and—as time would tell—ultimately subsume that larger culture.

While the distinction itself wasn't brand new, by 1965 it was suddenly more significant. "There are a great many more people who adopt the adversary program than there formerly were," Trilling noted. And a great many more of those great many people were youngsters. Since the Baby Boom, the seventy-nine million children born between 1946 and 1964, exponentially more children existed; since the expansion of higher education following World War II, exponentially more of those children went to college. In 1945, there were 1.675 million college students taught by 165,000 faculty. By 1970, there were between seven and eight million college students taught by 500,000 faculty. This represented a mass elite—something new under the sun.[18]

Irving Kristol assessed the change in 1968.

So long as the "adversary culture" was restricted to an avant-garde elite, the social and political consequences of this state of affairs were minimal. . . . The prevailing popular culture, however artistically deficient, accepted the moral and social conventions—or deviated from them in conventionally accepted ways. But in the 1960's the avant-garde culture made a successful takeover bid, so to speak, and has now become our popular culture as well. Perhaps this is, once again, simply the cumulative impact of a long process; perhaps—almost surely—it has something to do with the expansion of higher education in our times. In any case, it has unambiguously happened: the most "daring" and self-styled "subversive" or "pornographic" texts of modern literature, once the precious posession of a happy few, are now read as a matter of course—are read in required course—by youngsters in junior colleges all over the country. *The avant-garde has become a popular cultural militia.* [Emphasis added.][19]

One consequence is a steep decline in quality of the antibourgeois arts—a body of work which, in a provocative parenthetical aside, Kristol called "one of the great achievements of bourgeois civilization." The paradoxical fact is, this antibourgeois body of work—from Impressionism to Expressionism, from Strindberg to Shaw to Pirandello, from Debussy to Stravinsky to Ravel, from Yeats to Pound—couldn't have exploded onto the cultural scene without having burst from a bourgeois bottle. And the tighter and more airless that bottle was, the better those arts tended to be. In other words, no (bourgeois) pressure, no (antibourgeois) pop.

Little wonder, then, as the ranks of the avant garde shock troops swelled, the cutting edge became the shapeless middle. Suddenly, everyone was a Bohemian. Such popularity worried leftist intellectual Michael Harrington. "Bohemia could not survive the passing of its polar opposite and precondition, middle-class morality," he wrote in 1972. "Free love and all-night drinking and art for art's sake were consequences of a single stern imperative: thou shalt not be bourgeois. But once the bourgeoisie itself became decadent—once businessmen started hanging non-objective art in the boardroom—Bohemia was deprived of the stifling atmosphere without which it could not breathe."[20]

But it could change, as could the middle class. And while Bohemia as we know it now—an all-encompassing state of middle-class mind—may not be choking on its freedom, its reflexively tiresome shouts of defiance sound more than a little hollow. When U2's Bono promises Grammy night fans to keep "f——ing up the mainstream," as critic Mark Steyn has noted, Bono fails to see—or admit—that he *is* the mainstream, a bonanza to corporate stockholders, and well fit to perform at the official, ribbon-cutting opening of a presidential library in Little Rock.

The fact is, since the death of the grown-up, "f——ing up the mainstream" has become a mainstream occupation. Maybe the best way into an understanding of the phemenon is to revisit a time, maybe the last, when the wall between the mainstream and the counterculture was still in place, if crumbling. That would be back in 1970, on one of the last mornings of December when Elvis Presley arrived in Washington, D.C., to meet Richard Nixon. Or so the thirty-five-year-old rock idol hoped.

In a five-page letter to the president scrawled on American Airlines stationery, Presley introduced himself: "I am Elvis Presley and admire you and have great respect for your office." While Presley's sincerity may have grounded the letter's more atmospheric flights of fancy ("I have done an in-depth study of drug abuse and Communist brain-washing techniques. . . ."), what stands out years later is his instinctive awareness of his own tenuous relationship to both the bourgeois culture and the counterculture, specifically the culture of rock music—still two distinctly separate realms. Two decades later, of course, counterculture idol Bob "The Times They Are a-Changin'" Dylan would entertain at the first inauguration of the forty-second president. (And three decades later, profane rapper Kid "F—— You Blind" Rock, would be invited—then disinvited—to entertain at the second inauguration of the forty-third president.) In 1970, though, during the first term of the thirty-seventh president, the times hadn't quite all the way a-changed.

As Presley put it in his letter to Nixon, "the drug culture, the hippie elements, the SDS, Black Panthers, etc., do *not* consider me as their enemy, or, as they call it, The Establishment. I call it America and I love it." Hoping for some sort of "federal credentials" to add to his collection of law-enforcement badges, Presley offered to help with the nation's drug problem "just so long as it is kept very Private."

There was no need to explain Presley's reticence. To meet with the president, Presley knew he had to jump the then-unbreached wall between the antibourgeois rock culture and the antirock bourgeoisie. "If the rock 'n' roll world had known of this letter's contents," chides Patricia Jobe Pierce in *The Ultimate Elvis*, one of numerous volumes of packaged Presleyana, "it would have felt deeply betrayed."[21] And so "Jon Burroughs" checked into the Hotel Washington to await the president's pleasure, incognito if resplendent, in purple cape and amber shades emblazoned with the initials "EP."

Across the cultural divide, Richard Nixon, too, was content to keep the rock star "drop by" confidential. No flash-popping, full-press Rose Garden photo op for this president, no matter how many American citizens were loyal Elvis fans. The president seemed to know he and Presley made a joltingly odd couple, one that would be unacceptable to both men's still largely separate constituencies. In fact, during the thirty-five-minute Oval Office chat, as recorded in a slim picture book on the meeting by former White House assistant Egil "Bud" Krogh, Nixon repeatedly emphasized the importance of Presley's maintaining his "credibility"—i.e., independence from Establishment links. This, Krogh speculates, underscored Nixon's awareness of the hazards of guilt-by-association for both the king of rock 'n' roll *and* the anointed leader of the Silent Majority.[22]

Such a wall now looks medieval, particularly after the Clinton era, which began, arguably, with candidate Clinton's 1992 appearance on *The Arsenio Hall Show* where he donned Ray·Bans and trotted out his saxophone to honk "Heartbreak Hotel"—Elvis Presley's first number one hit. Not only was candidate Clinton not hiding his attachment to Elvis—indeed, his Secret Service code name would be Elvis—he was trying to broadcast it to as many millions of American voters as possible.

Maybe this is just a particularly sharp illustration of how times have changed. But it is also an illustration of how a people changes. This transformation is so thoroughly complete that we, as a people, no longer see it—or its implications. Thirty-odd years ago, it was clear to Michael Harrington that Bohemia was losing its identity; today, no one notices the mainstream has lost its Bohemia. What was once perceived as a threat by most Americans is now an icon. That certainly goes for Elvis, once known (and it wasn't a compliment) as "the pelvis," but he was just the beginning. A powerful brand more than twenty-five years after his death—he consistently tops *Forbes*'s macabre top-earning dead celebrities list—Elvis was just a simple pioneer overtaken by the legions who followed and, in Harrington's words, made the bourgeoisie decadent, a progression that made the mainstreaming of countercultural behavior possible.

This mainstreaming of countercultural behavior is probably the most significant marker of our own stretch of civilization. To be sure, the ebb and flow of decadence run through the ages, but it is only in our own time that it washes over us all like some giant fountain of youth that is not only hard to resist, but impossible to avoid. At essence, countercultural behavior—so pithily summed up by Bono as "f——ing up the mainstream"—is juvenile behavior: a range of indulgent actions taken to bug Mom, enrage Dad, and satisfy sophomoric appetites for sex, drugs, rock 'n' roll, and their variants, or even just appear to do so.

It is the pretense—faux-f——ing up that mainstream—that marks the perpetual adolescent. He may not be a punk, but he'll talk that way; she may not be a slut, but she'll dress that way. It reveals the choice, to borrow that phrase again, to define one's self down, to identify with the attitudes and behaviors of a countercultural youth movement grown not up, but old. And it has its roots—its real roots—not in the 1960s, or 1970s, but in the more placid decade before, the one, paradoxically, that conservative culture critics often invoke as the last days of American Eden. It was in the 1950s that the adult was pushed aside even before most Baby Boomers were even out of diapers.

The vast numbers of babies arriving during the Boom certainly riveted society's attention on the young, but it's worth noting, in a curious counterpoint, that the median age of the American population in 1960, 29.5, was still older than the median age had been in 1900 (22.9), 1910 (24.1), 1920 (25.3), 1930 (26.5), and

1940 (29.0). This means the new emphasis on youth we associate with the 1950s came along even as the general population had been steadily aging for decades. Indeed, after dipping down to 28.1 in 1970, our median age has been rising ever since, *even as the behavioral age of our society has plummeted.* (Remember the thirty-year-old video gamester.) In 2000, the median age in the United States was 35.3 years old—more than five years older than it was in 1950.[23] By striking contrast, in 1800, shortly after our Founding Fathers' work was done, the median age of newly independent Americans was just sixteen.[24]

Of course, something about the American sixteen-year-old had become radically different by the 1950s—not just from the previous century, but from the previous decade. To begin with, there was much more money in his pocket, and it didn't end up in the family kitty as it had, for example, during the Great Depression. The newly flush teen, born before the Baby Boom, was allowed, then expected, to buy himself a measure of freedom unavailable in the past, staking his place in a new subculture that arose beyond parental design and control, a place where teen taste and desire were king. So, too, not incidentally, was Elvis, and scores of other less enduring pop wonders. But there was even more to it than that.

As early as 1958, Dwight MacDonald took a crack at explaining the American teenager, who was not long on the scene but already the subject of intensive scrutiny. "Probably more books dealing with teenagers have been published in the last fifteen years than in the preceding fifteen centuries," MacDonald observed in *The New Yorker.* Such books, which represented a new genre of guidebooks for parents, included: *Facts of Life and Love for Teen-Agers, Milestones for Modern Teens, Understanding Teenagers, Do You Know Your Daughter?,* and *How to Live with Your Teenager.* He continued: "The list goes on and on, and it includes many titles that would have been puzzling even in fairly recent times, because *their subject matter is not the duty of children toward their parents but precisely the opposite.* [emphasis added]"[25]

It is hard to overstate the significance of this change. To say the tide had turned is to imply a temporary, cyclical shift. What had occurred—a cultural whiplash that twisted around a child's duty to his parent into a parent's duty to his child—has turned out to be permanent. This is not to suggest that parental duty did not exist before; it did, of course. In fact, maybe "duty" isn't precisely the right word to describe the phenomenon MacDonald noted. What changed was a sense of priorities. Long before the Baby Boom crested, adults—parents— were abdicating their rights and privileges by deferring to the convenience and entertainment of the young. Rather suddenly, adults were orbiting around their children, rather than the other way around.

This mid-century switch now seems not only irreversible but somehow eternal,

as though there had never been another way. The newness of this human reconfig-
uration may escape us, but it should become clear that without this parent-child
role reversal, without this human power shift, the structural failures that permitted
the behavioral revolutions of the 1960s to go forward unimpeded simply could not
have occurred.

Was the child-parent switch inevitable? It may seem so, given other changes. A
few years after MacDonald's essay, culture critics Grace and Fred M. Hechinger,
authors of a 1963 book, *Teen-Age Tyranny,* remarked on another significant and
related shift that had taken place within the family. "In the old days of an agrar-
ian economy, children were an economic boon to the family. The more children
there were, the more 'hands' in the field or behind the store counter. Today, the
greater the number of children, the lower must be the standard of living for the
parents."[26] This interesting, if icy, thought, is quite incontestable as any parents
struggling to pay for their children's upbringings well know. But once children—
teenagers, in particular—became an expense even as their role in maintaining
the well-being of the family had disappeared, maybe some new degree of generational friction was unavoidable.

And there was something else to consider: While the postindustrial-age child
doesn't assist his family economically, the postindustrial family doesn't train—
can't train—Junior to assist himself economically in society, either. This condition may be changing with the advent of homeschooling, but in the middle of the
last century, the family role was shrinking. Long ago, youngsters learned trades
or farming from their parents, but twentieth-century industrial society required
kinds of training that institutions, from nursery school to graduate school, were
set up to provide. In 1961, sociologist James S. Coleman took note of the implications.

> The family becomes less and less an economic unit in society, and the husband-
> wife pair sheds its appendages: the grandparents maintain a home of their own, of-
> ten far away, and the children are ensconced more and more in institutions, from
> nursery school to college.
>
> This age-segregation is only one consequence of specialization: another is
> that the child's training period is longer. . . . This setting-apart of our children
> in schools—which take on ever more functions, ever more 'extracurricular
> activities'—and for an ever longer period of training has a singular impact on the
> child of high-school age. He is 'cut-off' from the rest of society, forced inward to-
> ward his own age group, made to carry out his whole social life with others his
> own age. With his fellows, he comes to constitute a small society, one that has most
> of its important interactions *within* itself, and maintains only a few threads of con-
> nection with the outside adult society.[27]

These changes were still new when Coleman's book was published, part of the postwar reorganization of society around youth to the exclusion, or at least the marginalization, of adults. World War II had long receded into the Dark Ages, its epic heroes having vanished into civilian life as quickly as they had emerged. It is no exaggeration to say that their supreme triumph was also, in a very important sense, their final curtain. The so-called Greatest Generation, so dubbed in their dotage, had left the cultural stage as young men.

The impact of this exit was considerable, if not altogether understood. Something was palpably different, but what? Surveying beloved boy heroes in American fiction in 1958, the *New Yorker*'s Dwight MacDonald held up a literary model to illustrate the cultural change. "When Tom Sawyer and Penrod reached thirteen," he wrote, "they did not become teenagers but remained children, who accepted the control of grownups as something they could no more escape than they could the weather (though they could sometimes put up an umbrella)." Even in the case of the independent operator Huck Finn, MacDonald continued, "It was small-town respectability that stifled him, not adult life in general." And like Huck, Willie Baxter, from Booth Tarkington's presciently titled *Seventeen,* aspired to manhood rather than teenhood.

> His footling masquerades, his opalescent daydreams were all directed toward persuading others and himself that he was an authentic, full-grown Man. *The typical pre-teenage-era adolescent, in short, was part of the family, formed by adult values even when he was challenging the grownups who held them—perhaps most so then.* [Emphasis added.][28]

This—to contemporary ears—is a farfetched thought: that teen rebellion could ever take place within an adult context. But such a concept isn't just fiction. As MacDonald also noted, in both *Middletown* and *Middletown in Transition,* Robert S. Lynd and Helen Merrill Lynd's landmark sociological studies of life in a typical American city during the 1920s and 1930s, there was no mention of teenage problems even in the sections devoted to education and child rearing. That was because, he wrote, "the very concept was unknown."[29] Which is itself quite a concept. But then so is the whole notion of adolescence before the Teen Age—a halcyon time, no doubt, in which "hooking up" would be a crochet stitch and Britney Spears would peak as a Mouseketeer.

That was the time of the teen who moped at the moon, seeking solitude—not sex, not homies. In the words of psychiatrist Dr. Robert M. Linder—he who coined the title (and sold it to the movies) "rebel without a cause"—such solitude was the "trademark of adolescence and the source of its deepest despairs and of it dubious ecstacies." By 1954, Dr. Linder was already noticing that young people had "abandoned solitude in favor of pack-running, of predatory assembly, of great collectives that bury, if they do not destroy, individuality. . . . In the crowd, herd or gang, it is a mass mind that operates—without subtley, without compassion, uncivilized."[30]

I doubt the good doctor would have been a big fan of *Friends,* which, after 240 episodes, has ossified notions of the perpetual pack-running adolescence into ever-thus rigidity. Of course, long before *Friends,* the peer group had developed to upset a balance of power that had traditionally been anchored by the family. With the peer group attenuating, if not replacing, parental force in adolescent life, a new dynamic was emerging, one that helps explain why the parent lost his place at home and in the popular culture. By the 1950s, "Coming, Mother"—the famliar tagline from the Henry Aldridge radio serial, hugely popular in the 1930s and 1940s—was just an echo; what MacDonald described as the "dignified, wise, awesome father" of the equally popular Andy Hardy movie series, starring Mickey Rooney and Lewis Stone, was just a ghost. And so, too, was the character of Andy Hardy—the teenage boy who was always "innocent, lighthearted, and, whenever it came to a showdown, firmly under the parental thumb."[31]

Along with that "parental thumb," the dignified father character vanished like a dinosaur right about the time his real-life model by the thousands came home in triumph from Europe and the Pacific, having just won World War II and saved the world from the Nazi death machine. You would think that would have meant salad days for Dad. Not really. It was happy days for Junior.

And why not? It was a kiddie world. Offering a novel theory on the rise of Elvis, rock 'n' roll historian Phillip H. Ennis adds something quite illuminating about the demise of Dad. Presley, Ennis writes, was too young to have seen action in either World War II or Korea. As a result, he gained prominence as a peacetime idol independent of "the adults who guided the nation through the great war." This may have deprived the early rock 'n' roll star of the formative experience of the age—or, rather, what quickly become the previous age—but it also gave him a connection with the younger generation of children, kids whose fathers and older brothers had gone to war. Many of these youngsters, Ennis continues, had experienced the war as a period of uprootedness: "Shepherded by women, they moved through strange cities and new schools, with only their teenage scenes in which to make sense of the world." Elvis, he explains, would become "a lightning rod for all that dislocation and urgent need for identification." In the period of peace and prosperity that followed—the period in which not only Elvis, but all of rock 'n' roll evolved—"it is not too extreme an assertion to say that Elvis delegitimated the adults' command over these kids by making any authority conferred by World War II irrelevant."[32]

He certainly represented something new, something that took nothing from the era that had passed, leaving Benny Goodman, among others, washed up as an innovator and industry leader by age forty. All of which may help explain one of the great unsolved mysteries of the last century: why the World War II generation petered out as a cultural influence, handily overpowered by the lithe likes of pop music's Elvis Presley, fiction's Holden Caulfield, and movieland's James Dean.

Maybe more important than these three anti-adult Musketeers is the fact that the postwar period was a time when authority in general, including good, old-fashioned leadership, had a noxiously bad rap. At enormous cost, we had just vanquished the divine monarchy of Imperial Japan and the Nazi killing machine of the Third Reich—enemies characterized by their robotically vicious authoritarianism. In a sense, domestic trends toward more "democratic" modes of child rearing—including the relaxed discipline popularized by Dr. Spock, and "child-centered" schools that canceled the traditional diktat of parent and teacher—were as much the fruits of our victory as was budding democracy in Japan and Germany.[33]

And then there was the perhaps inevitable progression of modern liberalism itself. Judge Robert H. Bork explains that there are two leading characteristics of modern liberalism. The first is radical egalitarianism, which he defines as "the equality of outcomes rather than of opportunities." The second is radical individualism, which he defines as "the drastic reduction of limits to personal gratification."[34] Both creeds shaped the educational doctrines that first emerged in the 1920s, dominating our schools by the 1950s. The educational doctrine that nonjudgmentally prizes all forms of self-expression equally is perfectly compatible with the judge's definition of radical egalitarianism—a belief in equality of outcomes, rather than equality of opportunities. In other words: If it's all supposed to be wonderful, then it all *must* be wonderful—as if all self-expression is created equal. Meanwhile, the educational doctrine that drives child-centered education quickly becomes an exercise devoted to fulfilling the tastes and desires of the young. From this it is no large leap to Judge Bork's conception of radical individualism, with its emphasis on personal gratification.

As early as 1962, the Hechingers saw the problem with this approach, a genuine "root cause," if ever there was one. "Trouble came when the sound idea of the 'child-centered' school was combined with the permissive doctrine of extreme self-expression," they wrote. Sounds like radical individualism combined with radical egalitarianism.

From it follows the equation of individualism with selfishness. It is one thing to say that the purpose of the school is to teach the child, but quite another to let the child dominate the school and the curriculum. The early progressives insisted that the curriculum make sense to the child, and that the content of education be adjusted to age, maturity, and comprehension of the pupil. The perversion of this sound doctrine came when this was equated with the child's likes and dislikes.[35]

Crew cuts and pressed jeans notwithstanding, the youngsters the Hechingers had in mind were raised to rebel—long before anyone rocked around the clock, said they wanted a revolution, or was born to run. These children may not have meant to rebel, but their parents had left them to the devices of a system that almost completely segregated them from adult influence and guidance, from maturing lessons and the example of restraint, patience, and wisdom.

The impact of junior high school is a case in point. Created for social rather than educational reasons, its founders argued that because early teens have social problems that differ from both grammar school children and high school students, they should be separated—protected—from both. This isolated the youngsters, not only exaggerating but also perpetuating their concerns.

The Hechingers write:

> In many ways, this is typical of the American interpretation of the teen-age problem. Instead of making adolescence a transition period, necessary and potentially even valuable (if often slightly comical), it began to turn it into a separate way of life to be catered to, exaggerated and extended far beyond its biological duration. Eventually it became a way of life imitated by young and not-so-young adults.
>
> This normalized an abnormality. It gave teen-age an air, not of matter-of-fact necessity, but of special privilege and admiration. Instead of giving teen-agers a sense of growing up, it created the impression that the rest of society had a duty to adjust its way and its standards to teen-culture.[36]

Again, this was published in 1963, still several years ahead of the quasi-official "youth movement." The fact is, even before the first clenched fist or painted peace sign, youth had already moved, lock, stock, and barrel, to a place far from Henry Aldrich, Andy Hardy, *and* their parents, somewhere that ran— that was allowed to run—according to rules adults didn't make, couldn't understand, but were increasingly bound by. Early on, anthropologist Margaret Mead picked up on the change—the abdication of the adult. In a book published in 1949, she was quoted as saying: "When mothers cease to say, 'When I was a girl, I was not allowed . . .' and substitute the question, 'What are the other girls doing?' something fundamental has happened to the culture."[37] That fundamental happening was that adults, having been launched into their new orbit around children, were suddenly looking to those same children not only for guidance but also approval. In other words, long before the 1960s crack-up, American culture was no longer being driven by the adult behind the wheel; it was being taken for a ride by the kids in the backseat.

Where to? *Seventeen* magazine, celebrating its seventeenth birthday in 1961, gave its readers a general idea:

> When *Seventeen* was born in 1944, we made one birthday wish: that this magazine would give stature to the teenage years, give teen-agers a sense of identity, of purpose, of belonging. In what kind of world did we make our wish? A world in which teen-agers were the forgotten, the ignored generation. In stores, teen-agers shopped for clothes in adults' or children's departments, settling for fashions too old or too young. . . . They suffered the hundred pains and uncertainties of adolescence in silence. . . . In 1961, as we blow out the candles on our seventeenth birthday cake, the accent everywhere is on youth. The needs, the wants, even the whims of teen-agers are catered to by almost every major industry. But what is more important, teens themselves have found a sense of direction in a very difficult world. . . . Around the entire world, they are exerting powerful moral and political pressures. When a girl celebrates her thirteenth birthday today, she knows who she is. She's a teen-ager—and proud of it.[38]

Oh, brother. Just wait till she heads off to college, a member of the graduating class of 1970. Of course, what marks this editorial—no doubt written by no teenager—is the laughably spoiled brattiness of it all. The idea that 1944, the year of D-day, could be recalled as a time of forgotten, ignored American teenagers who languished in department stores reveals, as nothing else quite does, just how tightly focused and limited adolescent horizons had become—or, better, how tightly focused and limited adults had allowed them to become.

Meanwhile, just for the record, quite a number of teens, circa 1944, including my dad, had a perfectly healthy "sense of belonging," all right—to the United States Army. But there is something else that is equally striking about this absurd little teenybopper manifesto: the staggering truth of it. By 1961, the accent everywhere was indeed on youth. It still is. And it's time to say it's getting old.

2. THE TWIST

I can hear it now: "It was ever thus."

As in: The young have always rebelled against the old; it was ever thus. The old have always resented the rebellion of the young; that was ever thus, too. There's great comfort in such statements. They reassure us that we're part of one big happy continuum, motes in the sweep of generations, hurtling forward on the force of young rebellion . . . and there's absolutely nothing anyone can do about it. Any conceivable action to rein in or modify that rebellion, the theory goes, is as pointless as trying to stop waves on a beach. After all, time and tide wait for no teenager. Another thing about the ever-thus argument: It absolves adults, of generations past and present, of all responsibility for a calamitous situation.

In a review of *Huck's Raft: A History of American Childhood* by Steven Mintz, *Washington Post* book review editor Michael Dirda does a nice job of laying out the ever-thus school of thought when he writes that Mintz's history reveals both "how much childhood has changed over the centuries and how much some things never change."

Dirda notes that Cornelia A. P. Comer, a Harvard professor's wife, complained in *The Atlantic Monthly* that

today's youth were selfish, discourteous, lazy, and self-indulgent. Lacking respect for their elders or for common decency, the young were hedonistic, 'shallow, amusement-seeking creatures,' whose tastes had been 'formed by the colored supplements of the Sunday paper,' and the 'moving-picture shows.' The boys were feeble, flippant, and 'soft' intellectually, spiritually, and physically. Even worse were the girls, who were brash, loud, and promiscuous with young men. This was published in 1911, but it could be—old-fashioned diction aside—Tom Wolfe inveighing against college freshman in 2004. I suppose every generation of adults tends to feel, when regarding the young people around them, that the barbarians are at the gates. But really, there's nothing for us to worry about: One day our children will have children of their own.[1]

On its face, the ever-thus argument is fairly overwhelming. Like Mrs. Prof. above, adults have long thrown up their hands at "young people today"—"today" being any time since about 1400. But the outrage is gone, and certainly the shock. Adults might throw up their hands reflexively at the beserk doings of young people, but the overriding emotion today is an impotent sense of resignation because, after all, that's just the way things are and have always have been. End of circular argument.

Meanwhile, Tom Wolfe, whom Dirda singles out as the ever-thus voice of adult objection, is just a solitary scold whose roar is drowned out by a legion of critical voices.[2] These inveigh not so much against the vacuous promiscuity and drenching vulgarity of the college campus that Wolfe brought to light in *I Am Charlotte Simmons,* but against Wolfe himself for bringing such things to light in the first place; that is, for making such a big deal about about the numbing degradation and pointlessness of dormitory dalliances. Some denounce his reportage as a distortion of the facts; others, as a hackneyed reality, but it is Wolfe's alarmist judgmentalism that is today deemed antisocial, not the retrograde behaviors that inspire it. Besides, most critics add, it was ever thus.

But was it really? The grab bag of offenses held up at arm's length in 1911 by the indignant faculty wife sound familiar nearly a century later, but they also sound unremarkable, having become acceptable through common practice. Certainly no one from elite-seat Harvard is generating rip-roaring screeds about hedonistic youth these days. In fact—and this would really rock Mrs. Comer—in 2004 Harvard College extended official recognition to an undergraduate sex magazine featuring students posing in the nude. In our time, faculty, and no doubt faculty wives as well, quite expect and even encourage such behaviors as a first amendment exercise. They endorse them, condone them, and never, ever decry or—horrors—judge them.

This, in and of itself, indicates a clear-cut change between then (and by "then" I mean some point before the middle of the twentieth century) and now. Where there was once mainly indignation, there is now mainly abdication. What remains more or less unchanged is the younger generation's impulse to break with the past and take charge. But the older generation's reaction—the essential social counterbalance once provided by adult society—has been knocked completely out of whack.

In 1921, the morality of the "younger generation"—whose few surviving members are centenarians today—was the subject of an extensive survey by *The Literary Digest,* a leading periodical of the day. Only ten years had passed since Cornelia Comer's complaint in *The Atlantic Monthly,* but it had been a decade during which the world had shrunk, shaken, and accelerated through a global war and revolution, poison gas and the assembly line, air mail service, women's suffrage, and Prohibition. Bringing the machine gun into nations' arsenals turned international conflict into a new kind of slaughter; removing the corset from women's wardrobes gave sexuality a new kind of public intimacy. Long skirts vaulted to the kneecap, and long hair was bobbed to the chin. Women flouted convention by coloring their lips with lipstick they carried in handbags, and men flouted the law by sweetening their drinks with liquor from hip flasks. Revolution created the Communist Soviet Union in 1918, and inspired the founding of the Communist Party USA in Chicago the following year. A sense of anarchism was in the air. Soon, the casual lawlessness of an illegal cocktail would spread a newly criminal code of behavior that enervated, rather than salved, a war-burned generation.

"The older generation had certainly pretty well ruined the world before passing it on to us," wrote John F. Carter, sounding off in 1920, also in *The Atlantic Monthly.* "They give us this thing, knocked to pieces, leaky, red-hot, threatening to blow up; and then they are surprised that we don't accept it with the same attitude of pretty, decorous enthusiasm with which they received it, way back in the 'eighties."[3] Such were the sentiments Carter shared with some large number of his contemporaries, more than a million of whom had returned home from European killing fields. Pretty, decorous enthusiasm was out, along with a slew of customs and restraints that had once preserved it, or at least tried to do so. Little wonder *The Literary Digest* in 1921 was moved to wonder, "Is the Younger Generation in Peril?"

Its answer was yes. Morality among the young was decidedly in decline, this according to a vote of 107–81 by college and university heads and student newspaper editors. Adding in the votes of religious newspaper editors, the tally becomes a landslide for the existence of moral decline, 202–102.[4] More significant than the findings, though, was what the survey indicated about the extensive breadth of concern in the rest of society. Today, morality as a public good—and by "morality" I mean communal notions of decency in relationships and comportment—is valued mainly by conservative religious groups and institutions directly at odds with what we think of as the Establishment, or mainstream culture. By contrast, in 1921, morality was still a concern of groups and institutions that made up the Establishment, or mainstream culture. Big difference. Maybe this, as much as anything else, helps explain why the social explosions that put the roar in the Roaring Twenties did not also blow traditional society to smithereens. It would take the cultural minefields of the 1960s, laid in the 1950s, a decade of even wider and deeper social and cultural change, to do that.

In other words, it's no surprise that at a time when *The Literary Digest* was tallying its votes on youth and morality, the Catholic archbishop of the Ohio diocese was warning his flock against "bare female shoulders," not to mention the shimmy. But it's a revelation to learn about an Ivy League student editor (at Brown, which would later in the century earn an ultra-flaky left reputation) who entered a protest against "girls who wear too few clothes and require too much 'petting.'" Or about modesty-in-dressing campaigns launched by college women from the University of Nebraska to Smith College.[5] From *New York University News* in downtown Manhattan came the following moralistic manifesto:

> Overlooking the physiological aspects of women's clothing, there is a strong moral aspect to this laxity of dress. When every dancing step discloses the entire contour of the dancer, it is small wonder that moralists are becoming alarmed. The materials, also, from which women's evening dresses are made are generally of transparent cobweb. There is a minimum of clothes, and a maximum of cosmetics, head-decorations, fans, and jewelry. It is, indeed, an alarming situation when our twentieth-century debutante comes out arrayed like a South Sea Island savage.[6]

Young fogies of the world unite.

But it wasn't just young fogies. A *New York Times* fashion writer of the day was moved to report that "the American woman . . . has lifted her skirts far beyond any modest limitation."[7] In Philadephia, the Dress-Reform Committee made up of "prominent citizens," decided to determine what constituted a "moral gown" once and for all. How? The committee consulted 1,160 clergymen of all denominations in and around Philadelphia via questionnaire. In the tradition of dog bites man, "there was far from a unanimous verdict," *The Digest* reported. Hemline furor was such that a "group of Episcopal church-women in New York proposed an organization to discourage fashions involving an 'excess of nudity' and 'improper ways of dancing.'" And not just any "churchwomen"; this highly select group included Mrs. J. Pierpont Morgan, Mrs. Borden Harriman, Mrs. Henry Phipps, Mrs. James Roosevelt, and Mrs. E. H. Harriman—Manhattan matrons with money and power, or, as they used to say, "wealth and social position."[8]

Such as Caroline Kennedy Schlossberg, Aerin Lauder, and Blaine Trump in our day. Imagine Caroline, Aerin, and Blaine banding together to denounce MTV fashions, rap music, and freak dancing. It's utterly inconceivable. Society women still raise money for charity—and hooray for them—but they don't raise standards for anything. It is strictly physical ills alone—cancer, AIDS, battered women, the environment—that drive charitable work in our time. This isn't to suggest there's anything wrong with raising money to cure illness and ease penury. Rather, it's to note a telling difference: unlike in the past, charity work today isn't driven by moral concerns about modesty, sexual exhibitionism, or the value of marriage.

Meanwhile, it doesn't appear that Mesdames Morgan, Harriman, et al., pulled skirts back down to earth on their own. As *Vogue* reported in 1929, it took "Patou of Paris," who was tired of "ridiculously short dresses," along with the general gravitational pull of the stock market crash to do that.[9] But in their attempts, these pillars of society helped support and maintain the essential social tension that preserves and promotes what was once known as decent, or conventional, behavior. Such efforts actually have the bonus effect of making unconventional behavior that much more thrilling. But that's another story.

The point is, whenever a sneaking sense of moral decline clutches at us today with the newest assault on the most current notion of propriety, there's no such bouyant social tension to fall back on; nor is there any agreement on what constitutes propriety, or conventional behavior. We live with a social weightlessness that induces a state of moral freefall or paralysis at any new challenge. Consider the adult reaction to the fad for high school "freak dancing," that rhythmic, boy pelvis to girl buttocks pseudointercourse to "music" that makes the shimmy look like a minuet.

Forty miles from Washington, D.C., is the burgeoning if semirural region of Loudoun County, where things went smash, as they did in so many high schools across the country of late, when freak dancing at the prom, according to *The Washington Post,* left "some chaperones . . . so offended that they refused to take part again."

These days, the reaction is commonplace, and it says more about the chaperones than it does about the "dance." The adults in charge were *not* so offended by the spectacle of their daughters simulating rear-entry sexual intercourse with their sons that they felt compelled to (1) pull the DJ's plug, (2) flip on the house lights, and (3) call the town council into emergency session. They were only so offended that they decided to stay home and pull down the shades next time. By withdrawing in protest, they not only ceded their power, they vacated their rightful place in their children's lives. Just as bad, they did nothing to restore their own dignity, let alone their children's.

Where were Mrs. Morgan, Harriman, Phipps, et al., when you needed them? Suddenly, the school's principal was all but alone. In the run-up to the next dance, he asked his students to sign a pledge against bringing drugs, alchohol, and freak dancing into the campus-sponsored event. Mild enough. He didn't institute a dress code, which would have been appropriate; nor did he prohibit four-letter sex talk on the turntable, which would have made sense. He just asked attendees to observe the nation's controlled-substance laws, and to "face each other."

So what happened? The no-freak pledge, as *The Post* reported, "sparked a student-led protest about freedom and self-expression," with more than three hundred students signing a petition against this supposed abridgment of student rights. And this made some parents proud of their sons and daughters of liberty. "Civil rights are falling by the wayside every second," said Laura George, a mother who actually encouraged her daughter—her daughter!—and her class-mates to stand up for their "civil rights" to in effect simulate sexual intercourse on the gymnasium floor. "I've got to take a stand here for my kids. I've got to teach them that you question authority when authority's gone mad."[10]

Here we have society's guardians: The I-quit chaperone and the Right-to-freak mom; but it's "Authority" that's gone mad. Meanwhile, the Freak Three Hundred are learning not to "question authority," but to defy it as an obstacle to personal gratification—the ultimate goal, as Grace and Fred M. Hechinger wrote forty years ago, of child-centered education. In the lessons of Loudoun Valley High we may see the ABCs of modern liberalism as defined by Robert Bork—radical individualism and radical egalitarianism. The radical individualists of Loudoun Valley High School reject any limits to their desire to freak dance in the name of a radical egalitarian notion that equates sexual exhibitionism with free-dom of speech.

Meanwhile, poor, pathetic Mr. Authority-gone-mad—the principal—became so insecure and defensive about his dance instructions that he took to the school's public address system to reassure the student body that "we're not going to be the Gestapo" when it came to enforcing them.[11] By invoking nothing less barbaric and repugnant than Hitler's storm troopers, the principal reinforced a corrosive caricature of legitimate authority—in this case, grown-ups who wanted to uphold a minimal standard of decent behavior at a school dance. The kids and the parents cry "First Amendment!," the principal denies he's Hitler, and the terms of what passes for modern-day debate are set. Meanwhile, according to *The Post* coverage, no group of parents emerged to oppose freak dancing; no newspapers editorialized against the grossness of it all; not even a church group spoke out. Which begs the question: Where have all the grown-ups gone? It is a strange, and, I would argue, new state of affairs when rebels without a cause face off against reactionaries without a reaction.

Such is the unbearable lightness of being a grown-up today, a condition that belies the ever-thus canard that our social order is no different from the one our parents inherited. It may be natural to cling to this comfy thread of imagined continuity; after all, "it was ever thus" is a whole lot more comforting than "this is something new to the species." But our society, our "establishment," no longer has a solid foundation, and rests on random pillars that sway or even fall for lack of communal support. This is not as much a matter of saying, "It was better when . . ." as a matter of saying "It was different because . . ." And it was different because adults used to be repositories of cultural tradition—such as, the fairly pretty basic taboo on sexual exhibitionism in the high school gym. As pillars of propriety—even sobriety—today's adults are shaky at best, wholly unequipped to hold down their end of the once-mighty generation gap.

"Ever-thus" lore has it that such a gap has always isolated teens, permitting them to live a practically tribal life, virtually undisturbed, according to their own rules and appetites. In fact, it has never been "ever thus"—at least not until after World War II. In the wake of war and depression, an unprecedented swell of affluence swamped the family structure, providing children the means to live a social life in common with their peers. This marooned them, in effect, in a world apart from their parents and other adults. The common compass of the past—the urge to grow up and into long pants; to be old enough to dance at the ball (amazingly enough, to the music adults danced to); to assume one's rights and responsibilities—completely disappeared.

As consumerism became the postwar pastime, and as consumption, particularly consumption of entertainment, became driven by the yearnings of adolescents, the influence of the adult on taste and behavior rapidly diminished. At first, the focus on adolescence seemed to signal the emergence of a new, largely conventional subculture—a club of sorts, with the strictest limits on membership (age), that would eject its expired membership into the adult mainstream. But this did not prove to be the case. How could it? That mainstream had all but dried up.

But first, the fork in the river. In 1944, a little-known grandmother named Helen Valentine effectively launched adolescence with the creation of *Seventeen* magazine. A marketing visionary convinced of the unexploited bounty of the youth market, Valentine persuaded retailers and manufacturers to target teenage girls *for the first time*. The significance of this shift is profound. In 2003, the teenage market was a $70 billion-a-year industry, but half a century ago it didn't even exist. *Seventeen* gave it life. Profits came quickly; the revolution came later. The fact is, Grandma Valentine's *Seventeen* didn't make many waves. It promoted a vision of youthful desire grounded in personal responsibility, as Grace Palladino explained in her book *Teenagers: An American History.* By the 1950s, however, a younger generation of businessmen was ready to ditch the personal responsibility baggage in order to concentrate on the youthful-desire part.[12]

As Palladino pointed out, Eugene Gilbert, one of the more enterprising if unsung young men of the last century, made such desires his business—literally, inventing lucrative marketing strategies that relied on exhaustive and never-before-attempted surveys of teen opinion. In so doing, Gilbert found the key to understanding the adolescent. In a 1959 *Harper's* article entitled "Why Today's Teen-agers Seem So Different," Gilbert identified the adolescent essence: namely, the "role where he is most distinctly himself as a consumer."[13]

Eureka. Fixing the lens of the market on adolescence transformed society's perception of the teen age, magnifying its social importance to match its financial potential. As the teenager was finding his voice through his pocketbook—almost literally, with the advent of rock 'n' roll—the adult was losing his predominance and, even more significant, his confidence. Worth noting is that the first generation to lose its collective nerve this way and cede control of the mainstream to up-and-coming "youth culture" was the so-called Greatest Generation, the one that had just won World War II. There is a certain poignance, and even mystery, to the fact that these victors in an epic world war returned home to lose a domestic culture war that would climax in the 1960s. That is, these many millions of men may have returned from Europe and the Pacific to head traditional households and drive postwar prosperity, but they were also put to pasture culturally in no time. I think of my own dad, just turning forty when the Beatles arrived in 1964, balking at being directed to "nostalgia" bins at Tower Records on Sunset Boulevard in L.A. for any non–rock 'n' roll popular record albums.

But nostalgia—nostalgia of any kind—is not the issue. Generational power shifted, marking maybe not the end of a way of life, but certainly the end of a way of living—the end of growing up. The shift in confidence, obscured by victory in war and prosperity in peace, is key. For as British art historian Kenneth Clarke has noted, it is confidence, above all, from which civilizations rise.[14]

What kind of civilization, then, has arisen with adolescent confidence? The impact of rock music—the most vivid reflection of teen ascendance—can hardly be overstated. More than the simple addition of a new musical form, the development of rock 'n' roll (and varied offshoots) has both reflected and stimulated brand-new behaviors, attitudes, and aspirations.

Consider the following turn of events. In 1965, after a Beatles concert ended in mayhem, Cleveland's mayor banned all rock concerts from public venues, declaring that rock music didn't contribute to the culture of the city and tended to incite riots. By the 1990s, of course, another Cleveland mayor decided that not only did rock 'n' roll contribute to the culture of the city, it *was* the culture of the city; hence Cleveland's campaign to make itself the site of the new rock "museum." The shift was tectonic.

Designed by I. M. Pei, the $92-million complex was built to enshrine the memorabilia of a musical movement that, to put it bluntly, brought free love, getting high on drugs, and a reflexive anti-Americanism to the masses. While such practices are not usually associated with civic boosterism, the civic boosters were there on opening day in 1995, government officials and assorted Babbitts, to honor—and to be honored by—Yoko Ono, Little Richard, Jann Wenner, and other oligarchs of the antibourgeoisie.

Everyone smiled. Everyone clapped. Everyone stood for a Woodstock recording of Jimi Hendrix's amplified assault on "The Star-Spangled Banner" as Marine Corps Harrier jets performed a flyby salute. Middle America cheered, oblivious to the stupendous irony of the moment as the resounding clash of symbols—Amerika-bashers meet America-boosters—failed to arch any eyebrows.

The question is, how did we get from Cleveland, circa 1965, to Cleveland, circa 1995? What happened to that earlier mayor—not to mention the voters who supported him? Many, undoubtedly, simply changed their minds. Those who didn't found themselves in a cultural no-man's-land as the battle line between socially acceptable and socially unacceptable shifted and disappeared. Harvard's Harvey Mansfield has pointed out that the sixties revolution was a revolution in style more than in substance; in taste and manners more than in politics.[15] We see the fruits of that revolution, then, not in new political boundaries, but in new cultural boundaries—and perhaps especially in the lack thereof.

The choice of Paul McCartney to win one for the zipper at Super Bowl 2005 is revealing. What adult, back in, say, 1965, could have imagined, as Beatlemania was approaching its anti-Establishment crescendo, that the day would come—and easily within his lifetime—when the American people would applaud Beatle Paul for providing "decent half-time entertainment," fulfilling a virtual "guarantee he'll be innocuous," while not minding "his role as the Super Bowl's atonement for past excess"?[16] ("Past excess" refers to Janet Jackson's notorious "wardrobe malfunction" of the previous year.) Once, "decent," "innocuous," and "atonement" were not the first words associated with young Paul, John, George, or Ringo. Forty years ago, the Fab Four were still combustibly controversial with barely prevailing middle-class culture. They were still seen as the flying wedge of a rock culture that sundered families and propelled generations along separate tracks. Indeed, the Beatles were rather more likely to be banned from major venues (as they were in Cleveland) than credited with raising the moral tone inside them.

What would help 2005 explain to 1965 the transformation of Paul McCartney from barbarian at the gate to defender of the faith? Even after taking a gander at the 2004 "wardrobe malfunction," 1965 still wouldn't really understand 2005's decision to append the appearance of the Beatle to the appearance of the breast. That is, it's not enough to shine by comparison. But even if the People We Used to Be acknowledged that the People We Have Become regard Paul McCartney as mainstream-wholesome, it remains very hard to explain why this is so according to the ordinary logic of progress. Sure, at age sixty-five, Paul McCartney is older, and Queen Elizabeth has made him a knight. But it's worth noting that the songs Sir Paul played to be innocuous and decent early in the twenty-first century were the songs he played to be groovy and cool in the middle of the twentieth. In the 1960s, the reference to "California grass" in "Get Back" was unsavory at best, and downright dangerous, prefiguring the explosion in drug use that destroyed thousands of lives. In 2005, it's "decent," which suggest only one thing: He didn't change; we did. Which has left us at odds with our past.

This is probably where James Dean should come in. Or, better, "the James Dean legend," the screen persona that typifies adolescent angst—the brooding, surly, feckless animus toward powers that be, parents, society, whatever. Amazingly enough, it is this hormonal moodiness that revolutionized the culture, undermining not only adult authority but also adult confidence in adult authority.

The legend was born the day Dean died in 1955, age twenty-four, in a car wreck. It took place a few days before the October opening of *Rebel Without a Cause,* the movie that would give American juvenile delinquency "social significance." It also gave American psychiatry a poster boy for "troubled youth." (As Dwight MacDonald would put it in 1958, troubled youth "is never to blame; he just has Problems."[17])

Dean's was a separatist legend, the story of generational divide that later became known as the "generation gap." Fifty years later, with the overlapping of adolescent and adult aspirations and interests, that gap has closed—which probably helps explain the surge in parental popularity that shows up in recent polls of young people's opinions—but at the time, the rift was starting to resemble an open wound.

Aspirations and interests aside, it was money that first cracked things apart. After World War II, Dad was less likely to be the sole breadwinner, an economic development that diminished what it meant to be the head of the family. Many stay-at-home moms who had taken jobs in the war industries—leaving kids home alone where they established newly all-important peer groups—kept right on working in peacetime. Indeed, with the rising cost of 1950s living, both parents often found themselves moonlighting, even as more teenagers were entering the job market. But—and this is significant—no longer did these teens feed their wages into the family kitty as young people in earlier days had done; postwar teens pocketed the money. Moving up the economic ladder, postwar teens received hefty allowances. By 1961, *Seventeen* magazine would describe teenagers as "the most powerful, influential, affluential chunk of the population today." Glossy hype aside, this was something new, as *Seventeen* pointed out, writing: "'Twasn't always thus."[18]

A GNP's worth of new products suddenly appeared on the store shelf, items that had never before existed—45 rpm discs, hairspray, portable record players, transitor radios, Princess extension phones—all from manufacturers busy retooling their industries both to stimulate and meet the demands of the "youth market." Such a market was new; the term itself wasn't heard much before 1947.[19]

All this new stuff not only satisfied passing teen tastes, it validated them. It worked like this: If Western Electric manufactured Princess extension phones in "dreamy" colors, then teens should *want* Princess extension phones in "dreamy" colors. It also entrenched such immature tastes. That is, if manufacturers made Princess phones in "dreamy" colors, then, of course, teens should *have* Princess phones in "dreamy" colors. The retail relationship between consumer teens and their consumer dreams effectively derailed the adolescent trajectory toward adulthood, stalling and even blocking the transition to more mature tastes and interests.[20]

It also broke open the family circle, almost literally. Take the portable record player. Something like six million "kiddie players" were sold in 1952 alone, which meant that something like six million kiddies left Dad's hi-fi in the family room behind for the kiddie-player privacy of their own rooms.[21] There, they could play their own forty-five-cent singles beyond parental earshot and objection. Same goes for that dreamy Princess phone. A phone of her own gave "Teena," as *Seventeen* dubbed the prototypical youngster it pitched to advertisers, the privacy and ease with which to conduct a social life of her own. Like the portable record player, the extension phone promoted a kind of generational isolation and freedom that had never before existed when the family phone stood in the front hall or the kitchen, ejecting the young from the parental sphere into a world populated by peers.

Even family-friendly settings became teen-only turf. The drive-in movie theater, originally envisioned as a means by which the whole family could see a picture without hiring a babysitter or disturbing other moviegoers, further segregated the generations as it became dating heaven for unchaperoned youngsters.[22] Books for teens, too, reflected—promoted?—the growing solipsism of youth. "Instead of focusing on an adolescent's future," Grace Palladino observed, books "began concentrating on the teenager's everyday life. By the early 1950s, the social world of dating, popularity, and the never-ending search for a boyfriend had replaced more long-term, adult goals like discovering talents and choosing a career."[23]

Of course, none of this would have been possible without adult aid and acquiescence. After all, who wrote the books and movies? Who designed and sold the phones? And who really footed the bills? *Seventeen* magazine hammered the point home to its advertisers: "Teena has money of her own to spend . . . and what her allowance and pin-money earnings won't buy, her parents can be counted on to supply. For our girl Teena won't take no for an answer. . . ."[24]

Dear, dear Teena. I guess *Seventeen* had gone to her head—or *Dig, Teen, Teen World, 16 Magazine, Modern Teen, Teen Times, Confidential Teen Romances,* or any of the other adolescent mags that sprouted in the 1950s, brimming with advice about grooming, dating, and Mom and Dad. ("God's plenty in the age of specialization," was *Esquire*'s comment on the teen-mag explosion.[25]) More significant than the advice itself, though, was the unprecedented role these magazines had suddenly assumed: "They replaced, *tout court,* the advice that parents themselves were once expected to give their adolescents," explains Marcel Danesi, University of Toronto Professor of Anthropology and Semiotics, in his book *Forever Young.*[26] Little wonder parents were having a hard time making "no" stick; their voices were lost in a roar of competing authorities. Between Dewey and Freud, not to mention Spock, the traditional parameters of child-rearing and education were being redrawn, with command-and-control functions being ceded to institutions, authorities, and theorists outside the home. The 1950s may be remembered as being especially family-oriented, Steven Mintz notes, but "the most important development was the growing influence of "extra-familial institutions" such as schools, media, and the marketplace. These "fostered separate worlds of childhood and youth . . . from which parents, and even older siblings, were excluded."[27]

Not surprisingly, so were their rules, values, and experience. The counsel of *Ingenue* magazine is typical: "In a world changing so swiftly, the best-intentioned mother may actually be handicapped rather than helped by misleading memories of her own adolescence in the dark ages of only a few decades ago when life was simpler."[28] Ah, when life was simpler . . . exactly when was that? The pull of progress is such that every age grapples with new footings, the mastery of which later generations take for granted. I doubt Miss Ingenue really meant Mom's life was simpler; I think she meant Mom's rules were stricter. And what better way to undermine discipline—undermine anything—than by declaring it simplistic, naïve, irrelevant, and out-of-date? Not that these "modern" teens clucking over their poor, backward Mas and Pas were what you would call complex or superior. That is, a generation whose collective taste could be summed up as "all James Dean and werewolf stuff" (this, according to teen marketing guru Eugene Gilbert) wasn't exactly taking that giant evolutionary leap forward.

Whether Gilbert realized it, the two genres—Dean and the werewolves—were much the same. "Werewolf stuff"—the spate of low-budget horror flicks including *I Was a Teenage Werewolf* (1957), *I Was a Teenage Frankenstein* (1957), *Blood of Dracula* (1957)—took the old damsel-in-distress formula and turned it into a teenager-in-torment story. As in Innocent Adolescent suffers at the hands of Evil Adult—a scientist or teacher, or, worse, a science teacher. Or worst of all, a policeman or parent, as in *Invasion of the Saucer Men,* which also came out in

1957—a boffo year for teen B-moviegoers, just as 1939 was for A-list-loving adults. "James Dean stuff," meanwhile, may well have been an A-list proposition, featuring such big names as Elia Kazan, Elizabeth Taylor, Raymond Massey, Montgomery Clift, George Stevens, and, of course, Dean himself, but it exploited the very same theme as the teen horror flicks: sincere youth stymied by hypocritical adults. It was the sensitive against the crass, youth against age, child against parent. The movie ads for *Rebel* posed the question: "What makes him tick . . . like a bomb?" By 1955, the answer was obvious: his extremely creepy parents. It was the perfect teen movie.

Having brought Dean to stardom in *East of Eden,* legendary director Elia Kazan found himself uneasy about his unexpected role in creating the Dean legend. "It was a legend I didn't approve of," the late Kazan revealed in his 1988 memoir.

> Its essence was that all parents were insensitive idiots, who didn't understand or appreciate their kids and weren't able to help them. Parents were the enemy. I didn't like the way [director] Nick Ray showed the parents in "Rebel Without a Cause," but I'd contributed by the way [actor] Ray Massey was shown in my film. In contrast to these parent figures, all youngsters were supposed to be sensitive and full of "soul." This didn't seem true to me. I thought them—Dean, [Dean's character] "Cal," and the kid he played in Nick Ray's film—self-pitying, self-dramatizing, and good-for-nothing.[29]

Well, maybe so. But ever since Dean, self-pity, self-drama, and even good-for-nothingness have all too often passed for sensitivity and soul. And if Kazan's description sounds like the teenager next door, upstairs, or his antihero of the week, it's no wonder the Dean image remains fresh, a cultural touchstone for our time. The rebel without a cause is the Everyman of our age, the pretend maverick against the imaginary machine—the individual against conformity, the free spirit against the bureaucracy. It's rock culture against the Establishment. It's indie rock labels against corporate rock labels. It's the iconoclast against the bureaucracy, antiglobalists against the WTO, shock jocks against the FCC, freak dancers against "the Gestapo." And it's "cool" against "square" every time—the Manichaean split of our time.

Whether American rebels have causes—or just causes for emotion—doesn't even matter anymore. As the last half century tells us, phony American rebels inspire genuine American rebellions. The rebels even admit as much. After leading the sack of Columbia in the spring of 1968—the rampage through the university purportedly over the university's ties to the defense industry and the construction of a gymnasium in Morningside Heights, a poor, black neighborhood—SDS leader Mark Rudd urged Harvard- and Boston-area students to launch their own campus demonstrations, regardless of whether they had "issues."

> Let me tell you. We manufactured the issues. The Institute for Defense Analysis is nothing at Columbia. Just three professors. And the gym issue is bull. It doesn't mean anything to anybody. I had never been to the gym site before the demonstration began. I didn't even know how to get there.[30]

If the rebel without a cause is father to the protestor without an issue, he may also lay claim to every self-anointed maverick whose medium (rebellion) is his message. It is this pose that makes James Dean legendary, not those three movie credits of his. It probably also explains *Rebel* director Nicholas Ray's later fascination with 1960s radicals, which drew him back to the United States after ten years abroad. "For Ray, Abbie Hoffman, Jerry Rubin, and Black Panther Bobby Seale, among others, were the ultimate rebels," *Vanity Fair* informed its readers as the fiftieth anniversary of *Rebel* approached, an occasion the magazine deemed worthy of an article equal parts salacious and significant. Added his daughter Nicca Ray: "It was like putting James Dean on trial."[31]

Heavy. But she has a point. Dean was long dead, but his screen image had lived on to give adolescent rebellion its now-familiar shape and snarl. Which is a kind of genius, I guess. For even as the predominance of motion pictures was ending in the 1950s, screen-Dean was able to embody—and, in death, to embalm—the giant tantrum that was starting to roil the larger culture, a brave, new emotional world where perpetual adolescents would live on in churning opposition not just to adults, but to the idea of adulthood itself.

And, as *Seventeen* might have put it, "'Twasn't ever thus." With the apotheosis of James Dean, almost everything necessary to make the transformation from traditionally adult-oriented society to an adolescent one was in place. And that was long before the Beatles arrived on the American scene in 1964. In fact, the 1960s themselves, while understood as the era of cultural revolution and social change, were in a crucial sense only an epilogue to revolutions and changes that had already taken place in the 1950s. Just as there was "Victorianism before Victoria," as historian Asa Briggs observed, referring to the moral reformation that began in the eighteenth century under the influence of John Wesley but is associated with the British monarch of the nineteenth century, there was 1960-ism before the 1960s.[32] It took place in the 1950s, the decade regarded as rock-stable Republican, cookie-cutter conformist, and stultifyingly bland. The decade may have been all of those things, but it was much more.

A trove of literature survives from the 1950s and early 1960s about the adolescent world that had already taken shape before the authors' eyes. These include both academic studies, such as James S. Coleman's *The Adolescent Society* (1961), and more popular accounts, such as Willard and Marguerite Beecher's *Parents on the Run: The Need for Discipline in Parent-Child and Teacher-Child Relationships* (1955), Peter Wyden's *Suburbia's Coddled Kids* (1960), and, of course, the Hechingers' *Teen-Age Tyranny* (1963), all of which, in examining what was going on in the schools, the suburbs, and the culture, pinpointed the revolutionary changes.

"The homes of yesteryear were adult-centered. Today we have the child-centered home," wrote the Beechers in 1955.[33]

"What worries us is not the greater freedom of youth but rather the abdication of rights and privileges of adults for the convenience of the immature," wrote the Hechingers in 1963.[34]

"The mothers and fathers then explored . . . some of the causes that might be responsible for the obvious lack of brakes on the merry-go-round of their children's lives," wrote Peter Wyden in 1960. "Yes, they decided, the neighbors had something to do with it. Yes, and so did the teachers. And the various success-minded and promotion-conscious organizations that ensnare both youngsters and adults in Suburbia. But finally, Mrs. Roediger looked about somewhat defiantly and announced, 'It's the parents who don't say "no"!' "[35]

Such testimonies might sound like a reason to chalk one up for the ever-thus side of the argument—unless, of course, what the authors above were describing was something new in their own time. As indeed it was. In his landmark study of changing American character, *The Lonely Crowd* (1950), sociologist David Riesman took careful note of what he perceived as evolving child-centric trends.

> Children are more heavily cultivated in their own terms than ever before. But while the educator in earlier eras might use the child's language to put across an adult message, today the child's language may be used to put across the advertiser's and storyteller's idea of what children are like. No longer is it thought to be the child's job to understand the adult world as the adult sees it. . . . Instead, the mass media ask the child to see the world as [the mass media imagines] "the" child . . . sees it.[36]

What Riesman observed represented a colossal switch. Not only did cultivating children "in their own terms" cut the child off from the adult world, it *accustomed* the child to being cut off from the adult world; indeed, it made it unnecessary even to think about the child ever going there. It also drew the adult so deeply into a child's world that it became hard to leave—a condition that describes many grown-ups today. Consider, for example, contemporary attitudes toward play. "Play has historically been about recreation or preparing children to move into adult roles," Bryan Page, the chairman of the anthropology department at the University of Miami, told *The New York Times.* "That whole dynamic has now been reversed. Play has become the primary purpose and value in many adult lives. It now borders on the sacred. From a historical standpoint, that's entirely backward."[37] From a historical standpoint, that's also entirely understandable. Once the child-centric approach became the norm, youth culture was where it was at. Where else could adults go—and who would be there anyway?

The most significant expression of youth culture was, and is, rock 'n' roll. And while the history of rock 'n' roll is folklorically familiar, there are a few facts worth retrieving from myth's memory hole. After all, rock endures not simply as a broad musical category, but as the inspiration of a way of life—or, rather, a way to look at life. It is the worldview of the perpetual adolescent who sees constraint and definition as padlocks on self-fulfillment and self-expression, and not as keys to identity—and certainly not as a means to "making a life," as Lionel Trilling saw them.

Fifty years ago, rock 'n' roll was still just one pop form among many, a novelty that showbiz believed would probably come and go. Or so the Establishment hoped. Pre–rock 'n' roll rhythm and blues had—with such tunes as "Sixty Minute Man" (1951) and "Work with Me Annie" (1954)—introduced an unprecedented crudity into popular music, stripping sexual intercourse down to trite rhymes and a backbeat for the AM audience. This made most adults, even staffers at such music industry publications as *Cash Box* and *Billboard,* a little squeamish, at least at first.[38]

They were also unsure of what to make of the new phenomenon. Once the entertainment trade paper *Variety* had begun reporting on the R&B craze in earnest in the mid-1950s, it reviewed a concert in New York produced by disc jockey cum rock impressario Alan Freed—the "rhythm and blues evangelist," as *Variety* dubbed him—who was then just a few years away from being defrocked in a Manhattan grand jury probe into payola. Whether Freed brought R&B religion to *Variety,* he nevertheless brought in major grosses that, as *Variety* reported, were "bigger than any jazz concert ever staged anywhere in New York." Which inspired a certain amount of reverence right off the bat.

Indeed, it was that high-yield audience that drew as much of *Variety*'s attention as the featured acts, which included, among others, The Clovers, Fats Domino, The Drifters, and Red Prysock. "The kids were jumping like crazy in a pandemonium of honking and stomping that continued without intermission from 8 P.M. to 2 A.M," the trade publication reported. This, *Variety* decided initially, made the concert very much an ever-thus event. The "shattering repetoire of whistles, hoots, and mitt-pounding," it said, was

reminiscent of the days when the kids were lindy-hopping in the aisles of the Para-
mount Theatre on Broadway when Benny Goodman and his orchestra were
swinging there.

Like the swing bands, all the performers introed by Freed were characterized
by an insistent, unmistakable beat. Whether instrumental or vocal, the combos
based their arrangements on a bedrock repetitive rhythm that seemed to hypno-
tize kids into one swaying, screaming mass.[39]

"Reminiscent," maybe, but there were differences. Old pop was melody-driven,
not beat-driven. (Decca Records' old, almost taunting operating slogan,
"Where's the Melody?" as *Variety* noted in a separate 1955 story, had effectively
become "Where's the Beat?") Then there was the makeup of the audience. Rock
'n' roll concerts drew teenagers, mainly girls. Youngsters had been a huge slice of
the big band audience, but adults were there, too, adding up to what Grace Palladino has called "a generational mix that had insured a certain civility on stage."
While there just might have been something else besides the presence of adults
in the audience that kept, say, Benny Goodman from smashing his clarinet to bits
as an encore, their presence explains why, during a 1945 performance with the
Tommy Dorsey band, Frank Sinatra would tell the noisy youngsters in the audience "to keep quiet, there are other folks in the house." If prerock pop music
played for adults and youngsters alike, it played for them all according to adult
rules.[40]

After the war, both the adults and their rules began to disappear. By the middle 1950s, to borrow Sinatra's line, there were not "other folks" in the house—
and, equally significant, it didn't matter. "The bulk of the audience seem [*sic*] to
be girls under sixteen years of age," *Variety* reported in a review typical of the new
rock scene on August 24, 1955. "They shrieked at virtually anything as though
everything that transpires has hidden meanings that they alone understand, and
from the squeals that go on, it's pretty evident in what direction they lie."[41]

Variety was hinting, of course, at sex. And more than hinting at it. While the
write-up of a revue that included Charlie & Ray, Bo Diddley, and Captain Lightfoot still harkened back to old King-of-Swing crowds to do descriptive justice to
ebullient rock audiences, *Variety,* like the other music trade publications *Cash
Box* and *Billboard,* was beginnning to realize that grounds for comparison
stopped there.

There is little doubt that this kind of entertainment isn't the healthiest for
youngsters. . . . Swing . . . never had the moral threat of rock 'n' roll which is founded
on an unabashed pitch for sex. Every note and vocal nuance is aimed in that direction

and, according to the makeup of the present bill, should normal approaches fail to entice box offices in the future, there's the AC-DC set to fall back on.[42]

Institutionally, *Variety* was uneasy about this musical turn of events—this "moral threat." In an extraordinary front-page editorial published on February 23, 1955, entitled "A Warning to the Music Business," *Variety* spelled out the reasons why:

> Music leer-ics are touching new lows and if the fast-buck songsmiths and music-makers are incapable of social responsibility and self-restraint then regulation—policing, if you will—will have to come from more responsible sources.

This opening line—opening salvo, really—represented the considered opinion of the bible of the entertainment business. It was deliberate; it was confident. It did not mince words.

> What are we talking about here? We're talking about "rock and roll," about "hug" and "squeeze," and kindred euphemisms which are attempting a total breakdown of all reticences about sex.

The attempted breakdown itself wasn't new, but rather its newly prominent place in the culture.

> In the past such material was common enough but restricted to special places and out-and-out barrelhouses.

In other words, out of earshot of Teena and Junior, not to mention Mom and Dad.

> Today "leer-ics" are offered as standard popular music for general consumption, including consumption by teenagers. . . . The most casual look at the current crop of "lyrics" must tell even the most naive that dirty postcards have been translated into songs. Compared to some of the language that loosely passes for song "lyrics" today, the "pool-table papa" and "jellyroll" terminology of yesteryear is polite palaver.

And here *Variety* repeats its salient point of outrage:

> Only difference is that this sort of lyric then was off in a corner by itself. It was the music underworld—not the main stream.[43]

This distinction is significant. According to the showbiz chronicle, Old Man Mainstream didn't just keep rollin' along, it was abruptly changing course, flooded by currents from the "music underworld." *Variety* doesn't seem to have been balking at a new entertainment form so much as it was balking at the movement of an *old* entertainment form (crude sex ditties) from a place in the shadows to a place in the sun—from "out-and-out barrelhouses," whatever they were, to the Top 40. It was this pollution of the mainstream, more than the source of the pollution itself, that was of institutional concern. And as such it was something new.

Or was it? Long ago, the ever-thus argument goes, the emergence of jazz as a popular form, which dates back to the 1911 success of Irving Berlin's "Alexander's Ragtime Band," aroused similar antipathies and fears. In 1926, Paul Whiteman, an early jazz celebrity and impresario, published a memoir-slash-rumination called *Jazz* that cataloged some of these concerns. Whiteman is best remembered—when he is remembered at all—for staging the 1924 concert at Aeolian Hall that introduced the public to George Gershwin's "Rhapsody in Blue"; he also presided over a popular symphonic dance band that showcased the tender young likes of Bix Beiderbecke, Bing Crosby, Johnny Mercer, Frankie Trumbauer, Eddie Lang, Joe Venuti, Jack Teagarden, and Hoagy Carmichael. In his book, Whiteman explains he has been keeping a clip file on jazz alarmists for the previous five years. "Whenever I feel blue, I take it out," he said.

It is more enlivening than a vaudeville show. Ministers, club women, teachers and parents have been seeing in jazz a menace to the youth of the nation ever since the word came into general use.

. . . "Jazz music causes drunkenness," one despatch [*sic*] quotes Dr. E. Elliott Rawlings of New York as saying.

. . . The jazz spirit of the times was blamed by Dr. Harry M. Warren, president of the Save-a-Life League, in his 1924 report, for many of the fifteen thousand suicides in the United States.

. . . "The jazz band view of life is wrecking the American home," declared Professor Herman Derry, speaking in Detroit, Michigan.

Dr. Florence H. Richards, medical director of the William Penn High School for Girls, Philadelphia, based her opposition to jazz on a long and careful study of the reactions of 3,800 girls to that kind of music.

"The objection of the physician," she explains, "is the effect that jazz has on certain human emotions. . . . If we permit our boys and girls to be exposed indefinitely to the pernicious influence, the harm that will result may tear to pieces our whole social fabric."[44]

Drunkenness, home-wrecking, suicide, social chaos: The Babbittry attributed some pretty awful stuff to brass riffs, syncopation, and the piano pounders
of Tin Pan Alley—who, just as Whiteman was writing, were poised to usher in
what is even now remembered as the golden age of the American popular song,
the form perfected by Jerome Kern, Irving Berlin, Cole Porter, Rodgers and
Hart, Dietz and Schwartz, Harold Arlen, and others.

When rock 'n' roll emerged a few decades later, a similar cast of profession-
als, politicians, church leaders, and parents would chorus their disapproval. *The
New York Times* interviewed "noted psychiatrist" Dr. Francis J. Braceland, who,
after a brawl at a rock concert in 1956, called the music "cannibalistic and tribal-
istic," and a "communicable disease." Also in 1956, *Time* magazine interviewed
psychologists who saw in rock-generated hysteria "a passing resemblance to
Hitler's mass meetings." Said an Oakland, California, policeman, after watching
Elvis Presley perform: "If he did that in the street, we'd arrest him." But more
outspoken than anyone was Frank Sinatra, who, at the height of Presley's reign as
"the King," said rock 'n' roll is "the most brutal, ugly, degenerate, vicious form of
expression it has been my displeasure to hear."[45, 46]

Rock inspired a more heated invective than jazz, a fearful emotional intensity
that surpassed even the gravely bombastic concerns of the previous pop era.
Could it be that in the intervening decades a more passionate mode of expression had evolved due to that ol' devil loosening effect the Whiteman clip file
warned against? Maybe the cranks weren't really that far off the mark to begin
with. Over the top, sure, and ripe for parody. But it is an observable fact that jazz
and rock 'n' roll both have been keys to emotional release—the loosening of
strictures, an increasing deference to passion and quest for ecstasy—that has liberated an American personality distinctly different from that which came before.
Like all innovations, this is both good and bad. Along with creative vibrancy
comes destructive abandon; with emotional exploration comes self-absorption;
with musical evolution comes musical devolution. Music soothes the savage
beast—some music, anyway—but it also stirs the settled mind, arousing appetites
and passions that past civilizations more often than not hoped to restrain, not
unleash. Or at least direct through social channels—namely, the precision of a
marching band, the decorum of a box seat, the intricacies of choreography—that
prevented the communal musical experience from becoming the hedonistic bac-
chanalia that the modern-day rock concert, à la Woodstock, would come to epit-
omize. An almost atavistic concern for social order lay behind the fears of jazz
and rock in the more straitlaced among us; while derided and dismissed, such
fears were never entirely irrational.

This isn't to suggest that the advent of American pop, circa 1920, and the advent of American pop, circa 1950, were twin events with identical effects. And

not just because of the obvious musical differences in melodic, harmonic, and lyric competence and complexity. What matters more in this case are the striking distinctions between a pop culture oriented toward adults and a rock culture oriented toward youth. This may seem like a tricky argument to make, implying, as it does, that one form of loosening, or devolution, is okay, and one form is not; that Dr. Florence Richards was wrong in 1926 but Dr. Francis J. Braceland was right in 1956. But while the comparison may be subjective, it's still revealing.

With almost a century since the beginnings of jazz, and a good fifty years since the start of rock 'n' roll, the hard, nonsubjective evidence is in, and it comes down to this: People who listen to Jerome Kern (Ethel Merman, Duke Ellington, or The Hi-Lo's) don't want to freak dance; people who listen to Snoop Dogg (Linkin Park, U2, or 50 Cent) don't want to dance like Fred Astaire.

This is no small thing, no mere preference akin to a taste for, say, wheat bread over rye. It's an expression of culture clash separating one way of life from another. One mainstream expresses an ideal that draws on a longing-to-loving spectrum of human emotion related to romantic love; the brutish other wants to mash the male pelvis into the female buttocks—or thinks it's okay, or tries not to think about it. One public sees "a new sun up in a new sky" (Dietz and Schwartz), and the other wants to "do it in the road" (Lennon and McCartney)—or thinks it's okay, or tries not to think about it. This is no way to keep the toxins out of the mainstream that supports society's cultural health.

Here's a nifty culture health check story: One thing my dad found himself thinking about in his last years was a kid he served with in the army during World War II, a guy from New Jersey, eighteen or nineteen years old. One day, kidding around, this young GI started to dance my dad, a guy from Brooklyn, also eighteen or nineteen years old, around the barracks, singing "Cheek to Cheek"—a perfect, if quite complex and unconventional, standard by Irving Berlin that had been introduced eight years earlier by Fred Astaire in *Top Hat*. Now consigned to the rarified strata of "cabaret," this was the music of the enlisted man in 1943.

Again, such a fact is no small matter. It's not for nothing that Plato taught us to "mark the music" to understand an individual or his society. After all, people who hum Berlin or Arlen or Gershwin think they want to fall in love; people who hum (hum?) Mötley Crüe or the Ying Yang Twins think they want to have sex. People who listen to Mel Tormé (Nat Cole, Bing Crosby, or Ella Fitzgerald) don't want to pierce their tongues; people who listen to Eminem (Alanis Morissette, Kurt Cobain, or Public Enemy) don't want to pin on an orchid corsage. If the American popular song could idealize romantic love to a fault, rock 'n' roll degrades physical couplings to new lows—destroying not just the language of love and romance, but also the meaning of love and romance. And, I would sadly add, our capacity to experience both. The fact is, between a world in which romantic love is the ideal and a world where nonmarital sex is the goal lies a vast cultural chasm. And not simply in terms of aesthetics. There are salient differences between a civilization that sings of romantic love and marriage ("Have You Met Miss Jones?"), and a civilization that sings of lust and one-night stands ("[I Can't Get No] Satisfaction"). More than just the year has changed between 1937, when George and Ira Gershwin's "They Can't Take That Away from Me" was a hit,

We may never, never meet again
On the bumpy road to love . . .

and 1987, when George Michael's "I Want Your Sex" was a hit,

Don't you think it's time you had sex with me
Sex with me
Sex with me. . . .

In examining the impact of Judeo-Christian law on sexuality, columnist Dennis Prager inadvertently adds a significant religious and historical dimension to the comparison of pop and rock worlds: What we know as romantic love, which aspires to monogamous marriage, builds civilization up; what we know as free love, which aspires to a polymorphous sex life, keeps it down.

> It is not overstated to say that the Torah's prohibition of nonmarital sex made the creation of Western civilization possible. Societies that did not place boundaries around sexuality were stymied in their development. The subsequent dominance of the Western world can largely be attributed to the sexual revolution initiated by Judaism, and later carried forward by Christianity.
>
> The revolution consisted of forcing the sexual genie back into the marital bottle. *It ensured that sex no longer dominated society,* heightened male-female love and sexuality (and thereby almost alone created the possibility of love and eroticism within marriage), and began the arduous task of elevating the status of women. [Emphasis added.][47]

Sounds as if the emergence of monogamy five thousand years ago, and not the invention of the Pill in the 1960s, was the real sexual revolution. Having deliberately uncorked Prager's "marital bottle," society is once again dominated by sexuality, drenched in sexual imagery, and gagged by innuendo. From James Bond to Carl's Jr., from beer to jeans, from cars to computer servers, sex will sell it. And we will buy it—even, unbelievably, parents among us who purchase "pimp" and "ho" Halloween costumes for their trick-or-treaters. Picking up on the incessant sexual-messaging from the media that has turned our talk into one-track babble, freelance writer Sheryl Van der Leun cataloged the results: *Martha Stewart Living* is "homemaker porn" (CNN People); good fishing places are "bare-naked fishing porn" (*Men's Journal*); a British gadget magazine is "pure technoporn" (*Digital Living Today*); and gourmet recipes may be found at www.foodporn.com.[48] From cineplex sex flicks to checkout stand sex tips, we are now media-bathed in a red-light-district glow of sexual suggestiveness, as though there is no other light to show the way.

Worth marking is the prescience of *Variety*'s ink-stained wretches, who, without benefit of a crystal ball, writing in their showbiz-ese, instinctively recoiled at the mainstreaming of sexed-up pop. At the same time, though, there was little indication in 1955 that rock 'n' roll had staying power, that it would even surpass, say, the decade-long run of the big bands, whose heyday had ended by 1946. There was certainly no indication that it would become, in its varied permutations, an all-enveloping form that would still dominate the popular arts fifty years later. Maybe without quite knowing why, *Variety* drew a line on the culture map. The adult voice of industry experience and tradition was telling the music biz to clean up its act, or else.

> For the music men—publishers and diskeries—to say "that's what the kids want" and "that's the only thing that sells nowadays," is akin to condoning publication of back-fence language. Earthy dialog may belong in "art novels" but mass media have tremendous obligation. If they forget, they'll hear from authority.[49]

Fifty years later, it's that "they'll hear from authority" threat that's so interesting. *Variety* may not have held out much hope for the collective conscience of the music biz to honor its "tremendous obligation," but it professed an unflappable, and even serene, confidence in what it described as "the Governmental and religious lightning that is sure to strike." Don't say we didn't warn you, the paper said, tucking its head and bracing for the heavy barrage of Establishment artillery; the attack is coming. This ultimatum is now almost touching to read, based as it is on a guileless belief in the presto-restorative powers of men of the stump and cloth. The grown-ups were coming to the rescue. It's a bit like watching a little kid brag about the big brother you know will never show for the fight. The fact is, no such institutional bolts from the mainstream blue ever hurtled to Hollywood to wipe the leer off the face of rock 'n' roll.

That's not to say there wasn't Sunday sermonizing against "leer-ics" and their deleterious effects on everything from American womanhood to the space race. A censorship movement of sorts even got off the ground, briefly, pushed by such

groups as the National Piano Tuners Association, the National Ballroom Operators Association, and the Catholic Church. Meanwhile, Congress drafted interstate commerce legislation aimed at prohibiting the transfer of "obscene, lewd,
lascivious, or filthy publication, picture, disc, transcription, or other article capa-
ble of producing sound" across state lines.[50]

The legislation didn't pass. It wasn't long before the tuners, the operators,
and the Catholics went back to their pianos, ballrooms, and churches, leaving the
music industry to go about maximizing profits. This retreat, writes Glen C.
Altschuler, was "due, to a great extent, to the sanitizing of songs, but it was a response as well to the emergence of rock 'n' roll as a mass culture phenomenon."[51]
Not to mention a mass culture moneymaker.

Despite pockets of resistance—voices that grew increasingly shrill as they
grew increasingly irrelevant—the public that warmed to the front-burner sexuality of rock 'n' roll in the 1950s was very different from the public that had once
actually turned its back on a comparably torrid phenomenon: sex-scandal-ridden
Hollywood in the silent era. "Many fans boycotted anything that came out of
that slough," writes A. Scott Berg of the period in *Goldwyn*. After state legisla-
tors introduced nearly one hundred censorship bills in thirty-seven states in 1921
alone, moviemakers feared their nascent industry would die unless they could
somehow regain public confidence. "Hollywood decided to clean house," writes
Berg. This meant recruiting someone from outside the industry to regulate its activities. Having settled on Will H. Hays, an Indiana lawyer, former Republican
national chairman and then-current postmaster general, the heads of the
largest movie companies—Samuel Goldwyn and Louis B. Mayer among
them—petitioned Hays to ask President Harding to relieve him of his government duties so he might head up a "national association of motion picture producers and distributors."[52]

Decades later, it's hard to imagine anybody at Decca, Columbia, RCA—or
any of the other "major diskers"—petitioning President Eisenhower to relieve an
administration stalwart of his duties in order to save the music industry from itself. Unlike in 1921, there was no censorship legislation on the table in dozens of
states. On the contrary, there were increasing numbers of record buyers. By the
1950s, the music industry could afford to be indifferent.

Still, there were other concerns. In another round of hearings in 1958, Congress investigated the use of the public airwaves by government-licensed broadcasters to promote their own privately manufactured product—in this case,
music. This time around, Congress kept its hands off the sticky, mucky cultural
questions of public obscenity or cultural decline, confining itself to a more or less
sterile legal analysis. Which isn't to say the sticky, mucky cultural questions didn't
arise. The hearings drew the participation, in person and in printed testimony, of

many prominent composers, producers, and performers of the day, and they weren't getting involved for the sake of a legal point. Samuel Barber, George Jessel, Leo Robin, Dean Martin, Groucho Marx, Ira Gershwin, Oscar Hammerstein, W. C. Handy, Clarence Derwent, Harry Ruby, Johnny Green, Burton Lane, Mrs. Sigmund Romberg, Mrs. Fiorello LaGuardia, Morton Gould, Yip Harburg, Jimmy McHugh, Lillian Gish, Howard Lindsay, Sammy Fain, Richard Rodgers, Leonard Bernstein, Harpo Marx, Alan Jay Lerner, Tony Martin, Aaron Copland, and other entertainment industry notables weighed in with Congress to express their conviction, in effect, that the culture they had created wasn't just slipping away, it was being yanked.[53]

The legal point of contention was this: Should Congress pass a law to separate radio and television broadcasters from the music publishing and manufacturing businesses that they owned? Since the broadcasters were licensed by the government, they were trustees of public property; the argument against them charged that they shouldn't be allowed to use public airwaves to promote and sell the music they also published and manufactured. Should CBS and NBC, for example, be allowed to use the public airwaves they leased to promote the songs and records produced by their own subsidiary companies, Columbia Records and RCA Victor Records? Should the radio broadcasters be allowed to play the music catalog of Broadcast Music Incorporated (BMI), the song-licensing group the radio broadcasters themselves owned?

Not incidentally—and here we come to the culture question—the BMI catalog was mainly rock 'n' roll and country music. This pit the broadcasters and their music against the American Society of Composers, Authors and Publishers (ASCAP), home of the American pop standard. ASCAP charged that an unfair concentration of power—a financially interlocking network of broadcasters, disc jockeys, publishers, and networks—was purposefully keeping ASCAP music from the airwaves. But there was something else. ASCAP's underlying complaint— echoed by the wider arts establishment—wasn't only that the broadcasters were abusing the public airwaves by shutting out ASCAP songs in favor of BMI songs: It also believed the broadcasters were unfairly boosting the popularity of rock 'n' roll at the expense of "good music," thereby undermining musical taste generally. And not just musical taste: According to a slew of medical, theological, and educational witnesses who came before Congress in 1958, the six other lively arts were in jeopardy as well, not to mention the Constitution, Mom, and apple pie.

In the end, Congress was unmoved by the ASCAP lament, legal or cultural. But, before that, what a moment: Establishment America—the heart of the arts, an elite chunk of academia, and a major slice of our representative political body—was seriously debating musical devolution and cultural decline as if they were really happening and as if they really mattered. Their voices didn't prevail, but what they said wasn't distorted by a late-night culture of irony and ridicule, either. That's because so much of "them" were still so much of "us." In other words, Establishment culture had not yet gone countercultural. This is a big difference between then and now. Within a decade, as rock historian Phillip H. Ennis has pointed out, the culture war between ASCAP and BMI had ended, and "almost all those prestigious art leaders [and ASCAP boosters] would be replaced by a new set of faces and voices, who were only too happy to meet the rock stars of the day."[54] It's worth remembering 1958 as a year in which the arts and academia still thought there was something that could, and should, be done to stop the changing of the cultural guard.

This changing of the cultural guard is exactly how the ASCAP-BMI clash should be seen. One kind of music—ASCAP's pop standard born of the European melodic tradition, African rhythms, and New York wit and energy—was being supplanted by another kind of music: the BMI rock sounds emerging from the heartland strains of folk, rhythm and blues, and country music. And Congress wasn't the only place to prove the point. In 1953, a core group of ASCAP members led by songwriter par excellence Arthur Schwartz ("Dancing in the Dark," "That's Entertainment"), filed an antitrust suit against BMI. Asking for damages to the extremely loud tune of $150 million, Schwartz, himself a Columbia-trained lawyer, and thirty-two other musical giants—including composer Samuel Barber (*Adagio for Strings*), lyricist Ira Gershwin (everything with brother George), lyricist Dorothy Fields ("The Way You Look Tonight," "[This Is] A Fine Romance"), Broadway and Hollywood composer Victor Young ("Stella by Starlight," score for *The Quiet Man*), lyricist Alan Jay Lerner (*Brigadoon, My Fair Lady*), composer and impresario Gian Carlo Menotti (*The Consul,* founder of Italy's Spoleto Festival), and composer and critic Virgil Thompson—charged, in effect, that rock 'n' roll tastes were being cultivated in the radio-listening public at the expense of ASCAP composers by BMI-affiliated radio stations that unfairly "created" BMI hits through frequent airplay. *Schwartz v. BMI* would wend its way through the legal system for the better part of the next two decades—in true Dickensian fashion even outliving some principals—before being dismissed with prejudice in 1971.[55]

Whether there was merit to the ASCAP composers' allegations seems less important in retrospect than the question of whether more airplay of ASCAP standards—even a great deal more airplay—could have changed the cultural history of the 1950s. Could the magnetic forces in play have been neutralized simply by more Berlin, Jerome Kern, Cole Porter, and others (including Arthur Schwartz)? Even the plain fact, to begin with, that the songwriters had sought recourse in the courts and Congress over a matter of public taste and manners suggests how far the culture had already moved, from an ASCAP world—a place ordered by adult taste and behavior—to BMI land, a new landscape shaped by adolescent taste and behavior. Legal and hypothetical questions aside, this forgotten clash of the entertainment titans indicates the extent to which the culture war over rock 'n' roll was effectively over *before* the 1960s—the time we usually think it begun.

Rosemary Clooney, someone who found stardom in the old ASCAP world, knew things were different in 1959 when she came across a headline in a local newpaper about an upcoming performance at the state fair in her native Kentucky.

FABIAN, NEW TO MUSIC, HELPS
STIR INTEREST IN FAIR'S CLOONEY SHOW

I'd never expected to need a teen sensation to attract people to my show. I sang the hits people expected to hear: "Come On-a My House," "Botcha Me," "This Old House," and, for balance, "Tenderly" and "Hey There." The audience applauded warmly. But when sixteen-year-old Fabian took the mike, fans ran screaming down the aisles to the stage.

Fabian was cast, almost literally, in the teen idol mold: a critic called him "the star who was made, not born," a "musical Frankenstein" created by showbiz hustlers to pander to the tastes of teenage girls. Noted for his youth and looks, he was a lightweight piece of photogenic flotsam. But he was carried along on a powerful turning tide, and I was caught in the undertow.

There had always been various currents flowing through American pop music: "race" music and "hillbilly" music—politely recast as "rhythm & blues" and "country and western"—as well as the conventional pop that I'd come of age with. But beneath the glassy, placid surface of the 50s, it all began to come together in a turbulent stream of beat, sound and national mood. The timing was right as never before: A new generation of teenagers with a whole new kind of influence was coming along. *When I was a kid, we listened to grown-up music and bought grown-up records, the only records there were* [emphasis added]. But unlike my generation or those before me, these kids had their own money to spend. That meant that they had their own market, for the first time in popular music.

. . . I knew only one way to sing a song: The words had to mean something, and you had to be sure you knew what they meant before you started to sing. Then you had to hit the note and hit it true. As a singer, I couldn't have been less like Fabian if I tried. The review of the Kentucky State Fair called my performance "everything that rock 'n' roll is not."

That was meant as a compliment, but it also spelled a certain kind of doom—because the rock wave was cresting, about to break, and when it did, it would wash *my* kind of music right out of the mainstream.[56]

Clooney was thirty-one in 1959, and would be named Female Vocalist of the Year. Columbia, however, did not renew her contract—for reasons unrelated to Fabian frenzy, she wrote, but she didn't sign with another label, either. Freelancing some, she was soon making commericals for Remington Roll-a-Matic shavers ("Buy one and get a free record, *Music to Shave By*"). "Within a decade," she wrote, "nobody would be able to get a contract to record the kind of music I understood and loved: not Frank, who'd take a six-year hiatus; not Bing, who'd sign with a British label because he couldn't find one stateside."[57] Frank was in his mid-forties; Bing was fifty-five. In his mid-thirties, Mel Tormé considered leaving music altogether and becoming an airline pilot. At forty-three in 1960, Nat Cole could get a standing ovation at the Sands for singing "Mr. Cole Won't Rock and Roll" but that was a last hurrah. Meanwhile, Benny Goodman hadn't worked full time since he was in his early forties.

The baton had passed, all right. But the extent to which it was ripped from the old guard's hands may be illustrated by playing the children's game Mad Libs with the preceding paragraph and inserting modern names into Clooney's litany of cultural displacement. Like this: *In 2006, neither Snoop Dogg, thirty-five, nor Eminem, thirty-four, could get themselves recording contracts, and soon were making commercials for shavers ("Buy one and get* Rap to Shave By"); *Bono, forty-six, would take a six-year hiatus. Bruce Springsteen, fifty-seven, would sign with a British label, because he couldn't find one stateside. In later years, he would gratefully enjoy a comeback making TV Christmas specials.*

Just as Clooney predicted, a cultural tsunami had washed out the mainstream, producing a shift in taste and behavior that was remarkable for more than purely personal reasons. The culture changed beyond recognition, and adults could no longer find their way—unless, that is, they were the kind of adults who knew where the Peppermint Lounge was in New York City. There, in 1961, a very interesting thing happened on the way to the death of the grown-up.

It had to do with the Twist (as introduced by Chubby Checker and Joey Dee), which became a high-society dance craze in New York. Chronicled and photographed by *Vogue*, the Twist was suddenly everywhere, from New York Mayor Robert Wagner's victory ball at the Astor Hotel, to a Metropolitan Museum of Art benefit for its Costume Institute—whose director, *The New York Times* reported, "shook with dismay" when he discovered what was going on. According to Gay Talese, then a *New York Times* reporter:

> Members of Cafe Society approached Joey Dee with reverence, and one imperial gentleman, straight-spined in a tuxedo, hestitated before asking, "Joey, may I please have your autograph?" Many others begged Joey Dee to continue his music,

even if it meant holding up the rest of the show, which included dinner and a parade of historic costumes from the museum's collection.[58]

The poor Met director only knew the half of it. The amazing thing about the success of the Twist was that the dance ditty had already taken its turn on the "sub-teen" singles charts in the late 1950s, shooting briefly to number one on *Billboard*'s "Hot 100" before sinking down and out without ado. "By January, 1961," the Hechingers reported, citing *Billboard* magazine, "the same record had made it to the top spot a second time, its return performance the result of the adult craze. The adults had taken over where the sub-teens left off, according to *Billboard*'s research director, a 'first' in the record market."[59]

It was a "first" in more ways than one. The subject of various analyses at the time, the success of the Twist inspired Chubby Checker himself to write up an explanation of the craze called, "How Adults Stole the Twist." (He said he was "really dumbfounded" about the whole thing.) Leave it to the Hechingers to hone in on the essential grown-up/teenager connection: "Whatever the deep psychological reasons," they wrote, "the Twist and its history points up the new trend of society: instead of youth growing up, adults are sliding down."[60]

This was a twist, indeed.

3. CLASH

There is something somehow liberating about approaching the 1960s from the point of view that much of what our aging Boomer population takes credit for—retrospecting themselves regularly at five-year intervals—was already in the works before the tie-dye was dry.

"Most of the political/cultural business that late-sixties youth in America deluded themselves they were mobilizing around had *already happened*," notes writer Christopher Caldwell.

> Timothy Leary was ejected from Harvard for his LSD demonstrations in 1963. The Civil Rights Act passed Congress in 1964. Medicaid and other Great Society legislation became law in 1965. Even the vaunted "end of hope"—which the young radicals flatter themselves they bore so bravely in the wake of assassinations—was old hat. The "Port Huron Statement" bemoaned a loss of ideals in 1962, even before President Kennedy was killed.[1]

The list of pre-1960s Sixtiesiana goes on, both cultural and political. In 1948, the first Volkswagen Beetle rolled into the U.S.: That was the year the Baby Boom turned two. In 1953, *Playboy* magazine, porno-flagship of the sexual revolution, sailed into the mainstream; that same year, Sugar Smacks cereal became available to, among other tots, members of the classes of '68, '69, and '70.[2] Two years after *Brown v. Board of Education,* Rosa Parks boarded a bus in 1955, even as ten million Boomers donned Davy Crockett caps.[3] Sputnik put the Cold War into a deep-freeze funk in 1957. *Lady Chatterley's Lover* made its unexpurgated American debut in 1959. The Pill was introduced in 1960. James Meredith enrolled at the University of Mississippi in 1961. That same year, Lenny Bruce, born 1925, started beating obscenity raps.

All of which suggests that a lot of the "liberation" we tend to remember as being pushed, if not driven, by masses of impassioned students—everything from racial and sexual freedom to expletive-undeleted license—was already rolling along before the youth movement got in gear. Not even one lousy campus building was taken over before the very end of 1964, when the so-called Free Speech Movement began at Berkeley. Indeed, the dispassionate logic of the timeline makes a compelling, if politically incorrect, case for a certain measure of historical continuity: namely, that the brave, new, rebel world of the 1960s was actually an extension of, and not a break from, the boring old 1950s. In other words, the Ike-ian era was really where it was at. The 1950s "represented a period of far-reaching social transformations whose significance would become apparent during the 1960s," writes historian Steven Mintz, adding: "It was during the 1950s that teen culture assumed its modern form and that the civil rights movement's activist assault on school segregation got underway."[4] With this in mind, the revolutions of the 1960s begin to look like a mopping-up operation, a rearguard action to eradicate an already doomed ancien régime: the adults. Indeed, what other target of traditional authority, of social restraint, of corrupt repression was even left?

There was that matter of the Vietnam War, opposition to which directly and indirectly ignited student-stoked disruptions, violence, strikes, and shutdowns at hundreds of American college campuses. But when all is said and done—when all the boat people are counted, when all the victims of the communist bloodbath in Indochina are buried—we have to wonder whether this was about selfless politics, or maybe just self-politics. The synchronicity, post-1970, between a fizzling-out protest movement and a winding-down draft—even as the most intensive bombing campaigns of the war raged on—cannot be explained away as unrelated coincidence. In other words, it's tough to dismiss the fact that interest in the war as a political movement waned as self-interest in the draft became a nonissue. Concern about Southeast Asian "victims" of American imperialism vanished as those same Southeast Asians became targets of North Vietnamese and Khmer Rouge aggression. This reality ultimately struck David Horowitz, a famed thinker of "second thoughts" about both the antiwar movement and his own antiwar activism as editor of the New Left magazine *Ramparts.* Comparing two Washington antiwar protests that fell to either side of President Nixon's decision to "Vietnamize" the conflict and end the draft—one in June 1970, that drew close to one million people, the other on May Day, 1971, which only thirty thousand attended—Horowitz realized "the rationale for most people to protest was gone." He continued: "When this fact registered on me, the effect was devastating. The driving force behind the massive antiwar movement on America's campuses had been the desire to avoid military service."[5]

Between 1959 and 1975, the first and last years that there were U.S. casualties in Vietnam, about sixty million Americans turned eighteen.[6] Which is a lot of Americans turning eighteen. But the point here is not so much to second-guess the self-preservation instincts of a generation whose elders, after all, had tempted them with an arcane system of draft laws that could be beaten with little effort. Rather, it is to trade the myth of moral exceptionalism for some factual context. If history tells us that the antiwar movement was, as Horowitz has called it, an "antidraft movement," then history should be allowed to strip away the cloak of sanctimony so many of our ex-revolutionaries still like to wear. That alone should relieve the rest of us from that obligatory obeisance to Baby Boomer claims of moral purity. So what are we left with? What was it all about?

New Left leader Todd Gitlin found such questions perplexing as far back as the mid-1960s, when he was asked "to write a statement of purpose for a *New Republic* series called 'Thoughts of Young Radicals.'" In his 1987 memoir, *The Sixties,* Gitlin wrote: "I agonized for weeks about what it was, in fact, I *wanted.*" This is a startling admission. Shouldn't he have thought about all this before? He continued: "The movement's all-purpose answer to 'What do you want?' and 'How do you intend to get it?' was: 'Build the movement.' By contrast, much of the counterculture's appeal was its earthy answer: 'We want to live like this, voila!'"[7]

Build the movement *et voilà*? Pretty thin stuff, as things turned out. "When I look back, I can see that what the students were doing wasn't a movement that had much philosophical grounding, in terms of what lasted," J. Anthony Lukas said in *Coming Apart: A Memoir of the Harvard Wars of 1969* by Roger Rosenblatt. Such turmoil culminated in the 1969 SDS (Students for a Democratic Society) takeover of the administration building, University Hall, which then-president Nathaniel Pusey ended by calling in four hundred state and local policemen. The students' lack of "philosophical grounding"—the 1960s equivalent of "the emperor has no clothes," which Lukas noticed in hindsight—might have had something to do with what Seymour Martin Lipset pointed out in his landmark study of campus protest: In another break from tradition, the youth movement of the 1960s had no links to *adult* political parties.[8] But there was more—or maybe less—to it than that. As Lukas, once an admirer of the students and their protest agenda, explained: "The kids were driven by anxiety about the draft. They wanted to be heroes outside a war, so they made Harvard Square a battlefield. But," he added, flashing his liberal bona fides as if to ward off too many second thoughts, "I'm disappointed the New Left didn't have more legs."[9]

Philosopher and government professor Harvey Mansfield, one of a paltry few conservative professors at Harvard—in fact, maybe he's *it*—has pinpointed precisely why it didn't. In a 1997 essay called "The Legacy of the Late Sixties," Mansfield deftly put the tumult of the decade in its place.

> The sixties revolution was more a rebellion of children against parents than of cit-
> izens against the government. Its assertiveness was more in style than in substance,
> more longhair and workingclass duds than a new form of government. The New
> Left, rejecting the establishment, did not have an alternative; it lacked the organi-
> zational skills, the staying power, and the ruthlessness of the Old Left. It hoped to
> change politics by transforming culture rather than through the dictatorship of the
> proletariat.[10]

Lacking a bona fide "alternative," no wonder the New Left's Gitlin agonized for weeks. Empty pockets, theoretically and practically speaking, were as much a part of the movement as dirty jeans. These junior radicals were "Rebels Without a Program"—the title of George F. Kennan's January 1968 article about the movement. First appearing in *The New York Times Magazine* before being re-published as a book, it was a sober critique of the "virtually meaningless slogans" of student radicalism by a sober critic of the Vietnam War.

> When we are confronted only with violence for violence's sake, and with attempts
> to frighten or intimidate an administration into doing things for which it can itself
> see neither the rationale nor the electoral mandate; when we are offered, as the
> only argument for change, the fact that a number of people are themselves very
> angry and excited; and when we are presented with a violent objection to what ex-
> ists, unaccompanied by any constructive concept of what, ideally, ought to exist in
> its place—then we of my generation can only recognize that such behavior bears a
> disconcerting resemblance to phenomena we have witnessed within our own time
> in the origins of totalitarianism in other countries. . . . People should bear in mind
> that if this—namely, noise, violence and lawlessness—is the way they are going to
> put their case, then many of us who are no happier than [the student radicals] are
> about some of the policies that arouse their indignation will have no choice but to
> place ourselves on the other side of the barricades.[11]

Frankly, "the other side of the playpen" would have been more appropriate. If the youth movement was an all-style, no-substance rebellion of children versus parents, it was also the biggest temper tantrum in the history of the world. Fail-ing to overturn the political system, however, the 1960s youth revolution did ac-celerate and intensify the transformation of the culture, and to an extent beyond the scope of change projected by the political reforms and cultural shifts of the 1950s. But even this legacy doesn't belong to the kiddies alone. The fact is, the cultural transformation we associate with the 1960s could never have taken place without the aquiescence and complicity of their parents, along with every other adult in their lives. This dysfunctional symbiosis is the "strange conspiracy" that Roger Rosenblatt watched destroy Harvard.

> The odd thing is that none of the destruction would have occurred had there not emerged a strange conspiracy between those who wanted power and those who readily ceded it to them. The fact that student radicals wanted to take over Harvard, or all of America, for that matter, did not condemn them. However naïve much of their revolution was, for the majority of them it was sincere. Even most of those who for personal reasons protested Vietnam to avoid fighting there were sincere in their objective opposition.
>
> *Yet they never could have created so much chaos at Harvard had the administration and most of the faculty not allowed them to.* . . . There were certain critical moments in those two months when professors had the opportunity to instruct their students usefully merely by voting the right vote or by saying the right things—things in which they supposedly believed. Yet, for the most part, they offered no opposition to what they disagreed with, as if to tell the students: "If you want it, take it." Liberalism rolled over on its back like a turtle awaiting the end. I do not know why, but there was an impulse running under the events of that spring to let things go to hell, and it was acted on by young and old alike. [Emphasis added.][12]

Rosenblatt's mystery impulse may well have been acted on by young and old alike, but "young" wasn't the party in charge. "Old" was still responsible for "young," or supposed to be, along with liberalism, as well. All of which is to say that it wasn't "liberalism" that rolled over in the path of a lawless and antidemocratic youth movement, it was "old"—all the adults who were scared, cowed, or even thrilled by the juggernaut of spoiled young radicalism. It was the faculty at Berkeley who ignored the clarion warning of Seymour Martin Lipset: "Civil disobedience is only justified in the absence of democratic rights."[13] (As faculty adviser to the Young People's Socialist League, Lipset was hardly an "Establishment pig" plant.) It was all of academia who reinvented the term "political crime" in order to *justify,* not define, a crime by its political motivation; this, as Professor John Silber has written, has left society with a "contempt for law through inappropriate appeal to political motivation."[14] It was the president of Cornell, James Perkins, who, abjectly and unredeemably humiliated by student radicals, declared—addressing over eight thousand angry students after having been mocked and kept sitting cross-legged on a stage—that the campus insurrection was "probably one of the most constructive, positive forces that have been set in motion in the history of Cornell."[15] It was all the parents and teachers, administrators and government officials, who laid down their arms—their grade books and their transcripts, their allowances, their tuition, their scholarships, and their fellowships, their campus disciplinary codes and their local statutes, their democratic principles, their laws, and their dignity—at the first frisson of a Movement tambourine, at the first scream of "motherf————," at the approaching footsteps of this twentieth-century Children's Crusade to stop the war, stop bureacracy, stop corruption, stop the "pigs," stop racism, stop imperialism, stop poverty, stop ROTC, stop laws against illegal drugs, stop "hang-ups" about sex and start black studies on American campuses and a communist paradise in Vietnam. Writing in 1970, then antiwar activist and sociology professor Peter L. Berger commented on this mosaic of seemingly unrelated causes underlying student unrest.

> "The Movement" seems to be about specific social and political issues of the time. But "The Movement" also seems to be about sexual emancipation, about the "generation gap," about a new style of life, which, ranging from its religious interests to its tastes in music, stands in self-conscious tension with prevailing middle-class culture. . . . This is all more than a little confusing—even to individuals who regard themselves as being within "The Movement." After all, it is not immediately clear how the demand to "Stop the War in Vietnam!" relates to such other demands as "Legalize Pot!" or "Student Power!"[16]

At about the same time, a contributor to the SDS publication *New Left Notes* shed some light of his own on the kaleidoscopic spread of issues.

> You have to realize that the issue didn't matter. The issues were never the issues. You could have been involved with the Panthers, the Weatherpeople, SLATE, SNCC, SDS. It didn't really matter what. It was the revolution that was everything. . . . That's why dope was good. Anything that undermined the system contributed to the revolution and was therefore good.[17]

Thirty years later, Roger Kimball put all the pieces together.

> Students may have marched to protest the presence of the ROTC on campus, university rules governing political activism, or U.S. policy in Southeast Asia. But in the end such issues were mere rallying points for a revolution in sensibility, a revolution that brought together radical politics, drug abuse, sexual libertinage, an obsession with rock music, exotic forms of spiritual titillation, a generalized anti-bourgeois animus, and an attack on the intellectual and moral foundations of the entire humanistic enterprise.[18]

That about covers it. But there was something else: Virtually every list of student demands included one that always looks a little shrunken next to those living-large calls for destroying the fascist-pig-capitalist-complex. It is a demand that comes across more green eyeshade and bean counter than red eyes and icono-clasm. This demand, no less urgent than any other, was the demand for "amnesty": namely, that student protestors be exempt from punishment for their disobedi-ence, whether civil or criminal.

At Columbia, for example, SDS leader Mark Rudd, ensconced in the student-held administration building, pronounced any mediative effort that didn't include amnesty for student demonstrators to be "bullshit."[19] (He and his followers would occupy the administration building a second time to protest the university's mild disciplinary measures against four SDS leaders involved in the initial assault.) At Cornell, after nearly a week of violence and vandalism in the spring of 1969 that included the armed occupation of Willard Straight Hall (eject-ing thirty campus-visiting parents and forty campus employees in the initial 6:00 A.M. takeover) and radio-broadcast death threats against seven faculty members and administrators, a faculty voice vote passed "nullification" of all penalties against the student storm troopers by an estimated seven hundred to three hun-dred.[20] At Kent State—two years before the notorious 1970 riots during which National Guardsmen killed four students—charges against 250 black and white student protestors were dropped after several hundred black students left campus demanding amnesty.[21] It was as though all the revolutionary actions—the occasional hostage-takings, the frequent arson and building takeovers, the violence, extortion and intimidation, shutdowns, shout-downs, sit-ins, destruction, and strikes—were really just so many insurrectionary in-ternships that should be written off by campus elders; or, adding insult to in-jury, even accepted for credit.

Ronald Radosh, erstwhile leftist and former antiwar activist, was a faculty member at Queensborough Community College in New York during the student protest years. This period included 1970, when, after Kent State, many protest-paralyzed campuses across the country shut down their spring semesters a month early. In his memoir, *Commies: A Journey Through the Old Left, the New Left and the Leftover Left,* Radosh recalls an exchange over grades for revolutionaries with a philosophy professor and genuine grown-up named Katherine Stabile who "argued that it was cheating the students to let them grad-uate or be advanced without having done any of the work."

> She said she intended to keep her classes going, give final exams, and not cave in
> to left-wing tyrants who claimed to have all the virtue on their side. I, of course,
> had a sharp and nasty answer, which I gave in the best New Left fashion. "Some

kill students with National Guard bullets while others do it with grades." It was the worst of analogies, but my side carried the argument, and *no grades were required* that year at Queensborough. [Emphasis added.][22]

No students, of course, were ever killed by grades, but neither, it seems, were they even flunked by them. Campus authorities—"fathers in an anxiety dream," as writer and faculty wife Diana Trilling called them—rarely meted out appropriate punishments even as they frequently handed out passing marks, even high ones, to student provocateurs who themselves had either stopped attending classes or even shut them down.[23] Worse, academy elders did what they could to shield their parent-subsidized charges from all real-world consequences of their quadrangle rampages. At Columbia, for example, the new acting university president asked the New York district attorney to grant clemency to hundreds of students who had been arrested in the spring of 1968.[24]

More than anything else, it is this surrender of adults that accounts for the surrender of the American academy. It was a surrender as shocking to behold as it was widespread, as hard to believe as it was transformative. As late as the spring of 1969, Richard Nixon, then newly ensconced in the White House, could still express satisfaction at news of the SDS takeover of Harvard's University Hall. "Nixon told me that he was happy it had happened at Harvard," explained Henry Kissinger. "At first I thought he was gloating at the discomfiture of his enemies. In fact, he had something else in mind: 'Harvard is the leading university in the country. It will set an example for how to handle student upheavals,'" Nixon said.[25] It set an example, all right, but not the one President Nixon was undoubtedly hoping for. Notwithstanding his own antipathies toward the liberal establishment, Nixon obviously still assumed the grown-ups were in charge.

Why weren't they? This is the great ponderment behind the culture wars that have riven society for half a century. The answer lies somewhere between the abdication of the adult and the rise of the adolescent that took place as American society redirected its energies from realizing its destiny to raising its young. While children always were and remain any society's future, what had taken place was a cultural shift in emphasis from the distant horizon, from exploration, conquest, and settlement, to the family room; from the big picture to the good life; from looking out to looking within. Maybe, briefly, the 1960s were the real "end of history"—a pause, anyway, during which the upper end of the American middle class, and especially its young, took the opportunities offered by expanding leisure and unprecedented luxury to work on the real problem: its happy, indulgent, guilty, disaffected self.

In his magisterial history of Western civilization, Jacques Barzun makes note of "the loss of nerve typical of periods of decadence."[26] Barzun—who, incidentally, as a professor and former provost of Columbia played no role during the university's upheavals in 1968—was describing eighteenth-century France, but he could have been describing twentieth-century America, where the rotting heart of American academia revealed that same typical loss of nerve. Atypical, though, was the cause. In the American example, the ancien régime didn't shrink from an invading army, an invading people, or an invading ideology. It retreated from the ultimate "enemy within": its own children.

Peter L. Berger describes a "new cultural conception of childhood" that made the youth movement possible in the first place. It was linked, he writes, not only to the vast numbers of children born during the Baby Boom—seven or eight million of whom had matriculated by 1970 at rapidly expanding colleges and universities—but also to an "abrupt decline in child mortality." This, Berger maintained, transformed the parent-child relationship.

> Today, most children grow to maturity. One has to grasp the emotional conse-
> quences that this transformation has had *for parents* if one is to understand its
> staggering significance. Probably for the first time in human history, when a child
> is born today, the parents can bestow love on this child without having to reckon
> with the probability that, in the very near future, their grief will be all the more bit-
> ter for it. There is a new emotional calculus along with the new demographic
> one—and it is important to recall that all of this is very recent indeed.[27]

This "new emotional calculus" is crucial to any postmortem on the death of the grown-up. Once upon a time, more children living longer would have been a boon, say, to the family farm. In a technological economy, though, few kids feed chickens or bale hay. This has made childhood less useful to parents, even as it has made it more fun for children. At the same time, as the human condition has continually improved, childhood has also been increasingly buffered from the pain of illness and death. Additionally, according to Berger's thesis, there was one more new attribute to modern childhood: "Within this physical and social setting the modern child, not suprisingly, comes to feel very early that he is a person of considerable importance."[28]

Sure enough, self-esteem was not a problem with the occupiers of Harvard's University Hall—or Columbia's Hamilton Hall, or Berkeley's Sproul Hall. And occupying Harvard's University Hall—or Columbia's Hamilton Hall, or Berkeley's Sproul Hall—was not a problem for doting parents, not to mention doting professors. "Think of it as one of your own children who had been beaten like that!" cried a member of the Harvard philosophy department, "almost tearful" in his remarks at a faculty meeting about the "police brutality" that ended the University Hall takeover. Such empathy carried the day—the era, really. Sure, there was tough talk from the odd alum: "I don't give a damn whose head got bloodied. If you get mixed up in a thing like that, you deserve what you get," one told *The New York Times*. And sure, there was quiet anger in the occasional Harvard professor. After his "almost tearful" colleague spoke, Harvard professor John V. Kelleher recalled, "For the first and only time I wanted to get up and speak. I wanted to say that if it was one of my children, I could hardly wait to get him home so that I could give him a rousing kick where it wouldn't blind him. But I didn't, because an old friend was sitting in front of me; and his son had been in the hall." But such were the voices of the largely Silent Majority; they may well have voted, but they didn't make much noise.[29]

The fact is, general support for the Vietnam War under President Johnson, and, later, President Nixon, remained fairly solid during periods of student upheaval—although such support was going to be lower amid the increasingly liberal subset of society that sent its children to, or taught them in, college. But what did these supporters say to their children? It's not difficult to imagine long distance arguments over what was going on at school between Junior and the 'rents—liberal or conservative—but what harsh words ever led to harsh actions? That is, what collegiate revolutionary ever saw his dining hall contract canceled, or his bursar account closed? (As one historian remarked, he knew of no other uprising in history in which the revolutionaries had fellowships.[30]) The conduct of the war in Vietnam, the pace of civil rights reform, or university slumlordship wasn't ever the parenting issue. What concerned Mom and Dad—or should have—had to do with Junior's behavior. Dirty words. Shoving. Pushing. Cutting class. Cutting fire hoses. Waving guns. Taking things. Breaking things. Throwing things (paving stones, Molotov cocktails). Burning things (buildings, records, research). But it didn't—at least not in any consequential way. Indeed, at the University of Chicago, which may be the one campus where administrators acted swiftly to expel students who had occupied a building, "parents took out newspaper advertisements protesting the draconian punishment visited upon their darlings, thus providing a clue to what had gone wrong with their children."[31]

Central to the surrender of the adult, then, was the collapse of the parent. As much as any political, demographic, or economic factors, this made the ascendancy of youth possible, and possibly inevitable, first on campus, and, later, in the wider culture. So much for the World War II–winning Greatest Generation, whose own offspring, spoiled "youths" in the 1950s, became everyone's spoiled youth movement in the 1960s. Life may have been tough for the men and women whose formative years were marred by Depression and war, but theirs was the spawn of Dr. Spock's "permissive society."

Then again, there are those, particularly among our elites, who find the permissive society explanation—the spoiled brat theory—too simplistic. After all, the theory ignores the "real" issues in all their complexities: namely, that the Vietnam War was "immoral"; the American government was "corrupt"; our young people were "pure." It also fails to take into account that the North Vietnamese were good (all communists, of course, were good), and the South Vietnamese were bad (all anticommunists, of course, were neanderthals). All of which is, well, pretty simplistic.

Of course, simplistic or not, and even spoiled or not, the youth movement had an impact. In the fall of 1969, Richard Nixon addressed the emerging danger of mob influence. (Worth noting, for the sake of context, is that at no point in 1969 did any Gallup Poll show public support for Nixon's conduct of the war slip below 44 percent—at which point opposition stood at 26 percent. Even at the height of huge public demonstrations in the fall, 58 percent of the public supported the president, with 32 percent opposed.[32])

> In San Francisco a few weeks ago I saw demonstrators carrying signs reading: "Lose in Vietnam, bring the boys home."
>
> Well, one of the strengths of our free society is that any American has a right to reach that conclusion and to advocate that point of view. But as President of the United States, I would be untrue to my oath of office if I allowed the policy of this Nation to be dictated by the minority who hold that point of view and who try to impose it on the Nation by mounting demonstrations in the street.
>
> For almost 200 years, the policy of this nation has been made under our Constitution by those leaders in the Congress and in the White House elected by all of the people. If a vocal minority, however fervent its cause, prevails over reason and the will of the majority, this Nation has no future as a free society.[33]

The words of the Republican president essentially expressed the logic behind the liberal argument against the Movement—which, of course, is not to be confused with the liberal argument against the war. It jibes with what Seymour Martin Lipset said at Berkeley at the beginning; with what George F. Kennan said in the middle; and with what David Horowitz said two decades after it was all over: "In a democracy, where the people are sovereign, what justification can there be for self-styled 'revolutionaries' like ourselves? In rejecting the democratic process, we had rejected the people, setting ourselves over them in judgement as though we were superior beings."[34]

Of course, even superior beings could be touchy. In that same fall of 1969, during the semester following Harvard's spring revolt, Daniel Patrick Moynihan, then a Democratic member of the Nixon administration serving as counselor to the president, attended the annual Harvard-Princeton game. There, at Soldier's Field in Cambridge, Moynihan could see the biggest stumbling block to mounting a defense of the democratic process: the superior beings' parents. In *White House Years,* Henry Kissinger recalled the memo Moynihan sent to the president on the subject.

> It described a scene . . . in which the assembled graduates—worth, according to Pat, at least $10 billion—roared support when the Harvard University band was introduced, in a takeoff of Agnew's denigrating phrase, as the "effete Harvard Corps of Intellectual Snobs." Pat warned that while Nixon was right in resisting attempts to make policy in the streets, he should not needlessly challenge the young—*because of their great influence on their parents.* [Emphasis added.][35]

In the cheers of the crowd, Moynihan heard more than just the sound of parental approval. As Peter Berger might well have pointed out, parental regard for their young had merged into a sense of shared identity, or perhaps shared vision. Parent and offspring alike saw that children could do no wrong. Which, in its universality, was a new one on the human race. It's a safe bet that Ivy alumni at that same Harvard-Princeton matchup, circa, say, 1959—and certainly 1949 and earlier—would have slapped down any youth movement attempting to make policy in the streets.

But there was another factor in the emotional calculus that was changing the whole social equation: an increasing sense of self-awareness. This new state of self-consciousness was probably another tasty fruit of victory, relative peace, and rampant, increasingly technology-based prosperity. Indeed, such self-awareness had become a "chief characteristic of our culture," wrote Columbia's Lionel Trilling, high, low, and otherwise. From academia, journalism, entertainment, and advertising, he wrote, we learn "to believe not only that we can properly identify the difficulties presented by the society but also that we can cope with them, at least in spirit, and that in itself *our consciousness of difficulties to be coped with gives us moral distinction* [emphasis added]."[36]

What Trilling described was a perfectly phony brand of moral distinction, an ersatz morality, as in: I feel, therefore I am moral. Trilling found himself reflecting on it after reading the opening paragraph of the independent report on "the disturbances" at Columbia in 1968. These "disturbances" included: the seizure of five campus buildings; the overnight imprisonment of the acting dean of the college and his two assistants; an SDS manifesto from SDS leader Mark Rudd threatening Columbia's destruction addressed to the university president (ending, "Up against the wall, motherf————"); spitting at and punching senior faculty members; urinating in trash cans, urinating out windows; destroying faculty research and papers; and the paralysis of a thirty-four-year-old policeman caused when a student jumped him from above.

Four decades later, more memorable than the report's findings is the surrealistic, worshipful tone that was set in the opening lines by report author Archibald Cox of the Harvard Law School: "The present generation of young people in our universities are the best informed, the most intelligent, and the most idealistic this country has ever known." (Good thing—bad thing?—the report came out a few days before that best informed, most intelligent, and most idealistic young person Mark Rudd informed *The Boston Globe,* "We manufactured the issues."[37]) Trilling describes his "natural bewilderment" on reading Cox's words. Then he understood.

> In his high estimate of the young, Professor Cox accepted the simulacrum for the real thing: he celebrated as knowledge and intelligence what in actuality is merely a congeries of "advanced" public attitudes. When he made his affirmation of the enlightenment of the young, he affirmed his own enlightenment and that of others who would agree with his judgment—*for it is from the young and not from his own experience that he was deriving his values,* and for values to have this source is, in the view of a large part of our forward-looking culture, all the certification that is required to prove that the values are sounds ones. [Emphasis added.][38]

The phenomenon the professor is getting at sounds very much like an old boy riff on the Twist—the juvenile dance craze adopted and popularized by *adults*. In "deriving his values from the young," as Trilling wrote, Professor Cox and his fellow fact finders were defining their values down (to borrow Daniel Patrick Moynihan's handy concept again) to those embodied by student protest. In affirming the enlightenment of the young—and thus his own, according to Trilling—Cox was likewise defining enlightenment down, mistaking " 'advanced' public attitudes" (read: left-wing politics) for wisdom. This was a watershed moment. From this point forward, New Left values and "the enlightenment of the young" quintessentially defined the elites, effectively negating, and certainly downgrading, all experience and traditions that came before.

This elite embrace of youth-derived values and enlightened self-awareness became the basis of the 1960s legacy—and, thus, the basis of the so-called culture wars that would disrupt subsequent decades. In place of a hierarchy based on accrued wisdom, there would emerge a power structure based on accrued grievance. Authority and reason would give way to novelty and feelings. A new set of un-manners and non-mores would quickly overrun attitudes and practices that had evolved over generations by recasting refinement and restraint, honor and forbearance—virtues, not coincidentally, of maturity—as corrupt and phony, or, even worse, not "authentic."

In that bid for "authenticity," civility and decency, too, were quick casualties.

Not for nothing, as noted by Diana Trilling at Columbia in 1968, did a filthy stream of public profanity rush through the various student upheavals. Indeed, the most memorable words of the movement are four-letter ones.

> It was not alone President Kirk who was addressed as a motherf————. Vice-President Truman was a motherf————, Acting Dean Coleman was a motherf————, the police were—naturally—motherf————s, any disapproved member of the faculty was a motherf————. Rudd's response to the mediating efforts was "bull————." . . . At a tense moment on the steps of Low Library a Barnard girl-demonstrator jumped up and down in front of the faculty line—the faculty were wearing their white armbands of peace—compulsively shouting, "Shit, shit, shit, shit."[39]

Small wonder, as Trilling also noted, one pun-prone professor dubbed the student revolutionaries, "Alma Materf————s."

Oddly enough, these cataracts of obscenity were barely mentioned in the press, if at all, no doubt out of reflexive consideration for middle-class sensibilities. But, as Diana Trilling wrote, this phenomenon was "not of the gutter." It was out of the mouths of babes from the middle class; and, as it turned out, few of their middle-class parents were willing to wash out the little darlings' mouths with soap. "One discovered that a decent proportion of the decent American middle-class mothers and fathers of these young people, as well as other energetic spokesmen for progress, supported their offspring," she wrote. Among the proud parents were the Rudds, with Mama Rudd giving "the proudest and tenderest interview to the *Times* about how her-son-the-rebel planted tulips in their suburban garden." Up against the garden wall, motherf————, and all that. Indeed, roughly two hundred other mothers and fathers joined a Committee of Concerned Columbia Parents "to back their children and further harry the administration."[40] Strange conspiracy, indeed.

Not that everyone went along with it. The revolution on campus may well have successfully overturned the old order of the Establishment—and, more important, the established order of the old—but it didn't overturn everyone. The youth movement booted maturity and experience from all that was deemed, in 1960s parlance, "relevant" and "valid" to the life worth living, but some few scattered grown-ups were left standing. Looking back now, these adult remnants resemble ghosts and scolds, rattling cages and writing screeds as their world disappeared, lost to that same strange conspiracy. If the 1960s tell the story of capitulation, they also write the book on "clash," on frictions and collisions that to this day map out the shifting front in the so-called culture wars. Indeed, the culture wars themselves, from the university to the workplace to the family room, retain the basic aspects and patterns of that earlier clash—that strange conspiracy between young and old, child and parent, hip and square—that distinguish the 1960s from every decade that came before them.

Clash is key. Clash is pop versus rock; short hair versus long hair; restraint versus license. It was S. I. Hayakawa standing up to student militants at San Francisco State. It was Bosley Crowther of *The New York Times* crossing pens with Pauline Kael of *The New Yorker* over the amorality of *Bonnie and Clyde*.[41] It was Police Code No. 205 versus the mouth of Lenny Bruce.[42] It was any socially explosive face-off between hostile, if not actually warring, culture camps—the one established, the other revolutionary. Not that these two sides were evenly matched. In fact, all the Establishment ever did (ever does) was throw off a few sparks of reluctance to bear witness to cast-off traditions and subsiding sensibilities just as they were fizzing out. In the clash between Establishment (Nixon) and revolution (Elvis), revolution, it seems, wins every time. "We're going to bury you. We're gonna take over. You're finished," thirty-four-year-old Dennis Hopper (*Easy Rider*) said in 1970, poking a finger into the chest of seventy-one-year-old George Cukor (*What Price Hollywood?, Dinner at Eight, The Women, Philadelphia Story, Adam's Rib*). "Well, well, yes, yes," said Cukor. "That's very possible, yes, yes." A few months later, John Wayne in *True Grit,* not Dustin Hoffman in *Midnight Cowboy,* managed to take home the Best Actor Oscar, but it was still the end of an era.[43]

That's because it's always easier to release a genie than to coax him back into the bottle. Or, for that matter, stuff *Bonnie and Clyde* back into the can. It's easier to add women's, Latino, and gender studies to the curriculum than to remove black studies from the curriculum. It's always easier to be the first movie to use the word, "f——" (*M*A*S*H* in 1970)[44] than the next movie not to use it. Three esteemed professors may have resigned from Cornell in 1969 over the university's lack of intergrity, but the university still lacked integrity, not to mention the three esteemed professors.[45] In such cases, culture clash merely marks the fault line of change, an aftershock of wishful thinking that follows the initial trembler. Indeed, as Walter Berns put it, writing about Cornell's acquiescence to militant demands in 1969, "By surrendering to students with guns, [Cornell's President Perkins] made it easier for those who came after him to surrender to students armed only with epithets ('racists,' 'sexists,' 'elitists,' 'homophobes')."[46]

In July 1965, seventeen months after the Beatles entered living rooms across America via *The Ed Sullivan Show,* and six or seven months after the student protest generation debuted at Berkeley, *Esquire* magazine offered up what may now be read as the perfect clash issue on American youth. It is that rare cultural relic: an expression of a purely adult sensibility in a non-adolescent cultural mainstream before the sea change. In conducting a study of teenage life from an adult point of view, this issue stood as a bulwark, temporarily, against the adolescent deluge to come. Not having yet defined down either its sense of enlightenment or its values, *Esquire* in July 1965 was openly contemptuous of the new obsessions with "teen-agerism," and argued against it, albeit with an inkling that time was passing adults by.

> The traditional view, unfortunately discarded, was that you were sort of apprentice adults living through an awkward period, waiting and preparing to take your place in the real or "adult" world. There was a lot to be said for that view—one of the best things that could be said for it was that it was true. It still is, but the cultist teen-ager doesn't believe it anymore. He behaves as if he had arrived somewhere, as if he had already achieved his own sort of perfection, celebrating what he is (very little), instead of worrying what he may become (anything). His idols are only other teen-agers more or less like himself, which puts him in a rather static bind: we tend to become what we admire or at least move in that general direction. But the pro-teen is standing dead still, combing his hair and mouthing jargon. Hip or square makes no difference. He will never be anything but a teen-ager.[47]

Esquire also tried to show, not just tell, the folly of this philosophy in a fashion story—"Threads, or What the Well-Dressed Teen-ager Ought to Wear." The story went beyond just showcasing standard-issue chinos and loafers and camel-hair coats. The fashion spread instructed readers on how "non-adult" the new styles were, and it did so by contrasting the timeless look of the prepster with the mod look of the wanna-Beatle.

> So leave the tight pants and the boots and the pointed shoes and the latter-day zoot suits and the Martian getups to the idols. . . . Better yet, don't even dress like a teen-ager. Pretend you never were one. Pretend you couldn't care less. For instance, take the guy in the three-piece suit on the next page. It's a grey herringbone tweed (Cricketeer) worn with brown brogues, a button-down shirt and a paisley tie. Contrast this with the guy in the background sporting boots and a zany belted suit. He probably paid as much for his suit as the other guy. But notice which looks more comfortable. Notice, too, which one has the chick.[48]

Surprise, surprise: In *Esquire*-land—which obviously included a photo studio—the tweedy (mature) teen, not the zany (adolescent) teen, got the girl, and who could ask for anything more? This dream was nice while it lasted. In the real world of 1965 beyond the photo shoot, though, brown brogues were fast losing to tight pants. What *Esquire*'s editors hadn't quite grasped was the solidity of the emerging consensus on "teenagerism." The idea of never being anything but a teen wasn't a threat; it was an aspiration. Soon, it would be a promise, and one that *Esquire,* among other magazines, would ultimately try to keep. In an editorial already sounding like a blast from the past, *Esquire* tried to appeal to teen logic, revealing an understanding of the more or less irrational forces that good old American capitalism had unleashed.

> The danger is, though, that having become a matter of interest you will come to think of yourselves as therefore interesting, which is not quite the same thing. You have not created a valuable subcivilization merely by being too young to vote, although that is rather wise. Remember that no matter how many millions are spent catering to your taste in music, your taste in music remains very bad: even more millions are devoted to the study and treatment of your pimples, but that doesn't make pimples a good thing.[49]

Such caustic confidence was as doomed as the cultural establishment that inspired it. But it makes a good marker. In July 1965, a mainstream publication not only could, but did voice an adult point of view on adolescent culture. Indeed, that same *Esquire* issue ran a memoir of the day Benny Goodman met the Beatles. Written by Goodman's daughter, Rachel, the article chronicled a brief chat backstage—a cordial enough King of Swing making small talk with the Fab but clearly disinterested Four—and an even briefer review of the performance Goodman himself broadcast in exchange for publicity for an upcoming appearance of his own at the World's Fair. " 'There was a very a strong beat,' Daddy said, 'but otherwise the screams drowned out most of the sound. I'm afraid there's not much I feel qualified to say about it.' "

Rachel Goodman elaborated:

> In the tidal wave of screams that greeted them [the Beatles], I thought this was what the end of the world must be like. The din went past the painful, too loud for the ear to register. It was precisely the sensation of being behind a jet plane taking off: the same pitch and intensity. Flashbulb after flashbulb made the whole stadium white, the points of brightness popping everywhere, but giving the impression of a constant unearthly glow. . . .
>
> Daddy, [sister] Benjie and I watched the stadium with much greater fascination than we did the performance. Benjie turned to me and said, "Just think what people from another planet would think if they found themselves here." There was something so apocalyptical about it; pure frenzy, an almost mystical atmosphere of heavens opening up. I thought of the subtle element that held together these four boys performing not very well, and the incredible response of the kids. It was more complicated than sex alone or music alone. There is music and music. People

screamed at Carnegie Hall for Richter, and indeed for my father, but it was after the performance, and in Daddy's case, it had something to do with skill and rhythm which captivates in a different way.[50]

This reaction—the sensibility, the point of view—is not only antique, it is extinct, at least in the media mainstream. In our time, in our rock culture, such a critique of any leading music act would and could never appear. There is no one who sees things that way; no one, that is, who isn't regarded as irrelevant, anti-establishment, and downright countercultural—a subversive, who, Soviet-style, really should be sent to Siberia. This is more evidence of just how far the fault lines have shifted. As they move, we move, which is why all manner of clash is left behind.

In the end, the *absence* of clash becomes as telling as clash itself. In 1977, the year Queen Elizabeth II celebrated twenty-five years on the British throne, the Sex Pistols—remember them?—marked the occasion with the release of their dumb, if nasty, punk anthem "God Save the Queen," prompting what were still predictable clucks of outrage from defenders of the British institution. Indeed, the song was officially banned for a time from the land and the airwaves, prompting a live performance on the Thames that ended in a few cheap thrills and several arrests.[51] In other words, those were still the days when no rock star worth his authenticity would have dared cross the palace moat—nor would he have been invited to.

In 2002, when Queen Elizabeth II celebrated fifty years on her throne, Sir Paul McCartney, "First Lady of Soul" Aretha Franklin, and other bona fide rock icons marked the occasion by singing at the queen's invitation at the "Party at the Palace." Sex Pistol Sid Vicious may have been long dead of a drug overdose, but the spectacle offered a vivid juxtaposition of symbols: the amber-preserved trappings of monarchy versus the free flow of aging rock royalty, whose loyal subjects—fans—embody the image of mob rule. These rock 'n' rollers never went to culture-war against the monarchy as openly as the Sex Pistols, but they certainly attacked the manners and mores of the vast middle class—said manners and mores in Britain that included, for example, hanging the queen's picture in the parlor, sans irony, in reflexive obeisance to fealty, honor, duty, and other largely atavistic instincts stamped out in the rock revolution.

Given these seemingly natural cultural enmities, a golden jubilee invite to, for example, drug-addled, bleep-mouthed Ozzy Osbourne—at the time riding reality-show-high—should have struck a culturally significant spark or two somewhere in the realm. But no. As the aged Keeper of the Stiff Upper Lip and retinue prepared to receive the aging Advocate of Wild Abandon and mates at her own gala affair, there was no discernible tut-tutting, not a single letter to the editor wondering what the country was coming to. In the end, no one noted anything amiss about an event that brought together a man who bites bats with a woman who has a royal taster. Which goes to show the cultural revolution isn't just over; it's been forgotten entirely. This explains why, flashing forward to the 2004 Kennedy Center Honors in Washington, D.C., Billy Joel could celebrate Sir Elton John's Lifetime Achievement Award by performing "The Bitch Is Back" for a black-tie crowd including President Bush, his White House cabinet, and a national television audience.

This was another transgressive moment of pomp and punkiness, a mix of cultivation and coarseness, but no one noticed the clash *because there wasn't any.* Pomp is now open to punkiness, while punkiness will always tolerate a little pomp. The shared sensibility of a Richard Nixon and an Elvis Presley—both of whom knew better than to mix their cultural metaphors—is a long way in the past. In the years since, *The New York Times* has editorialized "in praise of the counterculture," which shows, as Harvey Mansfield has written, "by its very appearance in the nation's most prestigious newspaper how far the counterculture had become regnant."[52] The "bitch" isn't just back, it's here to stay.

To Mansfield, a paean to the counterculture in the "newspaper of record" has instantly, glaringly obvious implications. To almost everyone else—those who have become or were born insensate to cultural revolution—his words are meaningless. Either reaction tends to prove that the counterculture has become the establishment culture.

Sex toys and drug paraphenalia turn into Clinton White House Christmas tree ornaments, triggering the lonely ire of a solitary FBI agent on White House detail.[53] An elementary school principal in upstate New York has a child out of wedlock and townspeople castigate the anonymous citizen who publicly criticized her example.[54] The Erotica USA convention sets up shop in the Jacob Javits Convention Center in New York City, arousing zero complaints, but presumably plenty of customers. " 'For 35 years, I've been a pornographer, and we've always been underground,' said Al Goldstein, who—between signing autographs—was running a booth that displayed his [*Screw*] magazine . . . 'I never dreamed we'd be in the Javits Center. It is such a class place.' "[55]

So is the St. James Theater on West Forty-fourth Street. There, on the fiftieth anniversary in 1993 of the premiere of Rodgers and Hammerstein's *Oklahoma!*, then-seventy-six-year-old retired Broadway tenor (and father of Bonnie) John Raitt made a surprise appearance to sing the rousing title song, a melodious anthem of ascendant Americanism.[56] It must have been some surprise: The audience that night had paid to see *Tommy,* the 1969 rock opera by The Who ("Pinball Wizard," "The Acid Queen"), a fever dream of the drug culture. A half century earlier, *Oklahoma!* broke theatrical ground by bringing the folkloric

American characters of the Great Plains to Broadway; *Tommy,* on the other hand, made musical history by taking audiences along on an orchestrated drug trip. In other words, the 1943 season that saw the opening of *Oklahoma!* was, by 1993 when John Raitt opened his mouth to sing, a very long time ago. Then again, 1969 was itself nearly a quarter century past. The difference is the culture of the 1960s remains eternally accessible to contemporary audiences.

There's a reason: We live in a 1960s world, suffused with a 1960s sensibility that is informed, if not sustained by, the very contagious rebel-persecution complex. Writing in 1997, Todd Gitlin declared, "In the not-very-gay nineties, a president associated with [the 1960s], whether he likes it or not, has had to devote considerable energy to wriggle away from the reputation."[57] Maybe Gitlin was referring to Clinton's sidestepping of such age-old transgressions as draft evasion or womanizing. But to what extent, if at all, did our 1990s president ever have to distance himself from the 1960s era of his youth?

In answer, it's worth considering a little noted (i.e., clashless) excursion the First Family took back in 1997 to celebrate daughter Chelsea's seventeenth birthday. Flying to New York, the Clintons attended three of Broadway's most popular shows that year: *Chicago, Rent,* and *Bring in 'Da Funk, Bring in 'Da Noise.* In the course of their theatrical whirl, the Clinton family contemplated same-sex kissing, heterosexual intercourse (simulated), dildos, masturbation, marijuana, and twin blasts of black racism and cultural separatism. They were also mooned. (According to *The Washington Post,* the mooning incident took place "at an angle to the president and his family that was as decorous as allowed by the act of pulling down one's pants."[58]) That this juxtaposition of the (pre-Lewinsky) presidency—not to mention the (pre-Lewinsky) presidential family—with so countercultural a calvacade inspired little or no comment should lead us to rephrase the question. Rather than wonder how far the forty-second president wriggled from the 1960s, maybe it's better to ask, where else could he have possibly gone?

In so many ways, the same question may be asked of the rest of us. The answer is nowhere. This is true, but not because time has stood still. There is a link between our affinity for the adolescent culture epitomized by the 1960s, and our even older aversion to maturity. "I recall Leo Rosten observing long before Columbia that, so far as he could see, what the dissatisfied students were looking for were adults—adults to confront, to oppose, to emulate," Irving Kristol wrote in 1968. "It is not going to be easy to satisfy this quest, since our culture for many decades now has been plowing under its adults." He continued,

> I agree with Rosten that this is what is wanted, and I am certain it will not be achieved until our institutions of higher education reach some kind of common

understanding on what kind of adult a young man is ideally supposed to become. This understanding—involving a scrutiny of the values of our civilization—will not come soon or easily, if it ever comes at all. But we must begin to move toward it. . . .[59]

How? Almost forty years ago, Kristol suggested what he called a paradoxical first step that would encourage a "variety of meanings [of adulthood] to emerge." This sounds like one way to throw open the debate. But something else needs to happen first. Remember the child with the fearless clarity who declared the emperor had no clothes? We need to take a look at our adolescent culture and declare it has no adults.

4. PARENTS WHO NEED PARENTS

The deterioration in middle-aged adult behavior has driven virtually every major American social problem over the past 25 years.
—MIKE MALES[1]

Marco Andreoli was thirty years old in 2002 when Italy's highest court ordered Marco's father to pay Marco roughly €775 ($1,000) a month until Marco found a job that "fit his aspirations."

Alas, this could take a while. Marco had a law degree, a house on one of Naple's swankiest streets, and joint ownership of an investment fund worth more than £300,000 ($390,000). Clearly, not just any job would do. He also had zero relationship with his father, who was estranged from his mother. "How can you justify a decision like that?" his father Giuseppe Andreoli wondered after the court ordered him to pony up and support Marco in the style to which his son might never grow unaccustomed. "I would like someone to explain it to me."[2]

It's unlikely that the judges' rationale, as recounted in the British paper *The Guardian,* satisfied old Giuseppe. "The judges said that a parent's duty of maintenance did not expire when their children reached adulthood, but continued unchanged until they were able to prove either that their children had reached economic independence or had failed to do so through culpable inertia." The newspaper continued: "An adult son who refused work that did not reflect his training, abilities and personal interests could not be held to blame." In other words, little chick might well outgrow the family nest, but he certainly didn't have to fly away until he found that perfect perch—running Fiat? singing *Pagliacci?*— while Dad, poor sap, goes on playing early bird to catch Junior a worm.

If this court declaration against independence gives new meaning to the term "nanny-state," it also offers new insight into why Italy is a country where more than one in three Italians in their thirties lives at home with parents. Among Italian sons, ages eighteen to thirty, the number skyrockets to 85 percent, as compared to 20 percent of British adult sons and 25 percent of American adult sons.[3] "Unfortunately, we continue to be the mummy's boys of Europe," commented

Simone Baldelli, youth coordinator for the former prime minister Silvio Berlusconi's Forza Italia party. "The family, instead of being considered a fundamental cell for children's education and training, becomes a social safety net."[4]

No U.S. court is likely to venture this far, far out into child-friendly law. But the family-as-social-safety-net is nonetheless an American institution. And it is an ever-expanding one as educational costs, for example, continue to rise to insurmountable heights. Such costs are driving higher-educated sons and daughters in particular to rely on parental largesse well into adulthood, which so many now begin deeply in debt. The average college graduate leaves college not only with a diploma these days, but also debt amounting to $25,760. Little wonder Junior with his BA comes knocking on Mom and Dad's door, which seems to remain open to him indefinitely. One survey of recent college graduates found almost one-third still living at home more than a year past graduation—not exactly the surest way to "grow up."[5]

But not only do parents tend to support Junior no matter how old he is, but they also support him *no matter what he does*—and even as a minor. Instead of running that cell for education and training that the Italian minister mentioned, post–grown-up parents in America carry out the kind of nonjudgmental "duty of maintenance" that the Italian court cited in order to safeguard American children's increasingly high-wire lifestyles.

The very odd fact is, Boomer (and Boomer-plus) parents today expect, prepare, and even enable their youngsters to encounter and engage in a welter of antibourgeois, even criminal, activities. These range from a berserk kind of sexual adventurism, to the mortal dangers of mind-altering drugs and alchohol. They include a spectrum of rude, crude, and formerly socially unacceptable behaviors, such as what is still known as, even in these value-neutral times, "bad" language. Funny how these same habits and behaviors fit in with the fabled rock 'n' roll lifestyle of hedonistic abandon. Less funny is the realization that this same lifestyle—the one so many adolescents lead, or try to—is only made possible by Mom, Dad, and their underlying soft spot for the ethos of sex, drugs, and rock 'n' roll.

Certainly, it's not every kid who engages in such practices, any more than it is every parent who enables him to. But it's something to reckon with that every kid is unavoidably and indelibly marked by them. For example, even in rejecting drug use, the straightest-arrow teen is shaped and defined by his awareness of drugs. In taking a "virginity pledge" to remain chaste, a youngster has acknowledged mainstream notions about promiscuity in teen culture. Innocence has always been nullified by exposure, and good has always been defined, at least tangentially, by resistance to bad. But there is something new and disturbing in the modern-day incarnation of this age-old human condition.

For one thing, a state of exposure—not innocence—now coincides with the earliest stirrings of self-awareness that usually begin with life after Candy Land. Twenty years ago, Dartmouth College made shocking headlines for equipping incoming college freshmen not just with everything they needed to know about sex, but rather everything they needed to engage in it. And I mean everything. Along with various examples of drugstore birth control, the freshman sex kit included an "oral dam," a device I decided at the time I would probably prefer to avoid knowledge of, carnal or otherwise. Back then, a college setting up eighteen-year-olds for sexual experimentation seemed outrageous. Today, middle school students in Maryland learn "buying a condom is not as scary as you think."[6] In Wisconsin, they can pick them up for free at a "health" fair.[7] First-graders in North Carolina get primed on homosexual marriage with *King & King,* a storybook about a handsome prince who spurns a run of princesses for a handsome prince of his own.[8] New Jersey put together a sex ed kit that, among other things, gives elementary school students, the lowdown on masturbation.[9] Kindergartners in New York learn the mechanics of AIDS transmission.[10]

What happened to innocence? No longer considered a boon to virtuous behavior, innocence—of drugs, of sex, of homosexual princes, and of oral dams—is today deemed a handicap, an affliction to be cured as quickly as possible. Intensive treatment takes place both in the classroom and through the culture. Meanwhile, the notion of virtue itself—"conformity to a standard of right," *Webster's* says—is out altogether, replaced by the multifarious "values" of a relativistic culture. By definition, these values conform to *no* standard of right. This means that not only is virtue no longer its own reward, it's not even one of the door prizes.

As society spurns innocence in favor of exposure, and virtue in favor of values, it no longer sees any point in inculcating "good" or "moral" behavior in its young. Rather, it labors to encourage "better choices." Instead of virtues to live by, society provides "news you can use" about hygiene, about cliques, about tattoos, about sex, about STDs, about alchohol, about drunk driving, about rape, about gang rape, about date rape, about date-rape drugs, about other drugs . . . the list of vices to bone up on is endless.

Take the example of drugs. The object of drug prevention programs, obviously, is to prevent youngsters from using and becoming dependent on illegal and destructive drugs. To that end, they are given in-depth schooling on the drug world, from the finer points of freebasing cocaine, to the assorted hardware of drug use, to the lingo of the streets. A 2005 report out of Washington state brought news of a sheriff's deputy who routinely took classrooms of high school students through a cooktop recipe for producing methamphetamine.[11] This comprehensive and methodical demystification of the dark side is considered our greatest tool to deter drug use. And maybe it is. But it says something about our society that not only do we assiduously avoid making that dark side taboo, we also purposefully familiarize our kids with it without any regard for its impact on the sensibility of young people. That is, in order to teach our young to function "safely" in a culture of exposure, we have decided, as guardians, as educators, to jade and coarsen them *in concert with that culture of exposure,* the all-enveloping, virtually inescapable media that dominate the young in particular. Rather than instill virtuous behaviors based on the judgment that it is "bad" to use drugs, or "bad" to engage in premarital sex, we choose to build a logical case against vice based only on the risks involved. And these we neutralize by also, logically, teaching the young to "take precautions." It is a halfhearted argument at best for "healthy" behavior. Without making such behaviors anathema, society merely tries to talk its jaded young out of indulging in them—and for no "good" reason.

But why the ambivalence? Examining the malignant influence of Timothy Leary, the most notorious drug pusher of them all, Roger Kimball analyzed the high-flown bunkum Leary sold to American elites glamorizing drug use in his day: namely, the Leary creed that turning on, tuning in, and dropping out is the way to enlarge human consciousness, power, and desire. "What depths of credulity," Kimball writes, "must be plumbed before someone could mistake a deliberate pharmacological assault on the nervous system for an experience of divine truth?"[12] An excellent question. But even as the proselytizers of druggy wisdom have by now burnt out to pasture on society's edges, more or less, such credulity still energizes and directs the cultural mainstream.

The fact is, as Kimball points out, Leary left more than a chemical mythology behind him. While regarded as a semibeloved crank today, a gonzo kind of Uncle LSD—a status that is downright creepy—Leary, along with his fellow champions of "chemical emancipation," produced a legacy with lasting consequences. Together, Kimball writes, they "helped to acclimatize our entire culture to a demand for blind emotional transport." This unslakeable demand for sensationalist "highs" of every kind—from eardrum-blasting music, to "extreme" sports pursuits, to computer-enhanced screen mayhem—helps explain why as a society we acknowledge the perils of drugs, for example, but as a culture we fail to stigmatize the attraction. Indeed, we have even attributed to that attraction a large measure of moral superiority. It is as if the empty pursuit of release—"blind emotional transport"—is thought to absolve mankind of all complicity in the storied corruptions of a humdrum world. Such pursuit, even sympathy for such pursuit, allows one to avoid or deny the realization that limitations—of obligation, of responsibility, of ability, of luck—necessarily constrain the life worth living. Such pursuit, even sympathy for such pursuit, becomes a way to avoid the hard work of *making* the constrained life worth living. Little wonder the insatiable rock 'n' roll outlaw—not the clean-living lawman—inspires our cultural imagination. And little wonder we find the clean-living lifestyle such a hard sell to kids. Socially acceptable, it remains a cultural drag.

This fact as much as anything else explains why it is that parents in our day settle for keeping their children *safe*. "Innocent" and "good" aren't even on the table. Keep them "safe" from drugs. Keep them "safe" from sex—or, rather, "safe" in sex. Parents want to give their kids "a place to go," presumably to be "safe" from drugs and in sex (or vice versa). It's not exactly the language of the apocalypse, but the tremulous way middle-class parents talk about their ridiculously privileged, middle-class kids—threatened by no press-gang, slavers, famine, plague, or pestilence—has the overwrought sound of forced melodrama about it. Of course, these same parents who want to keep their kids "safe" with "a place to go" also want to make sure the kids "feel good about themselves" at the same time, which somehow takes the sting out of the Sturm und Drang.

That place-to-go-to-be-safe-while-feeling-good-about-themselves could be a library or tennis court, but it's more likely to be a rec room for a sexy coed sleepover, or a rousing round of prom night alchohol poisoning. This is parenting-by-containment, a strategy reminiscent of policing tactics that seek to restrict the vice world to a so-called red-light district. Red-light-district parenting tries to contain adolescent vice to the home. To whit: The Colorado mother who pled guilty in 2005 to charges of sexual assault and contributing to the delinquency of a minor for allegedly providing marijuana, methamphetamine, and alchohol to high school boys in her home reportedly told police she was always "responsible" in never letting them leave the premises intoxicated.[13]

Sometimes, red-light-district parenting extends beyond the family home. Patrick McNeill rented three $199 hotel rooms on New Year's Eve in Harrison, New York, to keep his son and his son's fifteen- to nineteen-year-old pals "safe" while they rang in 2003 unsupervised—at least, that is, until police showed up to make twenty-six arrests on charges related to the presence of beer, hard liquor, and marijuana. McNeill didn't speak to the press, but Robert Morabito, a family friend and Rye town supervisor, was reported to have argued that not only were the teens "safe" at the hotel, they were also "responsible."

> If I know [my children] are going to be someplace—either a hotel or a house—it gives me a sense of security. There's always a chance that alchohol will be involved at that age. Let's face it, you and I know it happens. I think these children chose to be responsible and, unfortunately, they got in trouble for it.[14]

"Someplace"—hotel, house—equals "security"? If underage teens drinking the night away qualify as safe, not to mention responsible, then I suppose these dads should star in *Father Knows Best*. Sure, so long as the youngsters were drinking and drugging "someplace," they weren't driving drunk or drugged on the road, but that's a pretty narrow definition of "security." And what happens when they leave "someplace" to go "someplace" else? One of the sadder, stranger ironies of this case is that the safety-conscious, room-renting father, Patrick McNeill, had earlier sued the Manhattan bar—its corporate owner, the stockholders, and several employees—where his older son, Patrick McNeill, Jr., had become greatly intoxicated before drowning in the East River one night in 1997. According to *The Journal News,* the law under which McNeill sued the bar allows courts "to impose liability for negligence on sellers of alchoholic beverages for sales to people under the legal drinking age or those who are obviously intoxicated."

Would that we could count on parents to meet, at least, the sort of standard the law sets for bar owners. But these are the parents who need parents. Unfortunately, they have children instead—children to whom they give a de facto green light for red-light activities not in the children's best interests. Because just as virtue is no longer a cultural given, neither are "best interests." Like society, parents just hope Junior will make "better choices."

Based on what, exactly? The fabled "better choices" we hear about are inspired by neither self-respect nor moral grounding, once building blocks of bona fide parental guidance. All Junior needs these days, so the theory goes, is "information," and plenty of it. In Fairfax County, Virginia, tenth-grade sex education students, for example, learn a most expansive definition of "abstinence," ranging from, well, abstinence, to all sexual activity short of intercourse. They are then "advised to choose which definition best suits their individual values." As one teacher put it, "We're not endorsing anything. We're just giving information."[15] But "information" doesn't tell the whole story. Remember the Spur Posse? In the mid-1990s, this gang of nice middle-class boys from Lakeland, California, had all the information they needed to practice "safe sex" when they competed with one another for the most "scores"—intercourse—with local girls. (The winner, on being arrested for molesting a minor, age ten, claimed a tally of sixty-three.) What, Posse members wondered, had they done wrong? "They pass out condoms, teach sex education and pregnancy this and pregnancy that," one of the boys said. "But they don't teach us any rules."[16]

Author Kay S. Hymowitz pinpoints exactly why preparing youngsters to embark on a life not so much well-lived, but based on "informed decision-making" is doomed to fail. "The decision-making model assumes that kids already posess the values, beliefs, and self-awareness that go into such decisions," she writes. "Experts never seem to consider where the values, beliefs, and self-awareness behind these choices come from. Though these are all clearly a product of gradual cultural learning, experts act as if they are magically part of teen identity."[17] They are not. But today's grown-ups, parents included, have forgotten this—if they ever knew it.

Guided by what Hymowitz has called an "ethos of nonjudgmentalism," such parents have become little more than caretakers, manning fairly useless stations along the social safety net. These stations include the rock concert "quiet room," those improvised hideouts many venues provide for parents who would like to accompany their children to a concert while remaining out of earshot. From just such a quiet room at a Marilyn Manson concert in Washington, D.C., "each time a teenager was wheeled past the room from the mosh pit to the first-aid station, the parents raced to the door to make sure the afflicted was not theirs."[18] This is parenting by process of elimination. Other stations include a freak-dance floor in Washington state, where parental "chaperones" pride themselves on keeping things, if not clean, then "safe."[19] And "safe" it probably was—as "safe" as any professional pole-dancing strip club. This is parenting according to OSHA. The ubiquitous cell phone is another safety-net accessory, a "virtual umbilical cord," as a Florida writer put it, between herself and her twelve-year-old in the mosh pit at a "punk-pop" festival. ("I'm okay," the daughter yelled into her cell phone. "I'm going to body surf now."[20]) Wireless parenting? It's not that such concern isn't genuine. But it's useless in warding off harm—bodily or mental—and it doesn't teach children to protect themselves. Without a resilient set of moral beliefs, the most intensive parental involvement and monitoring leave the parental safety net riddled with gaping holes.

Nothing better illustrates the failures of the safety net than what now passes for spring break. What originated as the Easter holiday cum school-sanctioned week off in the spring has morphed into an MTV-inspired, parentally supported debauch for teens without so much as a term paper for a fig leaf. Only a post-grown-up culture could go along with the bizarre ritual: Every spring, generally law-abiding, maybe churchgoing, and almost certainly PTA-belonging American Babbitts pack their unchaperoned, often underage boys and girls onto airplanes that fly hundreds, if not thousands, of miles away to a shore where alcohol flows, hallucinatory drugs are available, and rampant, often public sexuality—on a bar top, on the beach—is the main attraction. And almost invariably these parents do so against their will.

"It's not like we have a choice. They didn't ask. They pretty much told us they were going," said one mother to the *Detroit Free Press,* which in recent years has made parental spring break angst something of a perrenial spring break feature.[21] It is a study well worth undertaking, particularly as conducted in 2001 by reporter Tamara Audi. It illustrates a balance of family power that is absurdly out of whack. "We"—parents who raise, finance (such trips typically cost between $800 and $2,000), and generally sweat blood for their offspring—have no choice;

"they"—financially dependent, emotionally immature, undoubtedly spoiled minors—tell us what's what. And why not? If anything, this decision to fly away—the product of intensive research into MTV specials and beer commercials—is the quintessential "informed choice."

Such is the dubious triumph of adolescent desire untrammeled by rules related to virtue. And such is the concrete evidence of how deeply entrenched the primacy of the adolescent experience has become. There is, in our society, an innately reflexive deference to juvenile desires—in this case, a nightmare of booze and sex come true—and it reveals a startling absence of will in the adult population. So much for self-esteem—that is, Mom's and Dad's. Depravity may not be a family value, exactly, but due to their acquiescence, they have made it the universal experience, even the assumed right, of all too many children. Reporting on the run-up to spring break, Tamara Audi of the *Detroit Free Press* elaborated on the phenomenon.

"I'm nervous. I don't like it," said Beverly Boyd, whose son Charles [was going to Cancún]. When the travel agent told a story about a teen getting hurt by jumping from balcony to balcony while drunk, Boyd said: "I don't want him to go but he's 18. *I don't have a choice.*"

Even parents of 17-year-olds, parents who paid for their kids to go, said *they felt powerless to stop them. . . .*

When Ruth Goldfaden's 17-year-old daughter Alise Anaya approached her about a spring break to Cancún, "I said no way," the Dearborn mother said.

But after a few parents gave permission to their daughters, Goldfaden found it *harder to say no.*

"It's a dilemma. *One parent gives in and then you're all giving in* because you thought the other ones did, so I should too," said Goldfaden. She finally gave her permission for Alise to travel unchaperoned to Cancún with 10 girlfriends. [Emphasis added.][22]

None of which is exactly Churchillian. But parents aren't the only spinally challenged adults out there.

In the Grosse Pointe, the pressure to send a teen on spring break is so great, a principal acknowledged the phenomenon in a letter to parents this spring.

"I know it's difficult to deny your children this opportunity. There is considerable peer pressure to be involved in these trips," wrote Grosse Pointe South High Principal Benjamin Walker in his letter to parents.

"After the students return to school I hear stories that truly concern me. Stories of substance and alchohol abuse, unwanted sexual advances from other students and sometimes adults, and other experiences that you and I do not want for our students."

Yet despite that, Walker's letter concludes: *"I am not necessarily suggesting that you deny your children this chance to travel. I'm not sure I could do it."* [Emphasis added.][23]

Too bad this wasn't a resignation letter. The fact is, "To Cancún or Not to Cancún" is hardly a question to stump Hamlet, Dear Abby, or Yogi Bear. A week at the beach, where blowing up a condom on a "booze cruise" rates as a cultural event, just isn't on a par with the Parthenon by moonlight—a fact the *Free Press* report on teenage spring-breakers at the Screw Party at Club La Boom makes pretty clear.

> Well into the night at last week's party, drunken teenagers removed their clothes on the dance floor. A group of three boys danced on the bar and stripped naked. Girls dancing nearby spanked them. The boys reached for the faces of the girls below them on the dance floor and beckoned them to perform a sex act. A few did; others were repelled.
>
> Another girl in a blue-and-white halter top danced on the other side of the bar, switching from dance partner to dance partner, and kissing each one. She pulled her top down around her waist. Teenage boys swarmed her, kissing her face and body. Other boys undid her shorts. She threw her head back, as if gulping for air. A young man on the fringe stuck his finger in her mouth. With his free hand, he videotaped her.[24]

To their limited credit, most parents fail to find such "travel" broadening; but they let their children go anyway. In fact, to try to ensure that the kids keep things straight and narrow—or at least make sure they return "safely" to their rooms at some point—a sizable subherd of the cowed parental crowd is actually accompanying their young to Cancún these days, staying in hotels some distance from the kiddies.

> "There was no way we were going to let them go without us," said Tina Phalen, who chaperoned her 17-year-old daughter Katie on a trip to Cancún last week with a large group of parents and friends from Fenton. The teens, 50 friends from the junior and senior classes of Lake Fenton High School, stayed in a hotel next door to a group of 40 parents.
>
> The parents in the group said they expected their kids would drink, many of them to excess, at nightclubs and by the pool.
>
> "It's not that we like it. It's not that we're OK with it, but it's naive to think it

doesn't happen," said Donna Warren, whose 17-year-old son Jase [*sic*] was part of the Fenton group. "At least we're here if they need us."[25]

But so are paramedics. And paramedics don't intentionally place children at risk in the first place. Being "here if they need us" just isn't an impressive act of parenting, particularly when "here" includes places children should be nowhere near. Such as "Spring Break Jail," the local lockup for Cancún tourists. While parents hunkered down by the hotel phone—one mother instructed her daughter to call whenever she returned to her hotel room—the *Free Press*'s Tamara Audi checked out the action at the jail where some undisclosed number of spring-breakers end up every year.

> At 4 A.M. on Tuesday of last week, Cancun police officer Manuel Cervantes brought in a sobbing 17-year-old girl from Macomb County who was arrested while having sex on the beach behind a popular club. The teenage boy she was with, Cervantes said, "got away from us. He got up and ran, ran, ran. And she was screaming 'Come back, don't leave me!' He never looked back."
>
> The girl stood in the corner of the jailhouse office shaking. Sand was caked on her face, on her stomach and legs. Her clothes, a black halter top and shorts, were twisted. Her shoulder-length hair was matted and damp. Dark eye makeup was smeared across her cheeks. She cried into her hands, "I want to go home. I want to go home."[26]

Whenever I read this, I get angry all over again—furious at the adults who exposed this young girl to a nightmare of degradation she will wake up from but never forget. Not even a cell phone call to Mom-alone-by-the-telephone would have saved this kid, or others like her, from anything—not from alcohol poisoning, not from sexual assault, and not from the lasting mortification of the predawn arrest.

Strangely enough, though, having dispensed with all manner of sexual stigmas, society no longer takes such humiliations seriously. The experiential innocence of virginity and the mental delicacy of youth have long fallen into ill-repute, either discarded as forgotten trophies of sexual liberation, or designated expendable hostages to feminist success. But this doesn't mean that innocence and purity offer nothing of value to the young—particularly to young girls. Might not Cancún Girl have found in their retention a welcome protection—a virtue that really was its own reward? And even if the answer is no—mental delicacy is a tough sell in the age of oral sex on a school bus—isn't it extremely strange that her own mommy and daddy would fail to think so? Apparently not.

"There if they need us" they sit, the virtue-free, values optional, no-confidence, no-content, caretaker parents, offering nothing resembling parental guidance.

And these are the *conscientious* parents. At least they have a sneaking suspicion that, as Mme. Clavell put it in the old kiddie book, "something is not right." Others haven't a clue as to what right is. A few days before September 11, 2001, the stuff of a tabloid editor's dreams came true when Robert Wien, a fifty-year-old Wall Street broker—senior managing director of a firm—and his forty-eight-year-old wife, Rochelle, were arrested at their home in Chappaqua, the tony town outside New York City that both *Reader's Digest* and Senator Hillary Clinton call home. Neighbors had called police to complain about a noisy Labor Day weekend party at the Wien residence, an end-of-summer-training bash for the high school football team.[27]

It wasn't the stereo system that got these two parents into trouble. It was the $345-per-hour stripper lying on her back on the patio interactively "performing" with whipped cream and sex toys for fifteen- to eighteen-year-old boys, a few girls, and the Wiens—Mr. and Mrs. Mom and Dad. "We couldn't believe parents would allow this kind of thing to go on in front of a group of kids," Det. Sgt. James Carroll told the local paper. He continued: "We always want parents to support and encourage their children's endeavors, but there's certainly a limit to what a parent should allow."[28]

A limit, he says: such as, maybe, perhaps, licking refrigerated dairy toppings off a nude dancer's breasts? Sounds reasonable—but not in this household. "Jeremy's parents were right there, having a good time with us," one football player told the *New York Post*. They were "right there" for the youngsters, but apparently that wasn't enough. Or maybe it was too much. Det. Sgt. Carroll explained that the couple was arrested for child endangerment because "they were right there and aware it was going on" and did nothing to stop it. Maybe that makes the Wiens the perfect twenty-first-century parental chaperones: always there—but not all there.

The Journal News called the fact that Wien was also a "parental adviser" for the town's Safe Rides program a "sad irony." To be sure, everything associated with this story has a certain sadness to it, but there's no irony in Rochelle Wien's role with Safe Rides, a local volunteer service that provides transportation home for "stranded" (read: drunk or high) teens unable to drive home from a party—one of those "safe" "someplaces" in which today's parents find "security," no doubt. The program itself—with or without Rochelle Wien—is the perfect institutional expression of the modern-day parental voice of nonauthority that unquestioningly rationalizes adolescent vice, in this case teen substance abuse. Indeed, *The Journal News* did suggest that the Chappaqua stripper party, which also included alchohol and marijuana, might well be seen as an argument against the Safe Rides concept. That argument, wrote the paper, goes like this: Safe Rides "represents a kind of organized acceptance of teen-age alchohol abuse." "Organized acceptance" means organized enablement, and "organized enablement" means organized encouragement.

They're going to do it anyway, so let's keep them "safe." The youngsters at the Wien party were certainly "safe" as far as things went—safely lapping up the whipped cream the stripper sprayed on her body, safely inserting sex toys into her orifices. In their hostess, Rochelle "Safe Rides" Wien, they also had a "safe ride" home if the drugs and alchohol they imbibed at her home proved too much them. But how much *protection*—mental or physical—is there in being safe to do harmful things?

But maybe the Wiens should get one measly point for "being there," after all. While this little bash was hardly the first or last time teens in Chappaqua, or any other leafy American suburb, partied with drugs, alchohol, or strippers, what drew public scorn and condemnation was that the Wiens, as parents, could stand by, do nothing, and fail to see there was anything to do. But what about the parents who don't even stand by, do nothing, and fail to see there is anything to do?

The Wiens of Westchester were spared jail time after pleading guilty to the misdemeanor charge of endangering the welfare of a child, and sentenced to one year of probation and one hundred hours of community service. There were harsher consequences. As a result of this bona fide scandal, both parents lost their jobs—Robert Wien as senior managing director at Josephthal & Co., and Rochelle Wien as special-education teacher. (No word on whether her second job as a masseuse also suffered.) Insult to injury, the Safe Rides program dropped her from its roster of safe riders, and the couple also lost their membership at the Metropolis Country Club in Greenburgh.[29] In a therapeutic age of vacuous values and flexible forgiveness, the Wiens hit the wall. Is that because there still exists a moral standard—an accepted level of aspirational virtue—in their community at large?

One of the most fascinating stories to emerge in the wake of the party was the fallout at the high school, one of those overbuilt dream campuses that is consistently rated among the top public high schools in the country. But for all the high-tech labs, manicured playing fields, and cutting-edge media equipment, there suddenly appeared to be something lacking: a common sense of right and wrong. The local paper fit the problem into a headline: "It Was Like Stripper Party Was 'No Big Deal': Principal Seeks Help of Community in Teaching Teens Ethics."[30]

Lots of luck. On conducting an investigation into the incident, the principal

determined that no members of the football team had used drugs or alchohol at
the party; presumably non-team members who did so failed to rate administration attention. The administration also discovered that the team had hired and
paid for the stripper.

> [The principal] said she met with the football team last week and was surprised to
> find that the boys didn't think they had done anything wrong. She said one player
> informed her that he was 18 and could do what he pleased. Another said that no
> one was hurt, so he couldn't see any problem, she said. Yet another told her the
> stripper was just doing her job.[31]

And why not? Surely, Greeley's brave new kids have learned that "wrong" is up
to the individual, and that an eighteen-year-old has the personal autonomy to
hire what their enlightened world might call a "sex worker" so long as they keep
one commandment: Safety first.

> With that attitude, Mason said school officials decided not to mete out swift pun-
> ishment, such as the forfeiture of the squad's first game last Friday night. Instead,
> she said the school would work with the players so they understand what went
> wrong.
>   "We've got to instill a basic moral compass, to show them what is good and
> what is not," she said.[32]

Not that she was prepared to give them a punitive push in the right direction.
In lieu of "swift punishment"—quaint words—the principal settled on a sentence
of community service: namely, that team members design a community service
program. Maybe this made the team members "feel good about themselves"—
although this doesn't seem to have been a group suffering from too little self-
esteem. Still, it's difficult to see how it would give them any sense of moral
direction. Of course, where did the boys' sense of moral disorientation come from
in the first place? The answer is from the same sort of upper-middle-class parents
who cluck-clucked at the stripper bust, blackballed the Wiens at the club, and, all
too often, vacate the premises whenever Junior plans to party.

Or vice versa. That is, Junior may plan the party after his parents vacate the
premises. That's not good, either. If the story of "Chappaqua Chaperones Go
Wild" tells us that "being there" isn't necessarily the parental answer, neither are
nowhere-to-be-seen moms and dads. Parental absenteeism was the problem in
another notorious teen party that ended not in social scandal, but in the murder
of a fifteen-year-old girl.

It was another rich-kid party, this time in the posh Westwood section of Los

Angeles. The host was Howie Hendler, a sophomore at the private Milken Community High School. After he sent out an instant message (IM) saying his parents were going to Las Vegas for the weekend and he was throwing a party, about one hundred kids, many of whom were students at exclusive L.A. private schools, showed up at the Hendler home for the big bash. Before the night was over, Deanna Maran, a fifteen-year-old honor student at Santa Monica High School, had been stabbed in the heart by seventeen-year-old Katrina Sarkissian, a former student at tony Harvard-Westlake School. Rushed to a hospital by friends, Deanna died in an emergency room shortly after midnight.

The murder motive? Earlier in the evening, Deanna had chastised Katrina's younger sister, fifteen-year-old Sabrina Bernstein, for carelessly breaking some flowerpots at the home where the unsupervised party was taking place. There was some shoving, and the younger sister telephoned her big sister, Katrina, to come to the party. "Katrina, a blonde who looked like a starlet, drove up in a black Jeep Cherokee and asked, 'Who messed with my sister?' " reported Sara Davidson in O magazine. "Deanna stepped forward." In the course of the "bitch fight" that followed, which was egged on by a ring of cheering teens, Katrina fatally stabbed Deanna. Katrina committed suicide the following day.[33]

There is much to be said about the importation of the gangland mores—prison slang, prison clothes, even violence—into the prep school circles of the most privileged stratum. Indeed, in the course of a recent murder trial in Virginia for the 2003 killing of seventeen-year-old Brenda Paz, a former member of the brutal Salvadoran gang, Mara Salvatrucha (aka MS-13), *The Washington Post* made note of this phenomenon. Court testimony, the paper reported, revealed striking similarities between young gang members and ordinary adolescents, so many of whom pass their significant waking hours at shopping malls, multiplexes, and arcades, cultivating the same styles and attitudes down to the same baggy clothes of jailhouse chic.[34]

Such behaviors seem to take hold in the absence of a civilizing, mature dynamic—adult influence, adult rules, adult confidence. To be sure, the Westwood party lacked adults period. But even in the aftermath of the tragedy—the point at which adults reentered the scene to restore a semblance of order, mainly by shuffling around guilt and blame—these adults were unable to fill the vacuum.

From the district attorney came a single misdemeanor battery charge against the murderer's fifteen-year-old sister, Sabrina Bernstein, that resulted in a sentence of one hundred hours of community service and $100 in reparations. The murderer's mother, Angelique Bernstein, settled out of court with the Maran family for $300,000, rather than face trial for failing to contain Katrina, who had a long and even violent history of mental problems; Angelique Bernstein simultaneously brought suit against the city of Los Angeles and three policemen for Katrina's death by suicide. The Marans also brought suit—dismissed—against Shelley and Barbara Hendler, the Vegas-vacationing owners of the house where the fatal, underage party had gone off unsupervised.

> The Hendlers didn't know that 17-year-old Katrina Sarkissian would come to their home while they were vacationing in Las Vegas and stab Maran in the chest, [Santa Monica Superior Court Judge Linda] Lefkowitz found. They also didn't know that their 19-year-old son, Scott Hendler, would have an unsupervised party where underaged teenagers were drinking alcohol, the ruling noted.[35]

In other words, given that the Hendlers had no "heightened foreseeability"—read: no crystal ball—they were off the hook, simultaneously setting a dangerous legal precedent for the see-no-evil, hear-no-evil, speak-no-evil parenting model. Who was to blame? The entire community recoiled not only from taking responsibility, but from even assigning responsibility. "This was our September 11," one parent told a reporter, blaming "violence" for the crime. At a memorial service for Deanna, one of her teachers, Anoushka Franke, reportedly urged mourners not even to feel guilty. "No one here is responsible for our loss, and your guilt will only increase the tragedy."[36]

Frankly, a little guilt—a lot of guilt—and some profoundly regretful second thoughts about adolescent social life might actually decrease the chances of the next tragedy. On the very night of the murder, Deanna's mother, Harriet Maran, had begun to have second thoughts about her daughter's night on the town, leaving a note on the fifteen-year-old's pillow that said: "You are never going to leave again without telling me where you're going and leaving a phone number." As deeply concerned as she was, Mrs. Maran devised only mere containment strategies—a phone number, an address, a curfew—that wouldn't have have saved poor Deanna from her fate in this tragic case. Only the kind of strict parenting that keeps a kid home on a Saturday night, or on a parentally vetted (and quite possibly boring) outing, would have given her a chance. The fact is, parents can't count on other parents to "be there" to set the rules that keep children mainly "safe." Such chaperoning is outmoded in twenty-first-century culture. In the end, even Deanna's family looked elsewhere for answers to the senselessness of it all, eventually establishing the Deanna Maran Foundation for Non-Violence to teach "about the symptoms of violence, how to prevent escalation, and finally, how to stop it."

It wasn't poor "conflict resolution" skills that killed this girl. Deanna Maran died in a crime of idiotically misguided passion that erupted in a chaotic, adolescent milieu where a sharp warning about broken flowerpots became words to die for. On some important level, Deanna also died for trying to impose a sense of order lost in the absence of adults.

Writing in 1999 in *Commentary* magazine, Chester Finn, Jr., considered various trends in contemporary parenting, from aiding and abetting bad behaviors to the failure to shape good ones. Finn proposed that this de facto parental paralysis—the same syndrome that permits spring break madness to recur, organizes strip parties for minors, and sets teens free to roam into trouble—is an inherited cultural infirmity.

> Heirs or alumni of the 1960s counterculture, they [parents] tend to be ambivalent about the exercise of authority, fearful of upsetting their children or of quashing their self-expression, eager at all costs to appear "supportive." When faced with unsavory friends, or evidence of drugs or alcohol, they are reluctant to intervene, for did they not, too, "experiment" in their youth? This style of "passive parenting," as Hymowitz calls it, comprises equal parts incompetence, feel-good psychology, and the remnants of 60's ideology. The combination is deadly.[37]

Finn confines his main observations to the interplay among parents, children, and schools. At the same time, however, Finn, a former assistant secretary of education under Ronald Reagan, hones in on a colossal chink in the largely conservative argument against the spread of public education into domains once controlled by parents, churches, and neighborhoods: sex education, social services including drug counseling, and the teaching of ethics and politics now dominated by PC doctrine. Central to the conservative response has been the core conviction that parents should be setting more of the course of their children's education and that the state should be setting less of it. But, as the title of Finn's article asks, "Can Parents Be Trusted?"

At best, the answer is only sometimes—the dirty little secret of twenty-first-century life in America. Across the pond, in Great Britain, land of Oxford, Eton, and Hogwarts, the implications of parenting lapses have actually entered political discourse, with Prime Minister Tony Blair specifically calling on parents to lend their support to school disciplinary actions instead of taking their child's side without question. "When I was younger, if a pupil was in trouble with their teacher, they were in trouble with their parents. It is not always the case today, but it should be," he said.[38] In 2005, Britain kicked off an unprecedented program to improve basic social standards in children attending the country's twenty thousand elementary schools. The British Department of Education put school heads, or principals, on notice that schools should no longer assume that "the development of social and emotional skills is the responsibility of parents."[39] This prompted David Hart, leader of the National Association of Head Teachers, to say, "Once again, schools are being used to make good the deficiencies of parents. I think there's a distinct danger that we are drifting more and more into the

nanny state." On the eve of his retirement, Hart went on to lambaste the irre-
sponsibility of parents across the socioeconomic spectrum who have failed to instill either "basic social standards" in their children or respect for the authority
of a teacher in the classroom.[40]

This isn't to suggest that there aren't legions of stalwart mothers and fathers,
abroad and at home, successfully bringing up responsible, engaged, and decent
citizens of tomorrow. But while Britain has brought this issue into the political
open, we must rely on a range of anecdotal reports and headlines indicating a
similar problem: that teachers may no longer depend on parental support regarding even modest academic and behavioral standards. In Wisconsin, a parent
sues a school over a mandatory homework requirement for an honors math class.
In North Carolina, a father asks a judge to overrrule a teacher who gave his
daughter a bad grade. An Ohio teen sues her school district and eleven teachers
for $6 million, also for bad grades.[41–43]

These particular suits were dismissed, but that's not always the outcome. In
Tennessee, parents complained that the public posting of the honor roll "em-
barasses" the kids "excluded" from the list—so, on the advice of school counsel,
good-bye honor roll.[44] Then there are the honor students "excluded" from being
class valedictorian. Under parental pressure, some schools have abolished the
distinction altogether, while others have simply distinguished more students. (In
2004, Soquel High School in Santa Cruz, California, graduated no fewer than
eleven valedictorians.) In Arizona, a high school English teacher named Elizabeth Joice received a lawyer-letter the day before commencement exercises
threatening suit if a student she had failed didn't graduate with her class. "Joice
said the student plagiarized work, failed a paper and did not attend makeup ses-
sions," reported Fox News. "School officials caved and the student was able to
retake a test five hours before graduation and receive her diploma." Then there
was the Kansas biology teacher, Christine Pelton, who failed 28 out of her 118
students on a final project for plagiarism. Parental pressure drove the school
board to decrease the students' penalties and order the teacher to reduce the
value of the project toward the final grade. Pelton refused. And Pelton resigned.[45] All of which helps explain why the number of teachers buying liability
insurance has jumped 25 percent between 2000 and 2005.[46]

Manners and conduct, too, are deconstructed by postmodern Mom and Dad.
"For every parent who enthusiastically endorses school uniforms, there are many
more who object to even the most rudimentary dress code, like the families in a
posh New York suburb who protested collectively when a local middle school
tried to ban tank tops," Finn writes. Some parents in Modesto, California, even
signed a student petition in 2005 against a high school dress code proposing an
end to see-through clothing, among other sartorial distractions. Nor can teachers

count on parents to help them enforce minimal discipline, either. In wealthy Scarsdale, New York, two hundred intoxicated high school students, including five later hospitalized with alchohol poisoning, showed up for the homecoming dance. After twenty-eight students were suspended, a few of their concerned parents called the school to complain, but not about the binge drinking that left kids as young as fourteen "vomiting, incoherent, or on the verge of passing out," and not about the two families that hosted alchoholic pre-party festivities in their homes. They called to complain that "suspensions would mar their children's college transcripts." Principal John Klemme—a bona fide grown-up—held the line against the buck-passing parents, insisting, "There are consequences for what you do. That's a hard lesson, but perhaps the more important lesson a child can learn."[47]

But it's the hardest lesson to learn from parents who teach that consequences can be changed—or possibly avenged. The day after a teenage girl was removed from a Maryland school bus for rowdy behavior, the girl's mother blocked the bus's path, spat at the driver, pulled an ice pick from her purse, and then plopped herself on the bus's hood.[48] In Connecticut, a father (and art teacher at a Catholic school), angered that his daughter was suspended from the softball team for missing a game to attend a prom, beat the coach with an aluminum bat. The father was charged with first-degree assault and later sentenced to five years probation.[49] In Pennsylvania, a mother went to court to overturn her thirteen-year-old daughter's expulsion for having performed oral sex on a thirteen-year-old classmate while on a school bus. The mother reportedly maintained the suspension was unfair because the school "was not clear in its written policies that oral sex on a bus was unacceptable behavior." Case dismissed.[50] In Montana, parents of two eleven-year-old boys who cut class one winter day and died of exposure and alchohol poisoning sued the local school district for $4 million for failing to safeguard the boys. Members of the Confederated Salish and Kootenai Tribes, the parents further claimed in their lawsuit that the district had discriminated against American Indians by "failing to properly select, train and implement Native American staff who are sensitive to the disability of alchoholism."[51] A jury found the school district not guilty. In Pennsylvania, the parents of a fourteen-year-old boy who allegedly solicited funds on the Internet to hire an assassin to murder his algebra teacher reportedly sued the school district to overturn Junior's expulsion and seek monetary damages. The suit was dismissed twice.[52] And in northern California, in 2004, the parents of a fifteen-year-old who allegedly planned a Columbine-style assault on his high school cafeteria reportedly filed suit seeking "millions" from the school district for failing to provide counseling.[53]

Whether such parenting is purely cretinous or baldly opportunistic, or whether Mom and Dad, in therapeutic parlance, just don't have their priorities straight, it's not surprising that schools find themselves trying to pick up some of the moral slack. (This is a problem in a culture in which even a small number of teachers have been unmasked as sexual predators.) Such efforts by the schools take us back, circularly, to the basic conservative complaint against the education system. "With more and more children arriving in the classroom in obvious need of a moral compass, teachers, counselors, and administrators have willy-nilly taken on more and more nonacademic duties, reaching into every corner of their students' lives," Chester Finn writes. And this is exactly the problem—"exactly what conservatives have pinpointed," he adds. "Schools are no good at this sort of thing, and when they attempt it, they are apt to resort to politically correct fads of dubious merit, from AIDS prevention to training in self-esteem."[54]

Schools aren't alone in their attempts to fill all those empty parental shoes out there. We see legislatures across the country passing or considering bans on the sorts of minor behaviors and entertainments that were once quashed and controlled by reflexive parenting. No more. In addition to legal controls on the sale of cigarettes and alcohol, we now see legislation against body piercing for minors, bans on the sale or rentals to minors of sexually and violently explicit video games, even laws against junk food machines in school lunchrooms. We see schools devising dress codes that parents should be enforcing, and schools generating contracts with students to ensure minimal decorum on the dance floor. The lower house in the Texas legislature even approved a ban on "overtly sexually suggestive" cheerleading—the sort of moves that just the thought of Mom and Dad should chill.[55] Following a surge of teen traffic fatalities in Maryland in 2004, state lawmakers began considering new laws requiring more supervised teen time behind the wheel, and restrictions on when and with whom teens may drive—exactly the sorts of conditions parents should impose, but don't. As Patricia O'Neill, president of the Montgomery County Board of Education, told *Bethesda Magazine,* "Sometimes parents need laws to give them the moral backbone to do what's right."[56]

But shouldn't parents—above all citizens—be the ones lending the moral backbone to the laws? Certainly, but they're not doing it. This abject failure of moral will is one reason Power to the Parents is not the panacea we might traditionally expect it to be. The fact is, the parental backbone has joined the tailbone as an evolutionary remnant of what once was. Without such spinal support, no wonder it's so difficult for them to hold up an effective safety net for the kids. And no wonder a nanny state increasingly tries to pick up the slack.

Pondering what conditions might ever bring despotism to American democracy, Tocqueville imagined an America that would have seemed downright science-fictional in the nineteenth century—a nation characterized, on the one hand, by an "innumerable multitude of men, alike and equal, constantly circling around in pursuit of the petty and banal pleasures with which they glut their souls," and, on the other, by the "immense, protective power" of the state. In the twenty-first century, however, it begins to sound quite familiar.

> That power is absolute, thoughtful of detail, orderly, provident, and gentle. It would resemble parental authority if, fatherlike, it tried to prepare its charges for a man's life, but on the contrary, it only tries to keep them in perpetual childhood. It likes to see the citizens enjoy themselves, provided that they think of nothing but enjoyment. It gladly works for their happiness but wants to be the sole agent and judge of it. It provides for their security, forsees and supplies their necessities, facilitates their pleasures, manages their principal concerns, directs their industry, makes rules for their testaments, and divides their inheritances. Why should it not entirely relieve them from the trouble of thinking and all the cares of living?[57]

We may not have gotten all the way to Tocqueville's nanny state—just give us time—but it's within our sight. Maybe this is life's revenge on the Baby Boom, the generation perpetually in revolt but never its own master. Then again, maybe it represents the triumph of Baby Boomers who long ago decided not to grow up. The question is, will we always have to live with the consequences of their success?

5. SOPHISTICATED BABIES

What's going to happen to the children
When there aren't any more grown-ups?
—NOEL COWARD[1]

hen we talk about how "sophisticated" twenty-first-century children are—and we often do—we are describing youngsters with "a wisdom beyond their years," a knowingness that renders kid stuff, from Peter Pan collars to curfews, inadequate and inappropriate, sometimes insultingly so. This strangely touchy state of juvenile sophistication—if sophistication it is—is not to be confused with erudition, proficiency, or even, in most cases, experience. It is chiefly a condition of exposure to behaviors and tastes once relegated to the adult world—and often to its darkest corners.

How this came to be Adolescent's Fate is the story of our evolution from a mainly preliterate past, in which childhood didn't exist, to an increasingly postliterate future, in which childhood will cease to exist. In betweeen, of course, childhood has flourished, entering its golden age between 1850 and 1950. As a phase distinct from adulthood, childhood developed much earlier. Neil Postman argues convincingly that it was Johannes Gutenberg, who, in the middle of the fifteenth century, "with the aid of an old winepress, gave birth to childhood."[2] Prior to the development of literate adulthood, he writes, there existed no childhood; that is, no significant gap between old lives and young lives that physical growth alone wouldn't ultimately and effortlessly bridge. That's mainly because in the medieval world, "everyone shared the same information environment"— not to mention the same room—"and therefore lived in the same social and intellectual world."[3] Indeed, what we refer to as a "child" (in the Middle Ages, the word could also denote kinship, not age) entered adulthood at age seven, which, as Postman points out, is the age at which children have command over speech. In that preliterate time, no further command of language, of knowledge, was required.

But as the printing press played out its hand it became obvious that a new kind of adulthood had been invented. From print onward, adulthood had to be earned. It became a symbolic, not biological, achievement. From print onward, the young would have to *become* adults, and they would have to do it by learning to read, by entering the world of typography. And in order to accomplish that they would require education. Therefore, European civilization reinvented schools. And by so doing, it made childhood a necessity.[4]

Today, as the Age of Gutenberg has given way, rapidly and successively, to the Age of Television and the Age of Internet, the dynamic has changed again. It has reverted, albeit on a highly technological level, to a communal information environment more medieval than modern. Once again, children are privy to what Postman calls the "rapid and egalitarian disclosure of the total content of the adult world," this time disseminated through various electronic media. And once again, grown-up sanctums are increasingly turned over to the kids, as dining room tables give way to trampolines, and coffee tables lose precedence to dollhouses. More than two decades ago, Postman pointed out that "the six-year-old and the sixty-year-old are equally qualified to experience what television has to offer."[5] Today, more media only offer more experience.

Or, rather, more media *to* experience. Much of what "sophisticates" our kids is far removed from experience, or even reality—unless, that is, experience and reality exist within a cathode-ray-lit screen of glass, a studio-recorded song, a choreographed MTV video, or a special-effects-filled movie. Fashion megamogul Tommy Hilfiger's assessment of the contemporary juvenile condition is typical: "They are so much more sophisticated than when I was growing up—they're computer literate, they carry portable phones, they're bombarded with cool media from MTV to *Beverly Hills 90210*."[6]

"Bombarded" is right; but "cool"? "Sophisticated"? To be sure, MTV sets the pace of adolescence, with a massive young audience that includes 73 percent of all boys and 78 percent of all girls between the ages of twelve and nineteen. And what do they see? You think you know, but you probably don't. Over spring break in 2004, a conservative watchdog group called the Parents Television Council (PTC) monitored the music video channel for 171 long hours. The report dutifully tallied up 1,548 sexual scenes. These included 3,056 depictions of sex or nudity, and 2,881 verbal sexual references. The PTC went on to crunch the numbers: "That means that children watching MTV are viewing an average of 9 sexual scenes an hour with approximately 18 sexual depictions and 17 instances of sexual dialogue and innuendo." Behind the sterility of the statistics lies much muck: a boy and a girl searching sheets for semen stains; boys discussing the benefits of detachable underwear; boys and girls making "human sundaes," with boys eating cherries and whipped cream from girls' bodies . . . and that still leaves 3,053 more "depictions" to go.[7]

In those same 171 MTV hours, not too surprisingly, PTC analysts also recorded 1,518 uses of unedited foul language and an additional 3,127 bleeped profanities. Running the numbers, "that means young children watching MTV are subjected to roughly 8.9 unbleeped profanities per hour, and an additional 18.3 profanities per hour." This sort of decimal-point precision might provoke a hoot of *Saturday Night Live*–style derision, but the reality is way beyond satire. Song lyric example: "[Bleeped 'Fuck'] you, you [bleeped 'ho']. Another: "And love to get her [bleeped 'pussy'] licked by another [bleeped 'bitch']."

Whether such filth passes for "cool" aside, "sophisticated" is hardly the word for Hilfiger's child—if, by "sophisticated," we mean the twentieth-century connotation, as delineated by Roget's, of being "chic, disillusioned, tasteful, ungullible, worldly-wise." Chic? Tasteful? Please: Think assorted piercings and assorted *American Pies*. Disillusioned? These systematically demystified juveniles harbor few illusions to be dissed. Ungullible? Worldly wise? Not girls who believe performing oral sex ushers in a happy adolescence; and not boys who believe mommies should give them wake-up calls—in college. Hilfiger's "so much more sophisticated" child is, in fact, society's so much more exposed child— exposed to a numbing inundation of imagery and information once either unimagined entirely, or strictly withheld from public view.

Childhood as we have known it isn't compatible with such exposure. Postman explains why.

> One might say that one of the main differences between an adult and a child is that the adult knows certain facts about certain facets of life—its mysteries, its contradictions, its violence, its tragedies—that are not considered suitable for children to know; that are, indeed, shameful to reveal to them indiscriminately. In the modern world, as children move toward adulthood, we reveal these secrets to them, in what we believe to be a psychologically assimilable way. But such an idea is only possible in a culture in which there is a sharp distinction between the adult world and the child's world, and where there are institutions that express that difference.[8]

That sharp distinction, dulled by the time Postman was writing, is all but imperceptible now as our various and sundry institutions express no difference. They offer pedicures to preschoolers; they sell "pimp" and "ho" costumes for trick-or-treaters. They dispense condoms to fifth-graders (that's ten-year-olds)[9]; they eroticize preteen girls to advertise jeans. Postman points to a turning point in the law when, in 1981, the New York State Court of Appeals erased the distinction between adults and children in judging whether a film was pornographic.[10] In other words, the court saw no reason to distinguish between obscenity cases involving adults and those involving children. If a filmed sex act was deemed obscene, it was obscene. If a filmed sex act was not deemed obscene, it was not obscene. Big deal, the court in effect said, if it involved prepubescent "actors." The U.S. Supreme Court would ultimately strike down this appeals court ruling. But the 1981 ruling is significant nonetheless, indicating that in an important sector of American legal thinking on the regulation of pornography, the adult world and the child world were becoming one.

Once upon a medieval time, the lack of privacy in society—its absence both as an imagined concept and even as an achievable physical condition—made separate spheres for children and adults impossible. Today, a new lack of privateness—and a new lack of concern—has blurred the lines between the two domains. "The old adage that 'children should be seen and not heard' has been replaced with the presence of children in almost every previously adult-only situation," writes psychologist Mary S. Foote. She lists the workplace, exclusive restaurants, even decision-making processes as places the young are now routinely found. "An example is the five-year-old I know whose parents let him decide which preschool to attend," Foote writes, explaining: "Children who are allowed too much decision-making power too soon often suffer from high anxiety. This is because young children profit from the safety and security of knowing their parents are in full charge of their welfare."[11]

But maybe the notion of what it means to be in charge of a child's welfare has changed. Children attend R-rated movies—with their parents in charge (or with a parentally approved "R-card" that allows children in sans adult).[12] Children sit on sex education advisory committees—also with their parents in charge. One such committee in Montgomery County, Maryland, included among its advisers an eleven-year-old girl, someone still eligible to order from a kiddie menu (the controversial course it devised was ultimately ditched in 2005 under parental and legal pressure).[13] Society takes it on itself to rule out garlic and cayenne as being too spicy for her years (think: kids' menus), but not birth control methodology and polymorphous sexual experimentation.

Meanwhile, in Hollywood, child advocates have found themselves a sad, new cause: child actors in so-called risky roles that dramatize pedophilia, kidnapping, rape, voyeurism, and all manner of violence and menace. Almost invariably, their stage mothers and fathers bar their budding Barrymores from a "risky" movie's final cut—not buying, apparently, assurances from the likes of Nicole Kidman that her ten-year-old costar in *Birth* didn't understand his lines referring to sexual intercourse, or why he was crawling naked into the bathtub with her.[14] Such parental discretion after the filmed fact, however, hasn't checked the spread of a new form of depression afflicting certain child thespians in Beverly Hills.[15] Nor does it check the flow of other people's children into "risky" movie audiences. And that includes movies rated PG-13, which, despite what parents tell themselves to believe, routinely depict head-busting, throating-slitting violence and even torture, and include fluent, frequent references to sex and oral sex. They even feature lap dancing, pole dancing, and so much profanity (from "shit" to "fuck," from "bitch" to "slut," from "shit hole" to "asshole") that the *Washington Post*'s Liza Mundy, who made an in-depth study of the genre in 2003, wrote "it seems fair to say that kids will hear more bad language, and more forms of bad language, in PG-13 movies than they will in Rs." In Mundy's account, Nell Minow, whose father Newton Minow was an FCC commissioner, "says that her father always marveled at how parents will let Hollywood say things to their children that they would have an ordinary person on the street arrested for saying."[16]

But how do we get off the street? Where do we go for what is stultifyingly, if reassuringly, known as "decent family fare"? In a 2004 *New York Times Magazine* article about casual sex among young teens, writer Benoit Denizet-Lewis agreed to interview a fifteen-year-old boy at Hooters, the chain restaurant famous for waitresses who take orders from behind cascades of cleavage. Worried that he might be "aiding and abetting the delinquency of a minor," the writer phoned the restaurant to inquire whether there's an age requirement to dine at Hooters. "The woman who picks up seems annoyed I would even ask," he writes. " 'No, we're a family restaurant,' she says." But of course. And the Hooters bunny and her Hooters bosom are just another part of the family: "Welcome to the facets of adult life—and would you like fries with that?"[17]

Except for the part about violence—or, rather, meticulously staged depictions of violence—Postman's practically Tolstoyan list of adult experience (mysteries, contradictions, violence, and tragedies) is not at all what children are encountering in formerly adult venues. Instead, they enter a world of sensation in which a chaotic creed of abandon supercedes all civilizing sermons of restraint. It is a creed born of our mother motto of modern behavior—sex, drugs, and rock 'n' roll—and it continues to whet our appetites for the hedonism they promise.

And not just juvenile appetites. The world of sensation engulfs grown-up and child alike. And just as we have erased the boundaries that once defined the domain of traditional childhood, we have also erased the boundaries that once regulated the patterns of average adulthood. Such boundaries—long established according to religious commandments, the law, and related conventions of self-restraint—largely vanished from the courts and the culture by the end of the 1960s.

After a century in and out of the courts of law and public opinion, the civil libertarians of the Free Speech Movement, which author Rochelle Gurstein in her landmark study, *The Repeal of Reticence,* calls "the party of exposure," saw pretty much all forms of censorship outlawed. Finally, the law protected *Ulysses*; huzzahs in the academy. Of course, if the law protected *Ulysses,* the law also protected—to take rather less literary but no less victorious plaintiffs—*Trim, MANual,* and *Grecian Guild Pictorial.* Such porno magazines might not have received three cheers in the faculty lounge, but, along with such salacious, if unread novels as *Fanny Hill,* they did receive precisely the same protections as *Ulysses* from the Supreme Court.

These victories represented something new: not a new taste for pornography, which, as vaults at the Vatican reveal, is ancient; but rather an unprecedented respectability for pornography born of "going legit," of operating a newly lawful booth in Ye Olde Public Square. Remember *Screw* pornographer Al Goldstein's kvelling delight: "I never dreamed we'd be in the Javits Center. It is such a class place." After the courts had done their work, "class places" were increasingly X-rated accessible. As Walter Berns wrote in 1971, "the Supreme Court made pornography a growth industry by giving it a license to operate in the accessible and legitimate market, thereby bringing buyer and seller together."[18] The sluice gates had opened, and the once-filtered mainstream was instantly awash in fetid waters. Rochelle Gurstein describes the immediate and curious impact.

> The brazen appearance of pornography in places where it had not been seen before—in over-the-counter books and magazines, on movie screens, on the stage, and on the streets—was so outrageous and its crass commerical spirit so different from that of early targets of censorship that even some of the most distinguished free-speech advocates began to ponder the wisdom of their lifelong commitment. In 1964, Donald Friede, publisher of suppressed novels such as Radclyffe Hall's *Well of Loneliness* and Theodore Dreiser's *An American Tragedy* voiced second thoughts: "When I see some of the books published today, I cannot . . . but wonder if our fight against censorship in the twenties was really wise. . . . *Fanny Hill* in paper! And *Naked Lunch* in any form! But I suppose there are some people still willing to play the piano in the literary brothel. Certainly the pay is good."[19]

Morris Ernst, one of the twentieth century's foremost foes of censorship who had mounted a winning defense of *Ulysses* in 1933, also fell prey to a nasty bout of second thoughts, which he passed onto readers of *The New York Times* in early 1970. Having spent a lifetime striking, pushing, eroding the legal limits on utter freedom, Ernst suddenly looked around and declared, on the record, that he would "not choose to live in a society without limits to freedom." He was shocked, he told the paper, by the spread of "four-letter words out of context," and by "the performance of sodomy on the stage and masturbation in the public area." He continued: "I deeply resent the idea that the lowest common denominator, the most tawdry magazine, pandering for profit . . . should be able to compete in the marketplace with no restraints."[20] His admission was equal parts baffling and infuriating. Having done his yeoman bit to create that marketplace with no restraints, Ernst had decided he wanted no part of it—and, worse, no responsibility for it. Walter Berns summed up Ernst's absurd argument this way: " 'Ulysses,' yes, said Morris Ernst, but 'sodomy on the stage or masturbation in the public area,' no!"[21]

Having it both ways hadn't happened. How could it have? The arguments that destroyed the legal and moral bases for censorship of obscenity and pornography apply to trash as well as to art. By the time the courts, in effect, declared obscenity was dead, they had killed something vital to a healthy society: the faculty of judgment that attempts to distinguish between what is obscene and what is not obscene—the avowedly "grown-up" sensibility of an outmoded authority figure who had long relied on a proven hierarchy of taste and knowledge until it was quite suddenly leveled. From this leveling came another casualty: society's capacity, society's willingness, to make even basic distinctions between trash and art.

The lack of vision in Ernst and others on such crucial points blinded them to the inevitable toxic fallout of their culture wars. And in the end, what did they win? Ernst's beloved but impenetrable *Ulysses* remains the purview of a tiny elite; four-letter words are the language of the masses and elites alike; and on network television, masturbation is a laugh track punch line. To wit: Reporting from the primetime trenches, Brent Bozell describes a scene in a 2004 episode of ABC's lowercase (and lower-life) teen series, *life as we know it*. Teenaged Jonathan is in the bathroom when his mother knocks on the door. His father calls out, "God, Mary, give the kid a break. He's probably masturbating."[22]

Let freedom ring. "Having begun by exempting the work of art from the censorship laws," Walter Berns explained, "we have effectively arrived at the civil libertarian's destination: the case where the Supreme Court throws up its hands and concludes that there is no such thing as obscenity."[23] This conclusion has had massive, largely unintended consequences. Once the law balked at recognizing obscenity, the populace began to doubt the very basis for shame. With no legal, institutional support for consensus, little wonder the bottom fell out from under morality.

The resulting quagmire of nonjudgmentalism has marked a major turning point—a major reversal, to be more precise—in "the civilizing process." This phrase is the title of a groundbreaking 1939 book by Norbert Elias that identifies a connection between the development of shame—of sexual shame and embarrassment, in particular—and the evolution of civilized society. Very compellingly, Elias sketches shame's primary role since the Middle Ages in very slowly fostering the kind of self-control that became a hallmark of Western civilization, and may have reached its apotheosis in the popular imagination in the character of the British military man as played by such American movie stars as Gary Cooper in *Lives of a Bengal Lancer* (1935) or *Beau Geste* (1939). From the seventeenth century onward, "only very gradually . . . ," Elias writes, "does a stronger association of sexuality with shame and embarassment, and a corresponding restraint of behavior, spread more or less evenly over the whole of society."[24]

By the twenty-first century, shame and embarassment have zero association with sexuality—or so we are endlessly, numbingly instructed—and, correspondingly, an infantile lack of behavioral restraint may be observed in everything from freak dancing, to "super-size" eating, to McMansion-building. Without the concept of obscenity, without reason for shame, the "self" in self-control sees no greater, larger, socially significant point in holding back.

This helps explain a lot of things, from the exponential rise in crime over the past half century, to the ever-rising flood of obscenity, to the breakdown of the family. But shamelessness also sheds light on why it is that American matrons are more likely to host sex-toy parties than Tupperware parties; why the Major Leagues showcase Viagra ads at home plate; why a presidential fund-raiser for GOP candidates includes a well-endowing—that is, *contributing*—porn star and pornographer; and why at grocery store checkouts shoppers can check out "hot sex tips" along with a loaf of bread. We have all learned—or, at least we have all been taught—that the mental blush is superceded by the genital tingle.

The paradox is that less restraint doesn't necessarily deliver greater freedom. That is, our sexual freedom—licentiousness—is greater, but other freedoms may actually be at risk. That's because while personal restraint once curtailed public displays of sexuality, it also made democratic society workable in the first place. Already, we recognize and accommodate a more sexually unruly populace every time we don't let our kids play in the woods behind the park, or walk home from school alone. And already, we recognize and accommodate a more sexually unruly populace every time we sanction and enable the sexual promiscuity of these same kids with a line about how "they're going to do it anyway." Meanwhile, in a Dada-esque, if governmentally official, expression of this same mind-set, state Medicaid programs were buying Viagra for convicted rapists and other high-risk sex offenders in New York, Florida, Texas, and eleven other states until the federal government intervened in 2005. But there is more to it than that.

In a shameless culture—one that speaks trippingly of condoms, semen, and more—self-restraint is continually undermined, and in its absence there is political peril. As Walter Berns wrote,

To speak in a manner that is more obviously political, there is a connection between self-restraint and shame, and therefore a connection between shame and
self-government or democracy. There is, therefore, a political danger in promoting
shamelessness and the fullest self-expression or indulgence. To live together requires rules and a governing of the passions, and those who are without shame will
be unruly and unrulable; having lost the ability to restrain themselves by observing
the rules they collectively give themselves, they will have to be ruled by others.[25]

Berns made his case against pornography in 1971, a time when it was still
new to the public square. A quarter century later, Harvard Law School Professor Mary Ann Glendon could comment on its now-familiar presence. In a short
essay for *First Things* magazine, Glendon was addressing, with Tocquevillian
echoes, "the decline of the democratic elements in our republican experiment"—
namely, judicial usurpation of powers belonging to the political process; and the
ceding of powers belonging to individuals to the government. In the process,
she reintroduced the subject of pornography and democracy in a newly chilling
light. The sexual shamelessness and unconstrained passions that Berns said
would make democracy unworkable had become what Glendon called "the
democratization of vice," and she saw it as a way of pacifying the charges of the
nanny state.

When regime-threatening questions might come to mind, the oligarchs have authorized a modern form of bread and circuses, an array of new sexual freedoms to
compensate for the loss of the most basic civil right of all—the right of self-
government. With the democratization of vice, the man in the street can enjoy exotic pastimes once reserved to Roman emperors.[26]

This isn't to suggest that individuals don't still recognize obscenity, or that individuals don't still feel shame. But culturally speaking, obscenity is all but legally obsolete, and shame is a kind of secular sin—a symptom of "hang-ups," of repression,
of inhibition, of liberty lost. This point of view, by now consensus, also sees little
division between public life and private life. After all, any definition of obscenity
depends on an understanding that some things belong in public and some things
belong in private. "Activities that were once confined to the private scene—the
'ob-scene,' to make an etymological assumption—are now presented for our
delectation and emulation on center stage," Berns wrote, three decades before the
voyeuristic mania for so-called reality shows. "Nothing that is appropriate to one
place is inappropriate to any other place. No act, we are to infer, no human possibility, no possible physical combination or connection, is shameful."[27]

And so, the question that defines our age becomes: When anything goes, why shouldn't anything go? There is a compelling reason why not. "Repeated exposure to indecency," Rochelle Gurstein writes, "ultimately inures people and threatens to make all of society shameless, in the precise sense that it considers nothing sacred."[28]

Nothing sacred. This condition sounds unnervingly like the one in which the average twenty-first-century youngster is raised. Nothing is sacred when preteen pop concerts feature gyrating, crotch-thrusting boy bands who, as *The New York Times* reported, "tantalized the small girls who shimmied alongside their amused mothers, some of whom could see the attraction in the beefcake."[29]

Nothing is sacred when a media executive packs off his eight-year-old to a midnight premiere of R-rated *Matrix Reloaded*. Nothing is sacred, when, in the comfort of their parents' homes, teens turn into the raunchiest voyeurs this side of a raincoat by watching MTV. Nothing is sacred when, also in the comfort of their parents' homes, teens can start a syphilis epidemic, as in an upscale Georgia suburb where public health officials treated no fewer than two hundred teenagers as young as thirteen who had been leading orgiastic lives after school (thanks to the Playboy cable TV channel, paid for by Mom and Dad) before their parents came home. The public health investigation revealed that a number of the children had upward of fifty partners.[30]

And what about cell phones and the Internet? These hyperconnecting, yet depersonalizing modes of communication give "users"—the term itself is devoid of humanity—an effectively brazen anonymity, again, courtesy parental bill-payers. Teenagers "hang out online, asking questions they might not dare to in real life," says *The New York Times Magazine* in its report on the "underage sexual revolution," a revolution noted as much for its promiscuity as for its detachment. As one sixteen-year-old from New England put it, "Being in a relationship just complicates everything. When you're a friend with benefits"—that smarmy term for sexual favors—"you go over, hook up, then play video games or something. It rocks."

And if it doesn't, as another teenaged boy put it to reporter Benoit Denizet-Lewis, "Who needs the hassle of dating when I've got online porn?" In a world without obscenity, in a world without shame, in a world without self-restraint, that's a good question. But is it really "sophisticated"?[31]

In Montgomery County, Maryland, a teenage girl came to some measure of local prominence in 2005 as the anonymous "star" of a sex education video. It was for tenth-graders and it was produced by the county school board. The video, along with a new sex-ed curriculum, was ultimately scrapped in the controversy that ensued after it came to parental attention via the Internet. I watched the sex-ed girl online, as well, with her casual attire, her long hair and long fingernails, her too-many-ringed fingers, as she chirpily instructed viewers, in modified Val-gal speak, on the proper way to don a condom. "Oral, anal, and vaginal sex," she said, grasping her demo cucumber, looking straight into the camera—quite shamelessly—all require a condom, she explained. But what else do they require? Deviant behavior? Promiscuity? A superstash of sulfa drugs in case of "breakage"? An appalling lack of self-respect? Equal parts self-deception? Sadomasochistic tendencies? Stupidity? A pattern of duplicity? A scalding hot bath?

But what else besides condoms *could* they require? replies the education establishment that, of course, has charge of most children. A modicum of humanity would be welcome, although that doesn't come with the systematic demystification of human intimacy to which we purposefully subject the young of the species. "When sex is a public spectacle, a human relationship has been debased into a mere animal connection," Irving Kristol wrote in 1971.[32] And when sex education is a public spectacle, the human relationship has been debased into a mere mechanical connection. Stripped of the privacy it needs to flourish, human intimacy loses not just the intimacy but also the humanness, becoming a subhuman, degrading exercise.

But that's not all. As Gurstein notes, our very understanding of and sensitivity to matters of taste and judgment are lost as well. Instead of regarding moral and aesthetic questions as matters suited for public deliberation, we tend to exempt them as matters of "lifestyle choice," or, more often, confine them to "legal disputes, in which courts balance and weigh the relative rights of the individual against those of society." This recourse to the law, Gurstein maintains, "has made it impossible to address many vital issues that fall outside its narrow precincts." And this has led us to a distressing point in the course of our civilization: a point at which, as Gurstein puts it, "urgent differences over political, moral, and aesthetic matters are all but impossible to articulate."

By now, it seems, not even our thoughts stray beyond such strictures. Consider the great pseudo-obscenity cases of our day—the S&M snapshots by Robert Mapplethorpe, *Piss Christ,* "Dung Virgin," and the like. Rather than triggering debates over what belongs in the public square, and the relationship between art and the polity, they all devolved into unseemly squabbles over what is appropriate to spend public money on. Gurstein would likely label this "the balance-sheet approach," which omits all mention of the coarsening, contaminating impact of obscenity on the polity. Writing about this soulless debate over Robert Mapplethorpe's arty porno pics, Robert Bork highlighted the lack of moral courage: "To complain about the source of the dollars is to cheapen a moral position. The photographs would be just as offensive if their display was financed by a scatterbrained billionaire. We seem too timid to state that Mapplethorpe's and Serrano's pictures should not be shown in public, whoever pays for them. We are going to have to overcome that timidity if our culture is not to decline still further."[33]

I agree with Judge Bork, and would apply his argument to sundry works of piss and dung, I mean *art,* that have triggered similarly narrow debate. But in light of Cartoon Rage 2006, the cultural nuke set off by an Islamic chain reaction to twelve cartoons of Muhammad appearing in a Danish newspaper, I must digress for a moment to distinguish between arguing against the public display of various Excrement Icons of Christianity (or anything else, sacred or profane) as a matter of public abasement, and upholding the right to caricature or critique religion, Islam and Muhammad included, as a matter of press freedom.

While lumped together for purposes of public discourse, the two examples— Excrement Icons and Cartoon Muhammads—turn on different issues and here's why: Christianity and Islam are not interchangeable belief systems inspired by a generic divinity. One relevant distinction is the way they operate in relation to their societies. By modern times, Christianity had largely vacated the political sphere, abiding, de facto or de jure, by a deepening separation of church and state; Islam has never known any separation whatsoever. As a result, the theological teachings of Islam as revealed by Muhammad, which form the basis of the Islamic law (sharia) that drives Islamic societies, necessarily belong to the *political* sphere in a way that Christianity does not.

This is not to say that Christianity should be, or has been, off the table. Indeed, all the ink (not blood) spilled over assorted "artistic" assaults on Christ and his holy family have only enhanced their value, not to mention the reputations of their artists (using the word loosely). But the all-encompassing nature of Islam underscores a special need for open, critical examination of the Koran and Muhammad as political, and politically violent, forces that roil our times. Such examination should include analysis, commentary, and editorial cartoons. But it doesn't. (I explain why in chapter 9.)

Meanwhile, the kids are watching, learning, absorbing, like the little sponges they are, modern life's lesson: Nothing is sacred—except maybe taxpayer money and Muhammad. The law may still proscribe certain behaviors, but the morality has no bite.

Taking the example of the Montgomery County Public Schools sex education course a little further, it's true that under parental pressure the offending course was scrapped, cucumber and all, but mainly because it was so flagrantly in violation of the First Amendment. The curriculum went so far as to promote certain religions to the exclusion of other religions based on their teachings regarding homosexuality. In touting "the moral rightness of the homosexual lifestyle," the judge wrote, the curriculum suggested that "the Baptist Church's position on homosexuality is theologically flawed," as well as reminiscent of the racial prejudice of the segregation era. (At the same time, the curriculum applauded Reform Jews, Unitarians, and Quakers for their stands on the issue.) But since when did public schools weigh in, favorably or unfavorably, on religious doctrine? The answer is never. And that's what the court ruled.

The question is, if the school board had been smart enough to reel in those First Amendment red flags on which this particular sex-ed course was hung out to dry—religious favoritism—would Cucumber Girl be teaching Montgomery County teens how to make better choices regarding anal, oral, and vaginal sex? In this hypersexualized culture of ours, the answer is very probably yes.

But it's an answer that demands rethinking. Kudos to the parents in Montgomery County who banded together to stop this sex-ed train on its way out of the station. But after it has retooled, the same basic train will chug away again. Do we like where it's going, and, if not, how do we get off? Cases like this one should remind us there remains a spectrum of vital issues having to do with morality, modesty, privacy, taste, and judgment that schools are incapable of teaching and the law is incapable of recognizing. But neither, it seems, is anyone else. Such issues are never even articulated, let alone discussed. It's as if we have exchanged one "conspiracy of silence" about sexuality, as Gurstein writes, for another one about everything else—morality, modesty, privacy, taste, and judgment. One big difference: Past "conspirators" consciously or unconciously understood the power and importance of their mysteries; today's silence reflects the limitation of the modern mind that thinks only in terms of those pathetic dichotomies. Hip or square. Hot or frigid. Promiscuous or prudish. Safe or sorry.

When the Second Circuit Court of Appeals ruled in 1930 that sex education material could no longer be considered illicit, Judge Augustus Hand added an explanatory note: "It also may be reasonably thought that accurate information, rather than mystery and curiosity, is better in the long view and is less likely to occasion lascivious thoughts than ignorance and anxiety." That might have sounded logical in 1930, but in the intervening decades "accurate information" has done more (and less) than merely remedy "ignorance and anxiety." For one thing, "ignorance and anxiety" are only a small part of the human condition. "Equally important," Gurstein writes, "were considerations of the inherent fragility of intimate life, the tone of public conversation, standards of taste and morality, and reverence owed to mysteries. These defining characteristics of the reticent sensibility had been lost."[34] Also lost, it is crucial to recognize, is our ability to recognize, understand, discuss, and impart them.

Which is why, in the end, we have all these "sophisticated" children running around, tube-topped, buttocks-limned, birth-controlled, glossed, pierced, thonged—exposed. By now, it should be apparent that "sophisticated" is just a high-sounding euphemism for "sexualized." When this becomes clear, Tommy Hilfiger's line makes perfect sense: *They are so much more* sexualized *than when I was growing up—they're computer literate (Internet porn), they carry portable phones (hookup available), they're bombarded with cool media like MTV (one spring break sexual depiction every 6.6 minutes).* They are pornography's children.

In 1971, Irving Kristol made a courageously unapologetic and eminently sensible (if also universally dismissed) case for a kind of "liberal censorship" that would regulate, rather than repress, obscenity, much the way alcohol, drugs, and tobacco are regulated—along with their advertising, for example. The examples of "liberal censorship" he cited—the old British practice of staging plays judged to be obscene in "serious" theater clubs, and the old American practice of limiting access to "adult" material in public libaries—were practices made workable by a "grown-up" understanding of the need to cordon off obscenity from the public square. Of course, grown-ups are only human, and any system of controlled access is prone to the kind of error artists and art lovers deplore: namely, when a bona fide work of art suffers at the heavy hands of a censor. Kristol called this the price one has to pay for censorship—even liberal censorship. He went on point out—and quite persuasively, I would add—that liberal or not, the long-term impact of censorship on the arts had, in fact, been negligible.

> If you look at the history of American or English literature, there is precious little damage you can point to as a consequence of the censorship that prevailed throughout most of that history. Very few works of literature—of real literary merit, I mean—ever were suppressed; and those that were, were not suppressed for long. Nor have I noticed, now that censorship of the written word has to all intents and purposes ceased in this country, that hitherto suppressed or repressed masterpieces are flooding the market. Yes, we can now read *Fanny Hill* and the Marquis de Sade. Or, to be more exact, we can now openly purchase them, since many people were able to read them even though they were publicly banned, which is as it should be under a liberal censorship. So how much have literature and the arts gained from the fact that we can all now buy them over the counter, that, indeed, we are all now encouraged to buy them over the counter? They have not gained much that I can see.[35]

The rest of society, meanwhile, has verily lost its soul. Kristol recognized in pornography and obscenity the power to annul civilization as we have known it—to obliterate the culture of restraint, which, Norbert Elias argued, had developed in tandem with sexual shame and increasingly distinct spheres of childhood and adulthood. It was on that basis that he made his "liberal censorship" case.

The basic psychological fact about pornography and obscenity is that it appeals to and provokes a kind of sexual regression. The sexual pleasure one gets from pornography and obscenity is autoerotic and infantile; put bluntly, it is a masturbatory exercise of the imagination, when it is not masturbation pure and simple. Now, people who masturbate do not get bored with masturbation, just as sadists don't get bored with sadism, and voyeurs don't get bored with voyeurism.

In other words, infantile sexuality is not only a permanent temptation for the adolescent, or even the adult—it can quite easily become a permanent, self-reinforcing neurosis. It is because of an awareness of this possibility of regression toward the infantile condition, a regression which is always open to us, that all the codes of sexual conduct ever devised by the human race take such a dim view of autoerotic activities and try to discourage autoerotic fantasies. Masturbation is indeed a perfectly natural autoerotic activity, as so many sexologists blandly assure us today. And it is precisely because it is so perfectly natural that it can be so dangerous to the mature or maturing person, if it is not controlled or sublimated in some way. . . .

It is true that, in our time, some quite brilliant minds have come to the conclusion that a reversion to infantile sexuality is the ultimate mission and secret destiny of the human race. I am thinking in particular of Norman O. Brown, for whose writings I have the deepest respect. One of the reasons I respect them so deeply is that Mr. Brown is a serious thinker who is unafraid to face up to the radical consequences of his radical theories. Thus, Mr. Brown knows and says that for his kind of salvation to be achieved, humanity must annul the civilization it has created—not merely the civilization we have today, but all civilization—so as to be able to make the long descent backward into animal innocence.

And that is the point. What is at stake is civilization and humanity, nothing less.[36]

Thirty-five years later, it is fair to say that Kristol's fear—"this possibility of regression toward the infantile condition"—is our reality. It is hard to ignore—or repress, even—the signs of regression, sexual and otherwise, that mark our civilization and our humanity. Frankly, though, a state of "animal innocence" doesn't sound so bad next to the bestial decadence that a shameless culture has spawned, for children as well as adults. A popular singer raps: "He can get the bitch fucked, but how many can get the dick sucked";[37] a venerable publishing house, Simon & Schuster, brings out *Rainbow Party,* a book for young adults (read: twelve and up) whose premise rests on a teen party where girls prepare to leave a spectrum of lipstick rings on boys' penises; and schoolgirls, including Catholic schoolgirls, as young as eleven play a babyish but sex-charged game with schoolboys using cheap rubber bracelets—black for sexual intercourse, blue for oral sex, red for a lap dance, white for a homosexual kiss, green for sex outside, light green for using sex toys.[38] The very sad fact is, purity and innocence, sublimation and restraint, sensitivity and taste can neither be experienced nor learned among such "sophisticating" influences. Neither can childhood.

As early as 1969, *The New York Times,* one of those stalwart liberal champions of anticensorship, found itself quaking over the brave new world of "utter freedom" it had journalistically labored to bring into existence. In an extraordinary editorial, it turned in a practically reactionary fury on those who would sully the "great principle of civil liberties" by engaging in explicit portrayals of sexual intercourse on stage—"peep-show activity," as the *Times* called "the sodomy and other sexual abberations" in the theater that year.

> The fact that the legally enforceable standards of public decency have been interpreted away by the courts almost to the point of no return does not absolve artists, producers or publishers from all responsibility or restraint in pandering to the lowest possible public taste in quest of the largest possible monetary reward. . . . Far from providing a measure of cultural emancipation, such descents into degeneracy represent caricatures of art, deserving no exemption from the laws of common decency merely because they masquerade as drama or literature.[39]

Of course, those erstwhile "legally enforceable standards of public decency" that were "interpreted away by the courts"—to the hearty approval of *The New York Times* and its acolytes—turn out to have been the very last line of defense for the all-too-fragile "laws of common decency." Without one (the law), the other (decency) cannot prevail. Neither can the adult. Responsibility and restraint are not only bedrock virtues of liberal civilization, they are also hallmarks of the grown-up. Without them, civilization becomes anarchic, and the grown-up slips and regresses.

Going completely bitter, *The Times* forecast a dismal resolution: "The insensate pursuit of the urge to shock, carried from one excess to a more abysmal one, is bound to achieve its own antidote in total boredom. When there is no lower depth to descend to, ennui will erase the problem."[40]

Ennui may well do for the old, run-of-the-mill porn queen, or the odd syphilitic poet, but it's neither a condition of the state of nature nor a benchmark of civilization for the rest of us. Nor, I would add, is it anything like a state of grace for the young.

6. BOUNDARIES

What we're doing is f—— with the rules.
There should be no rules, man.
We're being honest to ourselves.
—PETER FONDA[1]

The first soldier to enlist in the Union Army during the Civil War came from Batavia, New York—or so the town claims. Batavia also claims the first home run NFL quarterback John Elway hit as a minor league baseball player. Between that first Union soldier, and that first Elway home run, probably the biggest event in town was a speech by Helen Keller in 1926 that drew a crowd of one thousand people. All of which tells us that Batavia—a town of sixteen thousand people about thirty-five miles east of Buffalo, where summer temperatures average a temperate 68.5 degrees Fahrenheit, and average home prices level off at $100,000—is no hot spot.[2,3] It's the kind of American town marked at its city limits by totem poles bearing the quasi-heraldic badges of Kiwanis, Rotary, and Lions that proclaim it to be the traditional stomping grounds of the enduring American burgher.

Enduring; but not unchanging. And in the Batavia burgher's changes, plenty revealing. Take the town chapter of the Rotary Club. Lampooned early in the twentieth century by the likes of George Bernard Shaw, H. L. Mencken, and G. K. Chesterton, the Rotary Club as an institution was definitively laid to rest as corny beyond redemption by Sinclair Lewis. While the Pulitzer-Prize–winning author's own standing isn't what it used to be, his efforts to skewer the boosters and belongers in small towns like Batavia live on. Americans may not actually read *Babbitt* anymore, but the eponymous character of George Babbitt, Rotarian, remains the indelible face of small-town commerce, small-town probity, and small-town prejudice: in short, the face of every social institution that artsy-woolly, misfitting freethinkers have always rebelled against—and have always *needed* to rebel against. Not for nothing was *Webster's New Collegiate Dictionary,* by 1930, defining a "Babbitt" as "a businessman or professional man who

conforms unthinkingly to prevailing middle-class standards." Less than flatter-
ing, this definition nonetheless stands as testimony to the accuracy with which
real-life Babbitts mirror middle-class standards.

And what middle-class standards do twenty-first-century Babbitts reflect? A
fascinating lack thereof, as demonstrated by the contemporary Rotary Club of
Batavia. It's not that club members aren't still pillars of their community, but, as
we have seen from Loudon County to Los Angeles, such pillars have grown hollow even as their communities have grown attenuated. In Batavia, this condition
became a matter of public record in 2004, the year the local chapter decided to
raise money for the town hospital by producing and marketing a calendar.[4]

This, of course, was a very Rotary thing to do—a practical, charitable act that
combined public-mindedness and public relations, enhancing the health of the
community, almost literally, along with the reputation of the club. Somewhat
more extraordinary, though, was the club's choice of calendar illustrations. From
January to December, the calendar would feature portraits of the shoe store proprietor, the banker, the warehouse owner, the printer, the insurance broker, and
on, each posed in his roughly half-century-old birthday suit, strategically fig-
leafed by a newspaper, a bouquet, a jackhammer, or some other handy accessory.
"There was one group shot," *The New York Times* wrote in its account of "Rotarians Gone Wild," describing the careful placement of privacy props. "Each
man held a cardboard Rotary symbol about the size of Frisbee."

In so doing, the calendar boys of Batavia revealed more than a passel of old
nipples, bellies, and dewlaps. They illustrated, in four-color splendor, the extent
to which the middle class—keeper of convention, repository of standards—has
been stripped of convention and gutted of standards. Or, maybe, the extent to
which the middle class has adopted a *new* convention—an adolescent-driven,
take-it-all-off, rock culture, no-boundaries convention—even as it has ditched
the old standards.

It's probably worth establishing that there was a time when, it's safe to assume, Rotary Club members didn't consider taking off their clothes in public,
period. The whole concept of naked Rotarians is one that even Sinclair Lewis,
without having experienced the eight decades that have bumptiously passed
since *Babbitt* came to life, couldn't possibly have dramatized without venturing
into the realm of science fiction with a detour through Freud. Rotary Clubs then
and now raise money for charity, but once-fixed reference points of common
convention—reference points on which Lewis's brand of satire once depended—
have vanished. It's as though magnetic north has lost its pull and the compass
spins directionless.

Interestingly enough, Batavia's Rotarians—the shoe store proprietor, the
banker, the warehouse owner, the printer, the insurance broker, and on—seemed

to have felt a little lost themselves when they first embarked on their calendar project. As Mr. July, aka Jim Isaac, forty-nine, a title search executive and former Rotary president, put it, "My first reaction [to the idea] was, what is Rotary International going to think about this?"

The Rotary ex-prez's first reaction is telling in itself, conveying his confidence—well-placed, it turned out—in having the support of the Batavia community. He didn't say: What will Batavia think of this? He was worried about Big Rotary. In his own community, there would be no local loss of face in Rotary's loss of clothing, no social sanction, and Mr. July knew it. But in seeking permission from Rotary International, the Batavia chapter was giving voice to its collective hunch that something wasn't quite right. Maybe it was the simple act of exhibitionism that troubled them. Or maybe it was a more complicated reaction to the strange homage that solid, respectable Rotary would be paying to the girlie calendar, a porn form designed to inspire a kind of private and sophomorically sexual gratification poles apart from the public philanthropy and civic improvement that Rotary supports. In other words, the aura around this Rotary fundraiser was always going to be more Playboy Mansion juvenile than public-square mature. Was it—and this is the operative word—appropriate?

Not to worry. "The response I got," Mr. Isaac said, "was, resoundingly, 'This sounds like a fabulous project, do it.' " I wonder if, secretly, he and the boys were just the slightest bit disappointed. Something had given them pause—some atavistic burst of forgotten moral code—causing them to wonder whether calendar portraits of what could still be called "town fathers" aping what could still be called "wayward daughters" was so tastelessly dopey (what was that archaic word, "vulgar"?) that if the local hospital really needed money maybe the club should just raffle off a Chevrolet. At least one man's wife put the kibosh on hubby's participation: She "took the decision out of my hands," said this one Rotarian who kept his shirt (etc.) on. "She said no."

Note the peer-appeasing, completely childish transfer of responsibility to the grown-up in charge—the *one* grown-up in charge—who bucked consensus to keep her husband's pants on. It was the adult thing to do, but she, apparently, was the only adult to do it. In short, Mrs. Rotary was a nonconformist who exemplifies the paradox of twenty-first-century life: the extent to which following once-reflexive middle-class manners and mores has become, weirdly enough, an act of rugged individualism—*the extent to which adult behavior has become the behavior of the maverick*. Meanwhile, the herd prevailed; it always does. With Big Babbitt's hearty approval, Batavia's boosters, rather than shoot for local pillardom through an inadvertently elevating if conventional act of philanthropy, set their sights a good bit lower. Large, Rotary-logoed pasties notwithstanding, they hit their target.

In this terror-shattered, shock-addled world, the Boys of Rotary produced no audible explosion—not even a puff of smoke. Indeed, our twelve bare Rotarians didn't even work up to a sizzle as sex objects; at worst, the old sacks were merely appetite-supressing. And no more so than the Pink Ribbon Men of Marin County, California, whose nudie calendar raised money for breast cancer,[5] or the Ladies' Bridge Club of Farmland, Indiana, which bared its seventy- to ninety-year-old bods in a bid to save a county courthouse that was even older.[6] But in mocking themselves as centerfolds, our fellow citizens ill-serve their communities. If imitation, even by way of comedy, is the sincerest form of flattery, Rotary et al were not only making pornography sweet and spoofable, they were also extending their venerable club's brand name, or just plain middle-class stamp of approval to pornography's presence in the life of the community. By sending up the girlie calendar in the back room, Rotary et al, were, in effect, pinning it up in the front office, or even family room. It would be interesting to see what stance all these centerfolds take the next time a strip club or "adult" video outlet tries to set up shop inside city limits. While it remains unlikely that these Babbitts would actively encourage X-rated establishments to open shop in town, it's also unlikely that they could even begin to explain why Main Street is, or should be, any different from the wrong side of the tracks.

In the creation of such calendars, however banal, something significant is lost: another length or segment of boundary that cordons off certain behaviors from the community at large, ruling them out as antisocial or just plain inappropriate. Famously enough, Boston once employed a censor to draw the line, although not against Rotary and bridge club. The censor's concerns were the traveling acts and entertainments that hit town. The last such official was Richard J. Sinnott (pronounced "sin not"). Between 1960 and 1980, Mr. Sinnott alone could keep a show from going on anywhere in his undoubtedly fair city by revoking the municipal license of theaters, nightclubs, and other venues for morally questionable presentations. His powers weakened as moral codes unraveled, but in an earlier era, the prospect of being Banned in Boston caused playwrights to gnash their teeth, producers to bite their nails, and assorted freethinkers to tear their hair over the Boston bubble. Whitman, Hemingway, even *Snow White* were all banished for a time from the city by Mr. Sinnott's predecessors, among them the Pilgrims, who, in the seventeenth century, banned Christmas celebrations in Massachusetts, undoubtedly for being too merry.

By 1960, though, no book no matter how salacious was subject to Boston's censor, and examples of obscenity and pornography, once beached on the seamier side of life, were beginning to make their splash in the cultural mainstream. As a government institution, censorship, even in Boston, was about to go under. In its last glugs, though, as Mr. Sinnott's 2003 obituary in *The New York*

Times points out, a rating like "banned in Boston" was in fact a money review that could turn even a real lemon into the showbiz version of forbidden fruit. The only stripper Mr. Sinnott ever kept off Boston's boards later thanked him for tripling her salary. When a dance company failed to draw Mr. Sinnott's stamp of disapproval for performing half-naked, producers were furious, later sending Mr. Sinnott a postcard from New York. "Thanks a lot," they wrote. "The show closed." Eventually, so did the censor's office.[7]

Looking back, Mr. Sinnott wasn't sure his roughly ten bans had been worth the bother. He thought they might have made Bostonians look like "party poopers." So they did, but what of it? While Boston's bluestocking statutes made the city the butt of jokes, could they also have served some public good? After all, neither Whitman, Hemingway, nor *Snow White* suffered much for being banned, and at least one stripper in the world ate better for a while. Looking back on decades of ever-more free speech that have made ever-more graphic depictions of sex and scatology ever-more ubiquitous, maybe now is the time to indulge in a little nostalgia for Boston's quaint attempts to put a lid on it. There was in the city's quixotic efforts a certain idealism; the city believed in the public good, and it believed said good should be protected by maintaining an obscenity-free zone within city limits. This notion, no doubt, had something to do with the legacy of such founding fathers as John Adams, a native of nearby Quincy, Massachusetts— where, by the way, Bostonians would travel in 1929 to see a proscribed performance of Eugene O'Neill's *Strange Interlude.*

As president, Adams specifically noted that the viability of the new nation depended on "a moral and religious people." If smut was threatening Main Street, what else were good patriots to do but clean it up? And how bad was it, really, to go to Quincy for Eugene O'Neill—and to New York City for anything else?

As the fates fixed it, Mr. Sinnott passed away around the time the mighty Wal-Mart chain announced it would no longer be selling the magazines *Maxim, Stuff,* and *FHM.* This British trio of dirty glossies—glossy dirties?—adds up to a male common denominator so low it's negative. In a kooky spin on the Victorian art of euphemism, however, publishers here and Over There persist in calling them "racy" or "lad" magazines—almost quaint terms that ring a bright-young-things sort of bell. This is a far cry from the bludgeon of dumb sex and crudity the magazines really wield. "Maybe they [Wal-Mart] think Tyra Banks should have been wearing pink instead of black," Stephen Colvin, whose company publishes *Maxim* and *Stuff,* told *The New York Times.* "For any men's magazine to put a woman on the cover seems a bit troubling to them."[8]

This is about as disingenuous as it gets. Wal-Mart, one of the last stretches of Main Street still in existence, banned the magazines just as it bans all pornography, soft and hard, which is only part of the story. Just because Wal-Mart stopped selling *Maxim* et al., doesn't mean the mags have disappeared in a black hole. Anti-obscenity crusades far more fanatical than Wal-Mart's have never pulled off such a trick.

And that's not the goal—or at least it shouldn't be. As Walter Berns has written, "the principle should not be to eradicate vice—the means by which that might be conceivably accomplished are incompatible with free government—but to make vice difficult, knowing that while it will continue to flourish covertly, it will not be openly exhibited."[9] In other words, temperance, yes; abstemiousness, no. Decency, yes; piety, no. Brown paper wrappers, yes; book burnings, no. Far better to drive the noxious stuff out of the mainstream and over to the margins than to eradicate it altogether. "Consumers should have the freedom to decide for themselves what they want to purchase," magazine publishers of America says. And so they do. Only sometimes consumers should have to turn off Main Street to do their shopping. The old boundaries we postmoderns have erased may never have eliminated vice in the past, but they certainly kept it at a distance, physical and imagined. Such divisions forced individuals to break from the Babbittry if they wanted to engage in it—secretly, if they were to remain in the middle class as "hypocrites," or openly, if they were to drop out into either artful "Bohemia" or chronic degradation.

Today, Babbitt qua Babbitt makes marginal behavior a mainstream activity, and the line of demarcation is lost. Goofy Rotary calendars aside, the mainstream publishing boom in explicit sex guides—"shiny paperbacks extolling the excitement [of] oral sex, anal sex, fetishism and S&M," reports *The New York Times*—bears this point out. The anonymous aspect of Internet commerce allows any would-be happy hooker or surreptitious sadist to shop unseen under the counter and buy "without the traditional embarassment," as Crown's Steve Ross put it, and without the risk of exposure.[10] Such anonymity erases the line altogether, and what was once well-charted and easily negotiable social territory reverts to a kind of cultural no-man's-land, a place where anything goes and nothing matters, not really. That's because when nothing is sacrilegious, nothing is sacred, either.

We have been famously taught, as a culture, to "let it all hang out." What isn't as obvious is that we have also learned, as a culture, to suck it all in: "it" in the latter case being the collection of instincts and habits acquired over centuries that once prevented us from letting it all hang out in the first place. Modesty, shame, fastidiousness, self-respect: These are the "hang-ups" of our time, the natural reactions we stifle in order to don the mask of the happy libertine—or the happy parent of the happy libertine. And stifle them we must to play the role, voices steady, manners nonchalant, amid the torrents of profanities and soul-shrinking depravities that bubble up in a mainstream without margins.

Why the inhibition over giving in to our inner modesty? In a coarsened, decorum-lite society, no one wants to be labeled a "prude." Given its very personal application, "prude" may be even worse than other such terms of opprobrium as "racist" or "sexist." But as hot-button epithets, such terms have something in common: Just uttering them is supposed to blast to bits all inklings, observations, or expressions of difference (for good or ill) that lead to division, to boundaries, and thus to hierarchies. It is these hierarchies—based, for example, on racial disparities in test scores that lead to a dearth of black students and a preponderance of Asian students in the Univerity of California system; or sexual differences in upper body strength that bar women from employment in fire departments—that are anathema to the wide-open society.

Let's stick with the scarlet "P." To be branded a prude is to be castigated and reviled for trying to reinstate, or even personally observe, any old boundary or defunct propriety that effectively walled off some aspect of marginal behavior from the mainstream. To be branded a prude is to be castigated for doing so, as though such efforts were the trivial expression of a mean mind. It is "prudish" to frown on bad language. It is "prudish" to avoid graphic depictions of violence. It is "prudish" to regret sexual relations out of wedlock. To be disturbed by skimpy teen fashions. To yank a kid from sex ed. Such "prudery," if that's really what it is, is understood as a retrograde effort to reimpose limits on human behavior, and as such is fervently, even religiously opposed by the mainstream muses of modern liberal culture—Judge Bork's radical egalitarians and radical individualists.

No one, then, wants to be labeled a "prude." We open the arts section of *The New York Times* one day and read about Mostly Mozart, ticket sales for Broadway musicals, and a photographer who "has photographed the sexual lives of sadomasochists since 1994."[11] We turn the page.

Rich Lowry of *National Review,* the conservative editor of the conservative (and historically Catholic conservative) magazine, goes to watch *Sin City*—an animated gore-fest of murder, decapitation, and defilement—and posts his thoughts online: "Interesting and well-done, but very hard to watch for those of us who don't have a high tolerance for torture and dismemberment."[12] He blogs on.

NBC's Katie Couric reports that three in ten children aged thirteen to sixteen are sexually active, with nearly half of them having engaged in oral sex and/or sexual intercourse.[13] She cuts to a weather report.

A national Republican organization banks $2,500 from porn star Mary Carey and lets her sup with the president—along with six thousand other donors, including her XXX-producer Mark Kulkis—at a congressional fund-raiser for the family-values candidates of the GOP. "They've paid their money. No matter what they do, the money is going to help elect Republicans to the House," said National Republican Congressional Committee (NRCC) communications director Carl Forti.[14]

So it goes. And so it flows—the mainstream, that is—carrying all that is marginal along with it. Incidentally, Mr. Kulkis, the pornographer, who made his stash filming unsimulated, unprotected sexual intercourse (or whatever), also happens to serve as honorary chairman of the NRCC's Business Advisory Council—a "small, prestigious group of conservative businessmen and women."[15] By belonging to this super-chamber of commerce, is Mr. Vice paying homage to Mr. and Mrs. Virtue? The answer is no. In this case, no act of hypocrisy has made the X-rated producer's participation possible—no shadings, no secrets, no fear of disclosure. He has taken his seat alongside other "conservative" businessmen and -women as a pornographer, full-frontally, as it were, unbowed, unmolested by the morally pliant Babbittry around him. His presence on the Republican business council may actually be flipped around and seen as the homage prudery-free virtue now pays to vice—the homage the mainstream pays to the marginal, Main Street to the red-light district.

The story of a one-day book ban on a national bestseller may be understood in similar terms. The book in question was *America (The Book),* a mock textbook in mock civics by mock anchorman Jon Stewart and the mocking writers of *The Daily Show.* Or maybe I should write: a "textbook" in "civics" by "anchorman" Jon Stewart and the "writers" of *The Daily Show.* The quotation marks, of course, convey the nudge-nudge nihilism that is comedian cum author Stewart's stock-in-trade. Not that it was Stewart's comedic commentary that brought on the ban, however brief, in a corner of southern Mississippi. Instead, it was a picture.

On page ninety-nine, the book features a photograph of the nine justices of the Supreme Court posed to reveal what the skin mags not so long ago taught us to call "full-frontal nudity." No strategically placed gavels or legal briefs here, à la Rotary. Just head-on, puckered, spreading nakedness.

The photos are fakes, of course, with bodies culled from a nudist Web site superimposed to match the famous faces of the court. Cutouts of the justices' black robes hang nearby, with a caption instructing readers to "restore their dignity, by matching each justice with his or her respective robe." Notably enough, this was over the line for good ol' Wal-Mart, which decided not to sell the book in its stores (although it was available at Wal-Mart Online). And it was over the line for the Jackson-George Regional Library System in the state of Mississippi, which banned the book.

"We're not an adult bookstore," said library system director Robert Willits, in the brief interlude during which the eight branches of the Jackson and George counties' library system managed to function without circulating the book. (More on the unfortunate corruption of the word "adult" later.) "Our entire collection is open to the public. If they had published the book without that one picture, that one page, we'd have the book."[16]

In a time when Babbitt takes it all off, it should come as no surprise that the plight of the stripped justices struck no sympathetic chord in the community at large. No hoisting of pitchforks, literal or figurative, materialized in defense of Homestead America. Nor was there even the passive acquiescence of silence. Quite the contrary; the public square clanged with calls supporting the book. *You can't tell us what not to read,* was the gist.

The library's more modest proposal, of course, was simply not to make a certain book available within the library system—to keep the mainstream free of the marginal, to uphold the basic dignity of the law of the land against pornographic ridicule. Libraries necessarily amass limited collections on limited funds. Whether personal whim, expert opinion, or ignorance, some criterion or other comes into play with regard to what books make it onto any shelf. This is fine with Joe Public, apparently, so long as the criterion that comes into play isn't based in a moral belief: in this case, the moral belief that a nihilistic attack on the custodians of the law of the land by exposing them in the nude is a bad thing. Over the line. Something that doesn't merit space on the shelf. "The people" thought otherwise, and loudly. After about one day, the Jackson-George Regional Library System made *America (The Book)* available to cardholders.

But it was nice while it lasted. The ban, that is. For a minute there, it seemed as if Babbitt were alive and well in a small corner of Mississippi, striking a quixotic blow for the kind of middle-class morality that once strived to mark off the public square in order to keep it neat and clean—quite sterile, even, in that wholesome way that once drove artists off into paroxysms of creativity. Or at least into paroxysms. What should be clear, though, is that it's not as if Babbitt *isn't* alive and well; he is. And he still embodies prevailing middle-class standards. It's just that the middle-class standards to which, as *Webster's* puts it in its definion of Babbitt, he unthinkingly conforms—from Batavia to Marin to Farmland to Jackson—have changed completely.

As it happened, the book-banning story coincided with the appearance of a *Vanity Fair* magazine profile of founding *Penthouse* publisher Bob Guccione. The story, an unblushing exercise in hagiography, depicted the seventy-four-year-old pornographer as "the fallen king," "one of the greatest success stories in magazine history," blah, blah, doomed by "Reagan-era censorship, the Internet, and a series of expensive dreams." No typography of irony here. No irony, period—all of it, presumably, having been used up on "democracy" in the Jon Stewart book. Just soupy gush. Lamented Guccione son Bob, Jr.: "He wanted so much to be acknowledged for something other than pornography." Alas.

But what a pornographer he was. Having launched *Penthouse* in 1969, "Bob outraunched *Playboy* by displaying genitalia and pubic hair in a magazine," as a former colleague approvingly told *Vanity Fair*. "That had never been done before."[17]

Balboa led the way to the Pacific. Edison turned on the lights. Guccione displayed genitalia and pubic hair. No wonder he gets the star treatment. In truth, of course, genitalia and pubic hair have been with us since Adam and Eve; they just never before made it into a magazine that plied the mainstream, both as a widely available mass publication, and as a mass influence on a wide variety of publications. Three or four decades later, thanks to Guccione and the wheels of progress, we get a full-frontal look at the Supreme Court in a bestselling book by a television star. As Rotary International might say: How "fabulous."

The Guccione article went on to allude to the greatest hazard of the porn trade: not censorship, which can actually spice things up, but jaded customers. This pornographer's nightmare began to come true as early as the middle 1970s. And now? Thirty years later, simply having lived through the intervening decades—or even through a description of the intervening decades—makes us all, to a very real extent, jaded customers. That's because it's hard to function in this world without a working knowledge of sexual depravity, bestial violence, and untoppable profanity, regardless of whether we are brothel owners or housewives, pedophiles or bird-watchers. We are all denizens of the same cultural no-man's-land that pop pornographers and other boundary-crossers have created even as we have willingly stripped ourselves of propriety's guidelines and signposts of convention. And that's why Batavia's Rotary Club could boldly—or, rather, banally—go where no Rotary has gone before; and why Mississippi librarians were repudiated in their efforts to hold a line that no longer exists.

And not just against birthday suits. In the Jon Stewart book, for one, there is also the, well, naked intention to level and degrade a pillar of democracy—the law—leaving vicious little snaps of humiliation, discomfort, and exposure in its place. This is a kind of pornography in itself, I would argue, but one Americans delightedly consume, absolutely smug in partaking absolutely of the First Amendment. Such destructive absolutism is another prevailing convention to which the modern-day middle-class conforms, and as unthinkingly as its forbears ever did to the morality of the past. The difference is, the middle-class reflex used to be to protect institutions, perhaps to a fault; today, it is to mock them, perhaps out of existence.

Maybe this is that "other" legacy Guccione Minor yearns for. Certainly, pornograhers are owed their due in creating a society in which all the lines— between speech and pornography, mainstream culture and adversary culture, middle class and Bohemia, bourgeois life and rock lifestyle, Us and Them, people who take their clothes off for the camera and people who don't—have been trampled out of existence and forgotten.

Or disguised. The Victorians have received much grief for their efforts to use language to cloak the corporeal, which must have reflected not only their moral creed but also their determination to rise above an intrusive physical side of life that still tied humanity to chamber pots, among other unpleasant things. In any case, Victorians, so they say, preferred "limb" to leg; "form" to body, and supposedly even draped shawls over the legs—sorry, the "limbs"—of pianos. That said, there is no euphemism more opaque and more absurd than our contemporary labels for the sex industry, from "gentlemen's clubs," where the paying customers are anything but, to "adult entertainment," which, of course, means pornography and the "mature" (eighteen-and-up) audiences that support it.

There is, in these terms, an explicit bar to children for which, I suppose, we should be grateful. At the same time, this language tells us that to reach "maturity" is to enter an R-rated—or X-rated, or NR-rated—world of mass voyeurism in which explicit, often depraved, depictions of sexuality, violence, and assorted barbarisms add up to "adult" behavior. Is someone who watches sexual intercourse on screen or buys a lap dance in a strip club "mature"? If so, is someone who doesn't watch sexual intercourse or buy a lap dance "immature"? Victorian euphemisms were more or less intelligible; our euphemisms mask the basest, most stunted behaviors in the guise of adulthood.

This lingo masquerade is by no means limited to the sex industry. When the scripts of the 2001 fall television season made (pre-9/11) headlines for including what *The New York Times* described as "every crude word imaginable, including one considered to be on the furthermost reaches of decorum"—wherever that is—*The West Wing*'s Aaron Sorkin had this to say: "Broadcast television can grow up as the rest of the country does. There's no reason why we can't use the language of adulthood in programs that are about adults."[18]

No, no reason at all. But Sorkin's idea of promoting "the language of adulthood" was to get a network okay for a character to "curse in a way that uses the Lord's name in vain." Producer Steven Bochco was engaged in a similar campaign to help broadcast television "grow up" by bringing American television viewers "a scatological reference that has never been uttered on an ABC series." In other words, we can forget *Bartlett's Quotations,* the *Federalist Papers,* and *War and Peace.* Finally, we're talking the "language of adulthood."

Obviously, there's no curse or "scatological reference" that's new to a culture rooted in earthy Anglo-Saxon civilization. What's new, though, is the promulgation of such raw references in the media mainstream—over our airwaves, into our homes, and throughout our casual lexicon—as an act of cultural elevation.

This probably started with Lenny Bruce, whose fame as a comedian (lasting) depended on the shock of profanity (fleeting) that he used in his stand-up routines. It is worth bearing in mind that it was a pornographer, *Playboy*'s Hugh Hefner, who first got Bruce booked at a mainstream venue in Chicago. It was "the big time at last," writes Gerald Nachman, in an admiring essay in his book *Seriously Funny: The Rebel Comics of the 1950s and 1960s*.[19] Interestingly enough, Nachman notes that Bruce's material, however startling to mainstream audiences, wasn't original then, either.

> His language was blunt street talk, but he was hardly the first dirty comic; others, like Belle Barth, Rusty Warren, Pearl Williams, Redd Foxx, and the notorious B. S. Pulley, rose to underground fame using filthy language (in some cases wearing a Yiddish fig leaf). The difference was that Bruce was in the public eye. Barth and company hid out, mainly in the Catskills, Miami Beach, and the saloon gulags. Foxx and his comic brethren were walled off in black ghetto rooms; Pulley (Big Jule in *Guys and Dolls*) was a harmless curiosity.[20]

This redefines Bruce's role: rather than a breaker of taboos, he was a popularizer or amplifier of broken taboos, notable for bringing trash talk from "saloon gulags" into ritzy venues. Sometime after BMI began broadcasting what *Variety* once called "leer-ics," and sometime before Bob Guccione stacked up "genitalia and pubic hair" at the corner newsstand, Bruce brought the blue streak to center stage. Maybe more shocking than the act, though, was its effect on the audience.

Malcolm Muggeridge, writing in *Esquire* in 1965, observed: "Every time he used an obscene word or expression you could feel the audience shiver with delight. It was what they were waiting for, what they had paid for, what they wanted of him. He met their requirement generously and contemptuously, spitting out the filth as though to say, 'Take that, you vile bourgeois scum!' " The critic remarked on "the spectacle of smart, rich people being lambasted and simply loving it. Please, please, Lenny, despise us again, spit on us again, insult us again!"[21]

From that masochistic midpoint in a small club, to that first "f——" in the nation's movie theaters from *M*A*S*H* in 1970,[22] to those 162 "s——" from *South Park* broadcast over cable television in 2001,[23] we have "progressed" to a point where profanity knows no boundaries. Funny how when you can say anything—cross any line, break any taboo—expression and communication fail to ascend to new levels of complexity or nuance. Or even to old levels of complexity or nuance. Rather, they revert to a broad and formless brutishness. Meat on a slab, rather than food for thought. Which suggests it wasn't only innate artistic virtuosity, then, that inspired Cole Porter, for example, to sculpt "Let's Do It, Let's Fall in Love" out of the prosaic muck of procreation in the animal kingdom with his electric eels that do it "though it shocks 'em I know," and those shad roe that do it, "Waiter, bring me shad roe."

It was also a deeply etched set of boundaries, which society had engineered, that drove a dazzling mind to use the language to transform the stuff of instinct into high art. It is said Porter was delighted that "Love for Sale" (1930) was banned from the airwaves, and no doubt double-banned in Boston. But that's called crossing a line (Porter) and keeping it, too (society). If Porter had written in the age of U2 ("keep f——— up the mainstream"), he would have made his mark, or not, as someone else, someone who never had to write his way out of a conventional box. This tells us that without social standards, there would have been no Great American Songbook standards. And without manners, there would have been no comedies of manners—no "Private Lives." Similarly, in a time of "no-fault divorce," there can be no *Anna Karenina*; in the era of one-night stands, no *Brief Encounter.*

Sticking with Porter's example, then, we can see that even when he wrote "Anything Goes" for the 1934 hit show of the same name—a show that also featured "I Get a Kick Out of You," "All Through the Night," and "You're the Top"—anything didn't go, not really, not so long as sex and drugs (not rock 'n' roll) remained frothy allusions in a theatrical score that played mainly to an elite, theater-going crowd. Not incidentally, "Anything Goes" (lyrics and book) went under the Hollywood censor's knife before it was filmed for a mass audience.

Today, a lifetime later, anything not only goes, but it goes unremarked upon. Take the oeuvre of 50 Cent, the artist behind that 2005 ode to (oral) sex, "Candy Shop" ("I'll take you to the candy shop, I'll let you lick the lollypop"). While it is impossible to compare Cole Porter, a highly trained theatrical composer from the upper echelon of American affluence, with 50 Cent, a fatherless former drug hustler turned rapper, a passing juxtaposition helps us gauge what is acceptable in the mainstream culture when it comes to treating love and romance. Dance bands under Paul Whiteman and the Dorsey Brothers helped make "Anything Goes" a pretty popular song in the 1930s. Five-million-plus Americans made *The Massacre,* the album that includes "Candy Shop," the second-highest seller of 2005 and helped its composer-performer rake in $73,351,514.85 for the year.[24] With 1.9 million sales, "Candy Shop" was also the number one song in a new musical product, ringtone sales for cell phones.[25] "Candy Shop"—"Get on top then get to bouncing 'round like a low rider"—was also one of biggest prom-trotting ditties of the season.

The song wasn't always played at the prom, of course, because there were some schools that drew some kind of line. Such schools restricted party playlists, barring the original lyrics of, say, "Get Low" by Lil Jon & the Eastside Boyz, allowing a somewhat sanitized version to play in the high school gym.

But nothing could keep the original lyrics out. "During one verse, when the edited versions says, "Till the sweat drop down and fall, till all these females crawl"—already organdy-and-lace-lovely—"the students shout the original line, which includes a graphic reference to male anatomy and a vulgar term for women." So reported *The Boston Globe,* which also quoted an eighteen-year-old girl, who said: "Sometimes people don't even know it's the edited version, because we're singing it anyway and we're louder than the music."[26] As in:

> *Till the sweat drop down my balls*
> *Till all these bitches crawl*

What is there to say, especially when no one wants to be labeled a "prude"— "Happy Graduation"?

It's not as if the world that's supposed to be these kids' oyster won't take them as they are. But rather than discovering those new frontiers people used to talk about, this generation is better suited for crossing any old lines out there that might still exist. Meanwhile, their elders are hardly through transgressing. While they don't throb to the beat of balls that fall and bitches that crawl, today's adults seem to be affected by the same impulse to strip away lingering strictures and culture codes, whether consciously or not. The conservative writer Peggy Noonan, she of the lyrical pen, opened a recent *Wall Street Journal* column with a joke that ended with the punch line, "bitch."[27] This has got to be some kind of first—but what next? Even the first lady of the United States hasn't held her ground during this cultural shift, as Laura Bush's monologue at a recent White House Correspondents' Dinner shows.

This annual media dinner, carried live on C-SPAN since the advent of cable, features the president delivering something of a comical command performance— thoroughly scripted by comedy writers and even more thoroughly vetted by political advisers. At the event in question, in 2005, Laura Bush "stole" the mike from her husband and told her own jokes—or, rather, told her own jokes thoroughly scripted by comedy writers and even more thoroughly vetted by political advisers.

As far as her press clippings went, the first lady was a hit, with kudos coming from left and right. But there were a few of us—in the media I can count them on one hand—who wished that a grown-up had happened by the East Wing to cut some of the first lady's jokes from the script, and replace them with some new video adventures of the president's beloved black Scottie, Barney, or something.

Why? Here is where boundaries and guidelines come back in—or should: When a lady happens to be first lady, "funny" at any expense isn't part of the job description, not when "funny" comes at the expense of her husband's image.

And I don't mean "image" as in the artificially spun, public relations product. I mean "image" as in public symbol: President of the United States. Commander-in-chief. Leader of the Free World. That's her fella. In these explosive times, with hundreds of thousands of soldiers under arms, such symbolism is a sobering thought, or should be, even during a night under the lights on the town.

In other words, feet of clay are fine, but there was no reason to bring the barnyard into it. During the 2004 election season, Whoopi Goldberg steered a Democratic fund-raiser into the gutter with a crude pun on the Bush family name, prompting Republican accusations that John Kerry didn't "share the same values" as the rest of America.[28] But what about the rest of the Bush family? Laura Bush is no stand-up comic, but that was all the more reason certain sorts of jokes should automatically, reflexively, and unquestioningly have been ruled out for her public delivery. Jokes that link the president's hands and the underside of a horse, for instance. Jokes that create a regrettably indelible image of the first lady, the vice president's wife, a Supreme Court justice, and the secretary of state—the diplomatic face of the United States—together at Chippendales, enthusiastically waving dollars bills at hulking, bow-tied male strippers. Even jokes that make a *Mommie Dearest* out of former first lady Barbara Bush.[29] Such material won't pull more than a PG rating these days, but a first lady in any era should be mature enough to avoid all so-called "adult" material.

Once upon a time, such discretion was a no-brainer, an almost autonomic response that came out of rules so reflexive as to need no articulation, much less conscious thought. No more—which is why so many more people, including conservatives, applauded Mrs. Bush than not. But "George," she said, "if you really want to end tyranny in the world, you're going to have to stay up later." It sounds like road company Jay Leno, but it was the first lady, and she was talking about a solemn if controversial goal her husband is pursuing, ordering hundreds of thousands of American military personnel into harm's way to accomplish it. The hilarity of her moment passes—the calendar turns, the book circulates, the centerfold fades—but something has changed. The first lady has crossed a line.

Laura Bush is not Joan Rivers. Splashing into the media mainstream to join the derisive fun of comedy today, decoupling fateful words from mortal purpose, is a risky proposition for the wife of a superpower leader. One day, "ending tyranny" is Mr. Bush's raison d'être—the high-flown focus of his second inaugural address. The next day, it is Mrs. Bush's punch line. The day after that—who knows? Even in an era that prizes the guffaw above all, the lingering air of uncertainty isn't worth the media snickers. Sure, the first lady managed to "humanize" her husband, as *The New York Times* so admiringly put it.[30] Certainly, she knocked him down some pegs, which in our age is much the same thing.

As an illustrative point of contrast, it's worth thinking back to other presidents and other first ladies, particularly ones who led in wartime. Would we have said Eleanor had "humanized" FDR by doing a stand-up routine in 1942 about Franklin always "fearing fear itself"? Or that Pat Nixon had humanized Richard by wondering in 1972 where the heck the peace was that Henry Kissinger had promised was "at hand"? Or that Nancy Reagan had humanized Ron in 1987 by teasing him about tearing down that old wall?

"Lighten up," I was told ad nauseam by readers of my weekly column presenting this same argument. This may be the password for Mrs. Bush, blazing a trail for first ladies to come, but where does it leave the rest of us? Lightened up, all right, having cast off one more weighty hunk of decorum. But is that a good thing? And what do we do now? And what does the first lady do next time? When the White House helpmeet, hostess, and christener of battleships fails to step on the brakes at the boundary of good taste, all the once-shared notions of public conduct are totaled.

I realize that the wreckage is in the eye of the beholder. And, if the tally from my own personal mailbag is an accurate reflection, at least 60 percent of the country robustly applauded Mrs. Bush's act, and would call for an encore. But from that 40 percent who cringed came a common point of departure: "I am not a prude, but . . ." was a frequent opening phrase. (A favorite variation: "I am a pretty coarse old cow, but . . .")

To be a prude is to be "excessively or priggishly attentive to propriety or decorum," a shallow figure of easy ridicule that a decorum-lite and lately coarsened society like ours holds in particular contempt. Hence, the letter writers' defensive posture: They were *not* paying excessive attention to a trivial matter of, say, which fork to use, and they knew it; they were concerned with a larger issue. But this was a distinction that the 60 percent who vociferously rejected any and all criticism of Mrs. Bush didn't see and, I believe, couldn't see. The line was lost to them. It's not that my 40 percent were offended as individuals by some person's jokes; they were offended as citizens by a first lady who forgot herself. The readers who bristled did so because they knew a line was there somewhere—or used to be there somewhere—that divided life between subjective notions of private fun and objective notions of public conduct, and they didn't like seeing the first lady of the United States even quasi-officially cross it.

In effect, these readers were themselves validating essential boundaries: between a private person and a public actor; a stand-up comic and the president's wife; childish behavior and mature conduct; good taste and bad; and between private life and public life. This is a hopeful sign. But it's also true they were expressing themselves as individuals who believed they were alone, even isolated, in their feelings. After all, three-plus decades ago, the Supreme Court, yet to be unrobed by Jon Stewart, collectively threw up its hands and declared there was no such thing as obscenity, thus eliminating the shelter of shame and modesty. Perhaps not suprisingly, then, these people seemed convinced there was no socially sanctioned place for them to go with their convictions.

As Walter Berns noted years ago, there had been a sudden change: "Nothing that is appropriate to one place is inappropriate to any other."[31] He was specifically addressing the impact of court decisions on obscenity; but ever since, in all areas of conduct and culture, communal notions of what is appropriate and when, what is appropriate and where, have sunk like a rock. Underwear-as-outerwear, pedicures for four-year-olds, Rotarians as centerfolds—why not?

Internet blogs and reality shows are the logical expression of such confusion, as the citizen-voyeur assumes his role in a society that is wide open. Bearing witness to a real-life range of behaviors that were once walled off from public scrutiny (from weight loss to pain, titillation, rejection, revulsion, and humiliation) still gives pause sometimes, but how can we not look? A sex partner sues a sex blogger for invasion of privacy for being "cruelly exposed to the world."[32] Some critics express genuine shock at a new reality show, *Intervention,* in which, as *The New York Times* reported, "viewers are invited to witness an addict's decline and then participate in the crucial moment when family and friends confront the troubled soul with a life-altering choice: rehabilitation or banishment."[33] Even so, such blogs are a way of life and such shows get a pass (unless, as in ABC's abruptly canceled show, *Welcome to the Neighborhood,* they offend PC sensibilities by eliminating Asian, Wiccan, and Latino contestants) due to the increasingly faint demarcation between public and private life, between appropriate and inappropriate behavior.

Are there any lines left? I came across a significant one in a story about a thirty-nine-year-old Brooklyn mother who found herself transfixed by the online revelations of her nanny's sex life.

As Helaine Olen, the mother, wrote in *The New York Times,* it was her husband who was not amused by the nanny's online "tales of too much drinking for [his] comfort" and catalog of sexual experience (among other things—and partners—the nanny wrote about touching her breasts while reading *The New Yorker*).[34] "This is inappropriate," Dad said. "We don't need to know that Jennifer Ehle makes her hot."

Mrs. Mom disagreed. Instead of screeching: *If she's in a lather over* The New Yorker, *what happens when she gives junior a bath?* this modern mother was composed, nonchalant. No prude, she. There was nothing about nanny, she maintained, not her flaunted promiscuity, her heavy drinking, or her parading these flaws in cyberspace, to disqualify her from caring for the couple's young, impressionable, defenseless, helpless toddlers. "Didn't she [the nanny] have a right to free expression? It wasn't as though she was [*sic*] quaffing Scotch or bedding guys, or the occasional girl, while on the job." At least, not according to the blog.

But then the nanny crossed that last frontier: She blogged "sarcastically" about her employers' home life. She judged it and found it wanting. This, to Ms. Olen, meant nanny "broke the covenant." How? Understand that drinking to excess and sleeping around are merely lifestyle choices and, as such, not to be judged—apparently not even by an employer whose children are potentially at risk. In return, however, the employer's lifestyle choices, however stodgy, however bourgeois, are not to be judged either. As in: *I don't judge you, you don't judge me.* In critiquing the household, the nanny was—sin of sins—being judgmental. "My issues, my problems, my compromises, my entire being," the mother wrote, "seemed to be viewed by her as so much waste." For this, finally, the nanny was fired.

But maybe there is another factor in this calculus. The mother reveals having been "more than a little envious" of nanny's wanton ways. On being ridiculed online by the younger woman, she experienced a terrible sting: As a wife and mother of very young children, the infinite debauch on the wild side was behind her. Perhaps on one level, then, this was a showdown between the perceived prude and the proud libertine. Ms. Olen saw herself stuck with the finite proposition of making a life. This gave her pause.

Living in a society that upholds the floozy as an "authentic" "free spirit" only reinforces such doubts and ambiguities. In a society without the boundaries that are the bases for judgment, the dutiful wife who makes a home and raises some kids really has nothing over the licentious lass who doesn't. Without moral judgmentalism, what's left is just the contrast between sensational excitement and grinding routine. No wonder Mrs. Mom felt stung. Nanny's promiscuity is just a lifestyle choice, as valid as motherhood. This helps explains why, when the XXX-porn star bought her ticket to the GOP fund-raiser, no eyebrows were raised. "No matter what they do," the Republican spokesman said, "the money is going to help elect Republicans to the House."

No matter what they do, the porn star sups with the president; the nanny cares for the kids (unless she critiques the missus); the Rotary twelve are pillars of the community. No matter what *Penthouse* or *America* contain, they rate space in the public square. A creed of nonjudgmentalism has erased all the lines we used to live by. But just because they *can* do these things, should they?

In considering the answer, it's worth recalling the Sensation art controversy which brought this question, however briefly, to light in 1999. The brouhaha was kicked off by that inelegant clump of elephant dung mooshed onto the breast of a portrait of the Virgin Mary by a British artist on display as part of the Brooklyn Museum's Sensation exhibition. Familiarly known as "Dung Virgin," this work of "art," which was also dotted with pornographic magazine cutouts, drew the wrathful judgment of New York Mayor Rudy Giuliani, who tried, in vain, to shut off city funds to the museum displaying it and other items from the Saatchi Collection. These included, as art critic Roger Kimball described them: "pubescent female mannequins, for example, studded with erect penises, vaginas, and anuses, fused together in various postures of sexual coupling . . . the portrait of a child molester and murderer made from what looked like a child's hand prints, [and] the bisected animals (pigs, cows) in plexiglass tanks full of formaldehyde."[35] While applauding Giuliani's efforts as "a courageous, heartfelt gesture," Kimball saw in the legal wrangle over the First Amendment that Giuliani initiated evidence of "an important public failure."

> For it brings the law to bear on a realm of activity that, in a healthy society, should
> be ajudicated in the court of taste and manners. To my mind, the controversy over
> "Sensation" has much less to do with free speech than with some basic questions
> about the kind of public life we want to encourage.[36]

Precisely. Because ours is not a "healthy society" with a functioning court of taste and manners, the law, for Giuliani, became the court of last resort. And he lost. But if the First Amendment guaranteed government funding of the "art" in question, it didn't really lay the controversy to rest. Legality aside, a more difficult question remained: Was "Dung Virgin"—not to mention chopped animals and cutouts of private parts—something worthy of public regard? To answer his own question, Kimball invoked the work of a British judge named John Fletcher Moulton, who, speaking on the subject of law and manners in the 1920s, noted that "there is a widespread tendency to regard the fact that [one] can do a thing"—as in display "Dung Virgin" or Mapplethorpe's snaps—"as meaning [one] may do it. There can be no more fatal error than this. Between 'can do' and 'may do' ought to exist the whole realm of which recognizes the sway of duty, fairness, sympathy, taste, and all the other things that make life beautiful and society possible."[37]

This realm between "can do" and "may do"—even a fine line between the two—has all but vanished. Lord Moulton described his realm as being suspended somewhere between the law of the land and the desire of the individual. He called it "the domain of obedience to the unenforceable." This is the domain of self-restraint, a place inaccessible to an adolescent society for whom "limit" is only limitation, and where little if any space ever shows up between the exercise of personal desire and the restrictions of the law. It is this absence of "unenforceable" behaviorial boundaries—self-restraint—that has made what one "can do" increasingly indistinguishable from what one may or should do.

Of course, much more than manners, arts, and letters have suffered from this lack of lines to live by. Our culture without boundaries increasingly reflects a larger world without boundaries—and it's a brave new world, all right. It begins with the increasingly amorphous proposition of personal identity (sexual, national, married name or not). It continues at home, permeable to the toxic seepage of television and the Internet. It goes to church, where the world's Catholics have had to confront line-crossing sexual crimes. And it extends to our national borders, which are increasingly porous to aliens and terrorists. Where there is no line, there is increasingly no will to draw any line. And that can be not only confusing, but also downright dangerous.

There is the temptation to see such perils only in the dry, quasicosmic terms of "civilization" or "culture." But a culture without boundaries—a society without grown-ups and a middle class without guidelines—can be a dangerous place to live. The shocking and tragic story of a young woman named Lyric Benson, a newly minted Yale graduate who was gunned down before her mother's eyes by her spurned lover, Robert Ambrosino, offers a particularly searing and unforgettable illustration why.[38]

She was nineteen when they met after her sophomore year; he was a New Haven "townie" pushing thirty and rough around the edges—that is, worldly-wise and real to an impressionable theater major. According to newspaper accounts, they moved in together, sharing a group house with other Yale students. They became "engaged" during her senior year, at which point, Ambrosino, according to *The New York Times,* "flew her mother and stepfather" to town from their home in North Carolina to celebrate. After graduation, with Lyric knocking on the door of the New York acting world, they continued to live together.

The rest of the terrible story practically writes itself. What seemed cozy in college was constricting in the real world. Lyric moved out. Ambrosino harassed her, stalked her. And then, one night in Manhattan, outside her apartment building, with her mother looking on, he shot her in her lovely face and turned the gun on himself, committing suicide.

It's a wrenching story of violence, pain, and waste. But how does this crime relate to broken barriers on artistic expression and social conventions? Maybe the best way to answer is to harken back to the past: In a culture *with* boundaries, in a society *with* grown-ups, in a judgmental, conventional, straitlaced world of reflexive manners and bourgeois mores, this tragedy might never have happened—and not just the murder and suicide, but also the relationship itself.

In our day, such a relationship, which seems to mismatch not just age and experience but also aptitude and opportunity, is quite unremarkable—and maybe therein lies the rub. No one dares to find, or even thinks to find, such a live-in arrangement in any way remarkable—as in worthy of remark, caustic or cautionary. Nonjudgmentally, society allows, and even enables, such a young woman to pass effortlessly into such a love affair with more emotional and sexual and professional baggage than she is equipped to handle. Our young women deserve more protection. Judgmentally, society should make it more costly, or at least a little more uncomfortable, for such a pair to perpetuate a relationship.

How? By throwing up the same old trip wires and obstacles that have blocked, or, at least, slowed lovers through the ages: punitive parents, outraged "dowagers" (that imposing term for old ladies), incredulous peers, college rules, moral codes, social stigmas—all the "artificial," "narrow-minded," "pointless" constraints society once mustered to try to quash what was once rather poetically known as "free love." From *Romeo and Juliet* to *Anna Karenina,* great (and not-so-great) literature is simply littered with such constraints; indeed, it relies on them for creative tension, plot, and character development. None of which is to say that traditional social conventions and boundaries of behavior alone offer any guarantee of happily-ever-after. But facing down family, answering to a college dean, even winning over suspicious friends provide critical tests of any affair, reaffirming a couple's desire to be together . . . or not. Maybe as reflected in the gimlet eye of a disapproving community, an unemployed barfly wouldn't look so great to a Yale undergrad. Maybe a few nasty stigmas in the mix would convince an older man that living with an inexperienced student isn't really worth all the trouble.

But no such disapproval, no such trouble, no such boundaries, no such grown-ups, exist any longer. Sadly, neither does Lyric. Society failed to mount a rigid defense of the young woman; instead, it provided the warm, slightly moist embrace of nonjudgmentalism that created a cocoon of unreality for the doomed affair. Society failed, period. As barriers and boundaries disappear, so, too, do our signposts, markers, and guides. We gain mobility, free rein, and lattitude, but we don't know where we are.

More dangerous still: We don't know who we are.

7. IDENTITY

*We must have but one flag. We must also have but one language. That must be
the language of the Declaration of Independence, of Washington's Farewell
address, of Lincoln's Gettysburg speech and second inauguration.*
—THEODORE ROOSEVELT, 1917

*I hope very much that I'm the last president
in American history who can't speak Spanish.*
—BILL CLINTON, 2000[1]

One day, a few years ago, when my girls were small, I read them *Mary
Poppins,* the notably bizarre but durably beloved 1934 fantasy by P. L.
Travers. Things were going along just fine, with Mary arriving on the
east wind to kick off a series of magical adventures for her charges. Then we got
to chapter six—"Bad Tuesday."

This chapter revolves around Mary's remarkable compass, which not only
tells which way to north, south, east, and west, but also sends Mary and the kids
there. Mary barks "North!" and they find themselves at the North Pole convers-
ing with a polar bear. The command of "South!" lands them in a steamy jungle
where they eat bananas with a hyacinth macaw. "East!" takes them to China and
a panda bear, while "West!" brings them to a beach where they encounter a
seaweed-serving dolphin.

It was the dolphin that did it. Maybe the exotic specificity of "hyacinth
macaw" should have made me wonder, but it was the dolphin, environmentalism's
poster mammal, that jerked my gearshift from doting mother to PC-detector.
Was it possible, was it plausible, that P. L. Travers—a British subject born at the
end of the reign of Queen Victoria, the high point of the British empire—would
choose a polar bear, a hyacinth macaw, a panda bear, and a dolphin to represent
the four corners of the earth? Not bloody likely. (Later, I learned that the panda
didn't even appear in the West until Ruth Harkness brought a cub named Su-Lin
out of China in 1936, two years after *Mary Poppins* was first published.) Another
hand, contemporary and clumsy, was at work, as indicated by the note to be

found in the 1997 edition's table of contents: "Chapter Six (Revised version)." A quick dip into the local library fished up a suitably old and unreconstructed copy of *Mary Poppins,* which revealed what drove modern-day editors to rewrite the thing.[2]

Turns out, Mary's original spin around the globe took her and the children not to visit animals of different species, but *human beings of different races.* To the north, in the original chapter six, Mary & Co. rub noses with "an eskimo man . . . his round brown face surrounded by a bonnet of white fur." This, of course, was not a face Inuit rights advocates were going to love. His "eskimo wife" goes on to make an offer whose generosity would be lost on PETA: "Let me get you some fur coats. We've just been skinning a couple of Polar Bears." In a southern desert, a black-skinned family offers, gulp, watermelon to the parched travelers—not only ballistically "incorrect," but also botanically improbable. ("My, but dem's very white babies," the mother, her tiny "picaninny" in her arms, tells Mary.) To the east, they encounter a punctilious Chinese Mandarin, whom P. L. Travers has dressed in a kimono—which, of course, is a *Japanese* costume, not to mention a fashion don't for Asian activists. To the west, they meet Chief Sun-at-Noonday: " 'My wigwam awaits you,' he said in a grave, friendly voice. 'We are just frying a reindeer for supper.' "

As benign, as hokey, as these travels are, they also hit just about every stereotype on race and enviroment there is. The significance of the modern-day editorial rewrite, however, goes beyond a contemporary compulsion not to offend. Lost in the shuffle between old and new is the author's point of view: the thoroughly Western, if specifically British, perspective from which Miss Travers, dimly enough, conceived of the world and its peoples. More than anything else, it is her singular vantage point (originally illustrated by a drawing of Mary Poppins and the children at the center of the world and its peoples) that has now become unacceptable, and hence defenseless prey to "revision."

Sometime between Mary Poppins's world tour in 1934, and her editorially forced march in 1997, a radical shift in outlook took place. As a society, we— "we" meaning we who are born of the West—no longer look through anything like a *Western* lens onto the *rest* of the world. Indeed, there really is no "West" and no "rest" by now, or so we are taught.[3] As we learn, beginning in preschool, there is now a "diversity" of "cultures," "voices," and "global perspectives." This shift has yanked us—again, we who are born of the West—from a reflexively Western viewpoint to a self-consciously multicultural one.

What was the impetus for this change? Taking into account the unprecedented movements, both legal and illegal, of nonwhite, non-English-speaking peoples into the United States (and also Western Europe) over the past four decades, it may seem logical to guess that the multicultural perspective reflects these new demographics. In America, these new demographics were the direct result of sweeping new immigration laws that Congress passed in 1965; they introduced entry criteria that effectively favored non-European over European immigrants, and weighed "family reunification" concerns over a potential immigrant's skills.[4] In Europe, meanwhile, as historian Bat Ye'or has documented, the past forty years have seen unprecedented immigration from Muslim countries into Western Europe, particularly following the oil crisis of 1973, and the subsequent creation of the Euro-Arab Dialogue, a political entity created by the European Economic Community at the behest of France and the Arab League to foster a kind of Euro-Arab civilization: a cultural and political "convergence between Europe and the Islamic states of North Africa and the Middle East."[5]

It would seem, then, that the multicultural outlook emerged as a reflection of multicultural demographics. To a great extent, however, the new outlook preceded and anticipated such population shifts. It turns out that there was something else that made us blink and redirect our cultural sights, something that has a lot to do with the same erosion of certitude, of cultural affinity and confidence, that led to the death of the grown-up.

As the authority of the adult diminished, so, too, did his totems of authority, from the "obvious" primacy of Shakespeare, to the "undoubted" superiority of the Bill of Rights, to the happily-ever-afterhood of the house in the suburbs—where, not incidentally, those "universal truths" of Shakespeare et al could be found in the inevitable set of encyclopedia in the equally inevitable family room. (Had Bob Dylan forty years ago revealed his secret longing for just such a house, complete with "picket fence," history might well have been a little different.[6]) Once there was no longer anything singularly precious about Socrates, Beethoven, or sliced bread, once these underpinnings that supported the Western hierachy of cultures buckled, the leveling impact of cultural relativism became the order of the day. Maybe it was French philosopher Claude Levi-Strauss who first sounded the call to arms to "fight against cultural differences hierarchically" in the 1950s;[7] by the 1980s, with a resounding multiculturalist victory in the so-called culture wars, this leveling mission was accomplished.

Amid a purposeful blur of cultural perspectives—among which only the anti-Western is deemed superior—the principles of multiculturalism have flourished and spread, undermining both our attachment to and confidence in Western culture across the land. Hence, Columbus's remarkable voyage of discovery to the western hemisphere is taught to fourth-graders through the eyes of a mocking West Indian girl (Chevy Chase, Maryland); the father of our country is deconstructed into a slaveholder unfit to name elementary schools after (New Orleans),[8] or hang portraits of in government offices (Brooklyn)[9]; and on the National Mall in Washington, D.C., the National Museum of American History showcases permanent exhibitions that emphasize American slavery, slaughter, and strife. (Just next door, interestingly enough, a permanent exhibition at the Natural History Museum called African Voices omits mention of African slavery, slaughter, and strife.)[10] In such a world, in such a culture, Mary Poppins and her compass just had to go. Under a multicultural sun, no one refracts humanity through a Western prism, not even a quirky character in a children's fantasy— maybe *especially* not a quirky character in a children's fantasy, given the impressionability of young readers.

The symbolism is striking. Like Mary Poppins, we have been blinded to our own perpsective. Conditioned by our academic, cultural, and political elites, we no longer regard the "rest of the world" as anything like the "Other." Having simultaneously embraced diversity and denied difference, we now find it, on the whole, just easier to save the dolphin. This is why sociologist Nathan Glazer could declare, "We are all multiculturalists now." Certainly, we are supposed to be. It can't be just a coincidence that this acquiescence to a state of cultural negation coincides with the cultural practice of nipping maturity in the bud. In other words, the loss of identity would seem to be linked to the loss of maturity. At the very least, the easy retreat from history and tradition reveals the kind of callow inconstancy and lack of confidence that smacks of immaturity as much as anything else. It seems that just as we have stopped "growing up," we have forgotten "who" it was we were supposed to grow up into.

In *Alien Nation: Common Sense about America's Immigration Disaster,* a bracingly unequivocal assessment of the cultural and political shambles that make up U.S. immigration policy—the basis of sovereignty—author Peter Brimelow opens his preface with a provocative statement.

> There is a sense in which the current immigration policy is Adolph Hitler's posthumous revenge on America. The U.S. political elite emerged from the war passionately concerned to cleanse itself from all taints of racism and xenophobia. Eventually, it enacted the epochal Immigration Act (technically, the Immigration and Nationality Act Amendments) of 1965. And this, quite accidentally, triggered a renewed mass immigration, so huge and systematically different from anything that had gone before as to transform—and ultimately, perhaps, even to destroy— the one unquestioned victor of World War II: the American nation, as it had evolved by the middle of the twentieth century.[11]

Brimelow doesn't elaborate on Hitler's revenge, but further consideration is illuminating. It's easy to imagine that in its revulsion at Adolf Hitler's genocidal anti-Semitism and obsession with Aryan racial purity, the U.S. political elite wanted to put as much distance between itself and any policy or practice smacking of the evils of the Third Reich. Ditto for the Nazi regime's rigid, if buffoonish, authoritarianism. Remember the Hechingers, with their astute observation that postwar American culture expressed an instinctive animus toward the autocratic classroom, its pedagogical authority, and the blind obedience of rote memorization. This old-fashioned model wasn't, as they observed, going to fly in the new postwar day. Having just triumphed over a German dictatorship and a Japanese divine monarchy, American culture was in a decidedly democratic mood; this, as the Hechingers demonstrated, played out in the widespread receptivity to new, nonauthoritarian, child-directed education theories, and a growing emphasis on self-expression.

Brimelow has picked up on another aspect of the postwar mood—the passionate concern of the political elite "to cleanse itself from all taints of racism and xenophobia." This, he maintains, culminated in the Immigration Act of 1965. By reconstituting the immigrant pool to accommodate non-Europeans and nonwhite peoples, this new legislation codified a policy of non-racism ("racism" understood as discrimination against nonwhites) within an official American embrace of non-Western cultures. The practical impact of this landmark legislation still hasn't been acknowledged; the emotional effect on proponents, however, was undoubtedly instantaneous as warm waves of self-satisfaction foamed with newly proven purity—not purity of *race,* of course, but rather purity of *intentions.*

Such idealistic trends, the one cited by the Hechingers, the other by Brimelow, were at heart emotional trends—part of the same national mood swing of postwar exhuberance. The "democratic" classroom that no longer saluted authority embodied the difference between the heil-Hitler bad guys and the power-to-the-people good guys; so, too, did "democratic" immigration legislation ("a national, emotional spasm"[12]) that sent Western European émigrés toward the back of the line for American entry. Just as we were now inclined to bridle at the traditional hierarchy in the classroom, we were also ready to reject the traditional hierarchy of cultures. This would ultimately, however, call into question our own place on top.

And therein lies Hitler's revenge—the cultural leveling that either emerged from, or was, in some crucial way, accentuated by natural outrage over the crimes against humanity committed by the Third Reich. Hitler, of course, was totally defeated, along with his tyrannical notions of cultural (Germanic) and racial (Aryan) "supremacy." But so, too, perhaps, were *all* notions of Western primacy regarding culture and race (which I take here to include nationhood)—even ones that supported, not supremacy in a murderous form, but judgment in a rational form. Grounded by notions of sovereignty and cultural affinity, such judgment determines the kinds of attitudes and choices—on everything from religion to law to literature—that are expressed in cultural identity. In the case of the

United States and its European allies, these attitudes and choices derive from a specifically Judeo-Christian identity forged in fire, ink, and steel by those whom our modern-day multiculturalists insultingly deride as "dead, white men."

Having failed to destroy the democracies by making Nazi war, then, Hitler may have unwittingly managed to destroy the democracies by effecting a post-Nazi peace in which the act of pledging allegiance to the flag itself, for example, would practically become an act of nationalist supremacism—racism, even; bigotry, too. Quite suddenly, it didn't matter whether the culture in question led to a reign of terror, or to liberty and justice for all. The act of maintaining or defending the culture, or, ultimately, even defining it—whether through unabashed opposition to communist expansionism, purposefully selective immigration practices, or even sticking to the Western canon—became confused with and condemned as an exclusionary and, therefore, evil chauvinism. In this way, having won the great victory, the Allies lost the will to survive. Writer Lawrence Auster has explored this theme.

> Having defined the ultimate evil of Nazism, not as the ultimate violation of the moral law as traditionally understood, but as the violation of liberal tolerance, postwar liberalism then set about dismantling all the existing ordinary particularisms of our own society (including, in the case of the EU, nationhood itself) in the name of preventing a resurgence of Nazi-like evil. This was the birth of political correctness, which sees any failure on our part to be completely open to and accepting of the Other—and thus any normal attachment to our own ways and our own society—as the equivalent of Nazism.[13]

Openness and acceptance on every and any level—from personal to national, from sexual to religious—are the highest possible virtues of the postmodern Westerner. This makes boundaries and taboos, limits and definition—anything that closes the door on anything else—the lowest possible sins. Judgment, no matter how judicious, is tarred as "prejudice" and, therefore, a neobarbarous act to be repressed and ultimately suspended. Patriotism has been caricatured out of polite society as boorish warmongering. Western civilization itself, which may be taken as the product of both judgment and patriotism, has been roundly condemned for being both prejudiced and warmongering. The overall effect has been to sap the culture's confidence in its own traditions, even—especially—in the classical liberal tradition that stiffened our spines against Hitler in the first place. The cultural anemia that began to take hold long ago has passively accepted the transformation of America the Western into America the Multicultural (and Western Europe into Multicultural Europe) as a good, or necessary, or even just inevitable thing. And thus—with the practical disappearance of the nation, or, perhaps better, the *culture,* that defeated him—Hitler's revenge.

Maybe this is the World War II Syndrome we never knew we had. As a touchstone in the twenty-first century, World War II evinces a nostalgia for unity in the face of adversity; such unity, however, is now irreclaimable for its having vanquished that specifically Hitlerian adversity that made unity itself—nationalism, nationhood, and culture—verboten.

The führer's revenge takes other forms. Consider the noxious "Bush = Hitler" equation. Senseless but pernicious, this comparison is a crude attack on the president's attempt to draw lines between Good Us and Evil Them. "You're either with us or you're against us," was the way Bush began his so-called war on terror—a declaration that is the very essence of national or cultural definition, and as such a multicultural no-no. It's necessarily "divisive," and thus, not "diverse"; it's by definition noninclusive, and therefore "intolerant." Never mind that it's noninclusive and intolerant of diverse people who singlemindedly want to kill you. Wasn't Hitler also noninclusive and intolerant? Ergo, "Bush = Hitler."

Seized upon by the antiwar movement, this slogan took hold in a culture without a core, inspiring proponents from former Vice President Al Gore, who repeatedly slandered President Bush's Internet supporters as "digital brownshirts," to ex-astronaut and former Sen. John Glenn, who tarred the Bush agenda as "the old Hitler business," to Sen. Robert Byrd (D-WV), who equated the Bush era with Nazi Germany—as did German Justice Minister Herta Däubler-Gmelin. Billionaire leftist George Soros, former UN arms inspector Scott Ritter, cartoonist Ted Rall, singer Linda Ronstadt, author and radio personality Garrison Keillor, and Nobel Prize–winning playwright Harold Pinter have all played the same Dadaesque, if malicious game.[14] The fact is—*all* the facts are—there is no historic or moral basis on which to make the comparison, period. Historian Victor Davis Hanson took the trouble to explain why.

> At first glance, all this wild rhetoric is preposterous. Hitler hijacked an elected government and turned it into a fascist tyranny. He destroyed European democracy. His minions persecuted Christians, gassed over six million Jews, and created an entire fascistic creed predicated on anti-Semitism and the myth of the superior Aryan race.
>
> Whatever one thinks of Bush's Iraqi campaign, the president obtained congressional approval to invade and pledged $87 billion to rebuild the country. He freely weathered mass street demonstrations and a hostile global media, successfully defended his Afghan and Iraq reconstructions through a grueling [reelection] campaign and three presidential debates, and won a national plebiscite on his tenure.[15]

Hanson went on also to note Bush's friendship with Israel—"in a world almost uniformly hostile to the democratic Jewish state"—and his efforts to introduce democracy to the Middle East, "with no guarantee that such elected governments will not be anti-American." In total contrast to Hitlerian policy, Hanson added, "No president has been more adamantly against cloning, euthanasia, abortion or anything that smacks of the use of science to predetermine supergenes or to do away with the elderly, feeble or unborn."[16]

Okay, so Bush does not equal Hitler. Where Hanson pegs the "Bush = Hitler" phenomenon to ignorance, arrogance, and even deflection (Senator Byrd, a former grand wizard in the Ku Klux Klan, and Däubler-Gmelin, a post-Nazi German justice minister, may be seeking some kind of cover or kudos by attributing Hitlerian evil to others), there is something else to consider. Or, rather, there is the lack of something else to consider, something missing from the wider society. What's missing is a connection to our own identity (dare I say cultural self-esteem?), that autonomic understanding that should tell us, unless we missed the coup d'état, that no American president—checked and balanced according to the U.S. Constitution, monitored and dissected by a free press—is going to be the hellish twin of Adolf Hitler, and unless we demand better, more decent ways to express dissent, our society won't remain civil, much less democratic. Lacking such a connection, lacking such confidence, lacking such understanding, lacking such cultural self-esteem, society is ill-equipped to rein in or laugh out the debased absurdity of "Bush = Hitler" in the first place.

Thus, the bogeyman of Hitler & Co.—I hesitate to make light, but the promiscuous invocation of Hitlerism and other racisms to shut down debate has created a ridiculous, extra-historical context—pops up in the most serious deliberations concerning sovereignty issues, bringing rational discourse to a screeching halt. A (thankfully failed) proposal to enable illegal immigrants in California to drive legally with a special driver's license is likened, by state senator Gil Cedillo, to "a scarlet letter that would invite discrimination, much like the star of David on Jewish people in Nazi Germany."[17] The Minutemen Project, the civilian group that patrols stretches of border to call attention to federal inaction on illegal immigration, is equated to the KKK by a U.S. Congressman, Rep. Lloyd Doggett (D-TX)[18]—and called "vigilantes," by the way, by President Bush. In Virginia, the proposals of a gubernatorial candidate, Republican Jerry W. Kilgore, to make the nation's immigration laws more enforceable are "tinged with nativism," according to the editorial page of The Washington Post.[19] Over There, in Europe, Margot Wallström, a senior official of the European Union (EU), took the occasion of VE-Day 2005 to condemn the concept of nationalism itself—not Hitler, not the democracies' appeasement of Hitler—for causing the outbreak of World War II. She accused Europeans reluctant to cede their sovereignty—or, as she put it, their "nationalistic pride"—to the supranational and antidemocratic EU bureacracy as risking a return to Nazism and the Holo- caust.[20] It's not just Bush that equals Hitler, national identity equals Hitler, too.

It's a simplistic, even babyish, argument, but that's no coincidence. Five or six decades of nonjudgmentalism and multiculturalism have taken their toll on edu- cation and knowledge. *Mary Poppins* aside, children's literature, also including educational material, is a festering hot spot for the syndrome. I say that not only having read such books as Sandra Stotsky's *Losing Our Language: How Multi- cultural Classroom Instruction Is Undermining Our Children's Ability to Read, Write, and Reason* (the subhead says it all), but also having watched, firsthand, the multicultural education process in my own children's classrooms.

Long before my kids went to school, the horrors of the Western world, ac- cording to politically correct indoctrination, were familiar past the point of cliché: *Columbus was a genocidal germ-carrier out-eviled only by plantation-owner George Washington and his oppressive band of white patriarchs, whose wigs we'd be powdering to this day—were it not for Molly Pitcher, the Iroquois Confederacy, George Washington Carver, and Yoshiko Uchida.* I knew this drill going into the game; what I didn't know was the strategy.

In other words, it came as no shock to learn, for example, that in our public elementary school in Westchester County, New York, third-graders devote a hefty part of a semester to studying Kenya. They don't know who discovered the Hudson River, who is buried in Grant's Tomb, or where the Battle of White Plains was fought, but they come home with plaudits for Kenya's health care system—which, incredible as it may seem, I had never heard of. This, I recog- nized, was par for the PC course, as were the stories that came home about cow's-blood cuisine and earlobe enhancement, which the kids found relishingly disgusting.

But the kids also came home with stories of how the teacher admonished them to modify their feelings about such barbarities; indeed, to coin a phrase, to shut up. Teacher says: "Who are we to say that supping on cow's blood is 'gross'? That's their culture." This is the pattern that has repeated itself in other years and other schools. In a public elementary school in Chevy Chase, Maryland, for ex- ample, fourth-graders study the Plains Indians. "Who are we to say that using a buffalo tongue for a brush is 'gross'?" the teacher asked the class. "That's their culture." What finally struck me is that teaching children to internalize these re- actions to one tribal custom or another is not a lesson in etiquette, akin, say, to table mannners that teach us not to spit out unfamiliar food at a dinner party to spare the hostess's feelings. It teaches children to sublimate the traditions and teachings of their own civilization—those that tend to regard buffalo-tongue brushes, for example, as being revolting or unsanitary. The repetition of this kind of instruction—who are we to say anything about anything?—impresses upon young minds the crucial need to adopt an attitude of painstaking neutrality when regarding other (read: less developed) cultures. In other words, it teaches children to suspend their judgment. This is an elementary lesson in cultural relativism that American and other Western children never forget.

Along the lines of Pavlov's dog, then, we learn as students to react to primitive customs or barbarous practices by reflexively suspending judgment. In the beginning, it's just weird cuisine and bizarre customs that get labeled neither weird nor bizarre. "That's their culture" becomes the mantra of accepting the Other. But it also becomes the mantra of denying the Self. And in learning to turn off the assessment process, in learning to stymie the gut reaction, we have learned to shut it down entirely. Such self-abnegation may be fine, sort of, in dealing with the more superficial practices of diet or dress—don't blanch at body "art"; do appreciate pendulous earlobes—but what happens in the face of less benign cultural phenomena, from censorship and religious repression to female genital mutilation (FGM), forced marriage, so-called honor killing, and suicide bombings?

First of all, words fail. Literally. After a 2005 terrorist attack on a Baghdad school in which five teachers were lined up against a schoolroom wall and shot to death, columnist Clifford D. May pointed out that leading newspapers such as *The Washington Post* and *The New York Times* described the terrorists as "gunmen" and "armed men."[21] Such euphemistic restraint is typical. Middle East expert Daniel Pipes compiled a list of twenty euphemisms used by the news media to avoid using the term "terrorist" in stories describing the, well, *terrorists* who murdered 331 civilians in Beslan, Chechnya, 186 of them children.[22] The word "militant," he observed, usually serves as the media's "default term" for terrorists everywhere, although it would seem that the heretofore unimagined heinousness of the atrocities committed at Beslan School No. 1 challenged the media's collective imagination. From "assailants" (National Public Radio), to "fighters" (*Washington Post*), to "perpetrators" (*New York Times*) to—Pipes's fave—"activists" (*Pakistani Times*), the euphemisms, he noted, betrayed the kind of frantic thesaurus-thumbing on the part of journalists that may actually induce calluses. Pipes explains the quest for synonymity this way: "The origins of this unwillingness to name terrorists seem to lie in the Arab-Israeli conflict, prompted by an odd combination of sympathy in the press for the Palestinian Arabs and intimidation by them." Worth considering also is the idea that such sympathy and/or intimidation may be something we learn in school, a way of thinking linked to a widespread moral paralysis born of the conditioned response to suspend judgment.

In the case of the Beslan atrocity, for example, we're talking about the ski-masked, explosive-belted bastards who seized more than one thousand innocent people, children, parents, and teachers who came to school to celebrate the beginning of a new year, not to be imprisoned in a school gymnasium booby-trapped with mines and enmeshed in trip wires. Terrorists, no? Not so fast, according to the fourth estate. They were "militants," or "rebels." It's not that journalists were necessarily endorsing the Beslan terrorists and the jihadist cause of their leader, Shamil Basayev, to establish an Islamic caliphate in the Caucausus. (Basayev, killed by Russian forces in 2006, also made noises about reviving the Islamic caliphate with the capital city in "Al Kudsa" [Jerusalem].[23]) But the media's studied nonjudgmentalism on this and other atrocities gives jihadist terrorists a perpetual benefit of the doubt. Such doubts—raised in the language of "neutrality"—reserve a crucial moral space for the possibility of sympathetic judgment, enforcing the notion that blamelessness for terrorism is just as possible as blame. This implies that terrorism is not beyond the pale, which, in a civilized society, is no longer exactly a "neutral" position to take. Treating terrorism with an evenhandedness accorded to competing tax plans creates an atmosphere that is amoral to a point of immorality. Besides staving off condemnation and leaving room for approval, the act of suspending judgment—and this is what may be most significant—delivers terrorism and terrorists from the nether realm that all civilizations reserve for taboo, anathema, and abomination. This begins to explain why the practice is so dangerous.

Reuters (Beslan terrorists = gunmen) says its doesn't "characterize the subjects of news stories, but instead [reports] their actions." To do so, the wire service follows "a policy to avoid the use of emotive words." But "terrorism," which may usually be defined as attacks on noncombatants in civilian settings, is employed by terrorists specifically to create emotion—terror—for political or strategic ends. "Terrorism," then, is not only an emotive word, it is an emotive practice. Repressing the word not only mischaracterizes the action, it also serves to supress, and even numb, society's natural reaction of salutary abhorence.

Not that most media would agree. The *Chicago Tribune* (Beslan terrorists = "militants") defends eschewing the "t" word as a way to provide "unbiased" coverage. "No intellectually honest person can deny that 'terrorist' is a word freighted with negative judgment and bias," writes Don Wycliff, the newspaper's ombudsman. "So we sought terms that carried *no such judgment*" (emphasis added). This is as good an introduction as any to that hoary cliché: One man's freedom fighter is another man's terrorist. Or, as *The Boston Globe*'s ombudsman Christine Chinlund put it with a gratuitously feminist twist: "One person's terrorist is another's freedom fighter."[24] The real question is, if the killer is a terrorist to "Us," who cares if he's a freedom fighter to "Them"? But I am forgetting: We are supposed to have learned that there is no "Us" just as there is no "Them." Even in the face of terrorism, there can be no such consensus—"no such judgment," as the *Tribune* editor put it, no such Western-based belief in the sanctity of pizza parlors, commuter trains, and the first day of school. This shattered consensus helps explain why, when the first raw shock of the latest terrorist barbarity fades away—discos, skyscrapers, hospitals, yawn—so, too, does sympathy for the victim. Or at least it must now jockey for space with sympathy for the terrorist.

On some level, this is the latest incarnation of the age-old encounter between the West and the rest—specifically, the non-Western Other encountered during various periods of Western exploration, conquest, and colonization. Age of Exploration Europeans liked to talk about the "noble savage," acknowledging or projecting a nobility onto the primitive peoples of the New World that canceled out, or compensated for, their obvious savagery. A striking parallel seems to exist in contemporary analysis of the Islamic terrorist—sorry, "militant"—and his assault on heretofore Western civilization. Just as apologists have seen in white man–scalping redskins the desperation of the primitive in the face of an advanced and encroaching civilization, apologists today see in the suicide bomber a similar desperation, a plight in which a terrorist's life and limbs are his only weapons against a technologically superior and encroaching civilization. What sounds like an apology for Islamic terrorism against Israeli, American, and other Western targets also sounds like a variation on the traditional theme: enlightened society meets primal scream. And who's to say . . . whatever?

We can trace the first more or less flowering of this relationship with the Other to the sixteenth century, writes Islamic history scholar Ibn Warraq. That was when the noble savage theme emerged as a rhetorical device European writers used to critique their own societies. Warraq points to the writings of Peter Martyr Anglerius (1459–1525), who contrasted the greed and cruelty of Spanish conquistadors with the "happier" Indians who peopled an Edenic paradise "free from money, laws, treacherous judges, deceiving books, and the anxiety of an uncertain future."[25] Under Martyr's influence, Montaigne (1533–1592) would go on to "develop the first full-length portrait of the 'noble savage' in his celebrated essay 'On Cannibals.'" Warraq pinpoints this essay as being "the source of the idea of cultural relativism." (In a nutshell, Montaigne lays it all out in his assessment of Brazilian Indians: "I am not so anxious that we should note the horrible savagery of these acts as concerned that, whilst judging their faults so correctly, we should be so blind to our own. . . . [We] surpass them in every kind of barbarity.") The noble savage myth endured through the centuries, taking in not just indigenous peoples of the Americas, but also other non-European peoples, including Muslims in the Ottoman East.[26] By the eighteenth century, Warraq tells us:

> The noble savage was simply a device to criticize and comment on the follies of
> one's own civilization. . . . By emphasizing the corruption, vice, and degradation

of the Europeans, eighteenth-century writers exaggerated the putative superiority of the alien culture, the wisdom of the Chinese or Persian or Peruvian moralist and commentator. They were not really interested in other cultures for their own sake; in fact, they had very little knowledge of these civilizations.[27]

In this era of the ideal Other, it was the antimaterialist, anticlerical likes of Voltaire, Gibbon, and Carlysle who used the Other like a goad to poke and prod their own societies. "Europe has always needed a myth for purposes of comparison and castigation," historian Bernard Lewis writes. As Lewis tells it, after Europeans became disillusioned with the stereotypically "wise and urbane" Chinese, "there was a vacancy for an Oriental myth. Islam was in many ways suitable."[28]

And even necessary, although not simply to energize what Lewis aptly calls "Western intellectual shadowplay." Historian Bat Ye'or sees the myth of Islamic tolerance as piece of propaganda born of nineteenth-century political expediency. Such a myth was engineered, she says, to maintain the great powers' balance of power in Europe, which was at the time anchored in the East by (Muslim) Turkey's block against a (Christian) Russian advance to the Mediterranean. She credits the British with primary authorship: "To justify the maintenance of the [Muslim] Turkish yoke on the [Christian] Slavs, this yoke had to be presented to public opinion as a just government. The [Muslim] Ottoman Empire was painted by Turkophiles as a model for a multi-[ethnic], multi-religious empire."[29]

But a tolerant Turkey was always a fraudulent model, given its foundation in sharia (Islamic law), which codified harsh inequities between men and women, Muslims and non-Muslims. These didn't go unnoticed. Despite the machinations of geopolitical mythmaking, the work of such nineteenth- and twentieth-century scholars of Islam as Sir William Muir, David S. Margoliouth, Thomas Patrick, Arthur Jeffrey, and many others cataloged copious evidence of Islamic repression and intolerance of non-Muslims. Still, the myth survived. Besides taking its place in the narrative of European diplomacy, the myth was increasingly perpetuated, perhaps paradoxically, by devout Christians. Their Islamic knowledge was deeper than the intellectual apologists of a century or two before, but, as priests and missionaries, their motives were different because their times were different. Ibn Warraq explains: Rather than use Islam "as a weapon against [European] intolerance, cruelty, dogma, clergy, and Christianity," as seventeenth- and eighteenth-century intellectuals had done, these Christians of the nineteenth and twentieth centuries increasingly believed "that Christianity and Islam stood or fell together." In an age of rationalism, skepticism, and atheism, Christian scholars took it upon themselves to protect Islam and its totalitarian dogma from deconstruction, just as they protected Christianity from undergoing similar deconstruction. "Thus, by the end of the twentieth century," Warraq writes, "Christian scholars of Islam had become the unwitting guardians and perpetrators of the myth of Islamic tolerance."[30]

The above is a brief explanation of how the myth of Islamic tolerance—noble Islam?—became lodged in the mind of the West. But there's a crucial difference in the contemporary incarnation of this Other. Where the Other used to live, vividly imagined if dimly understood, in the Western imagination, the Other now lives, quite literally, in the West itself. If the Other was once a remote star by which the West liked to see its own failings, proximity has changed the light completely as a massive demographic shift has brought Islam, chief among clashing civilizations, deep into Europe. The Other is still vividly imagined, if dimly understood; but where he once provided intellectuals with a theoretical foil against modernity, the Other—in this century, in the guise of Islam—now manifests itself as a concrete bloc. The Other-inspired tradition of self-criticism is no longer adequate in these circumstances. Instead, the Other demands and receives a kind of cultural accommodation that is nothing short of revolutionary. In the real-life endgame of multicultural "inclusion," then, this would seem to make the West's dismantlement inevitable.

The story of France and the hijab offers an inkling as to how this is taking place. In 2003, when the French government determined that Muslim girls, draped in the hijab, or head scarf, were inserting religion into the state-run and avowedly secular French classroom, it passed a law. The new law barred Muslim dress in the public schools. This ban on the hijab—a form of dress, like Muslims, that is relatively new to France—came at a very high, Judeo-Christian price. Also banned by law were the star of David and the yarmulke (Jewish skullcap), "large" crucifixes, along with the turban of the Sikhs. In other words, all these religious symbols, which, in modern times, had coexisted as easily in France as their religions had, were suddenly stripped and hidden away from the public square. Why? The reason was to save Islam's face: to make it appear as though the hijab hadn't been singled out as an offending symbol, despite the fact that it was. And why was it so singled out? The answer has something to do with the fact that the hijab—unlike the star of David, the yarmulke, the cross, and the Sikh's turban—symbolizes a Muslim way of life that makes sharia the law of the land, any land. Allowing the head scarf, goes the argument, creates a climate hospitable to other special, extra-Western demands, from the insistence of Muslim men that their wives be treated by female doctors, to a refusal to tolerate certain Western texts in the classroom, to the institution of sharia-compliant (no-interest) loans, forced marriage, and polygamy, to the toleration of jihadist treason in the mosque, to, the Islamic hope goes, universal submission to sharia in a global caliphate. No other religious symbol on earth packs this totalitarian punch. But France—and this has happened elsewhere, including Germany, where school hijab bans have also stripped nuns of their habits—has decided to pretend otherwise. Thus, for the government to bar a symbol of religious oppression, all other symbols of religion were judged oppressive also. In the name of tolerance, they were deemed equally provocative; in the name of inclusion, they were all banned.

In such a way is traditional (pre-Islamic) society dismantled, symbol by symbol, law by law. Are all religious symbols, and thus all religions, equally prone to incite trouble, if not terrorism? And are all religious symbols, and thus all religions, equally imperialistic, and thus incompatible with an ecumenically based secular democracy? Of course not. But for France to admit Islam's violent past, present and, to date, unreformed future, is to advance a case for discrimination—in this example, to justify a ban on the hijab of resurgent Islam, while justifying the acceptance of the cross of quiescent Christianity, the star of David of beleaguered Judaism, and the turban of nonbelligerent Sikhism. Such a judgment is a multicultural impossibility. Rather than resist the bigotry of the hijab, France (and by extension, the West), without even the courtesy of a show trial, will always plead guilty, admitting to the catchall culpability of itself and its symbols—and hence, its beliefs.

This could only happen in an era of Western identity-decline, a time in which cultural relativism has wedged itself between the West and those original and defining beliefs. The extent of the estrangement comes into focus in a story of a brief but intense identity fight that broke out at Harvard in 2002 over what constituted the acceptable bounds of a specifically Christian identity on the multicultural campus. The point of contention was whether the college—founded in 1636, let's recall, as an institution for Puritan ministers—would renew its official recognition of a tiny campus Christian group, the Harvard Radcliffe Christian Fellowship. Here was the deal: While any student could join the Harvard Radcliffe Christian Fellowship, the group drew its leadership from among candidates who actually believed in the Holy Spirit and the resurrection of Jesus Christ.

This was unacceptable discrimination, according to the brave, new editors at the *Harvard Crimson* student newspaper; indeed, they argued, it violated Harvard's antidiscrimination policy. As one editorial put it, Harvard was "in error for not demanding that the club remove its discriminatory policy from its constitution. All students should be free to participate in College activities without being discriminated against because of belief."[31]

Zounds. Given that a Christian fellowship is one big college activity uniquely dependent on belief, it would seem that Muffy and Jason and Savonarola went a little far this time; ultimately, the College thought so, too, because it continued extending recognition to the Christian group. But the case laid out by the opposition made clear the extent to which that basic Christian identity was not only nothing sacred, but that the manifestation of its very existence was open to "liberal" censure. According to this next generation of sensitivity trainers and diversity consultants, any student who wanted to lead the Christian Fellowship "should not be excluded because of a reluctance to accept certain tenets." Moreover, they wrote, Fellowship members should be "forced" by Harvard to eliminate these "certain tenets"—you know, Christ, the Holy Spirit—from their leadership requirements "or lose College recognition."[32]

In their totalitarian zeal, these best and brightest types helpfully crystallized the obvious threat and the apparent contradiction at the core of multicultural groupthink: in the name of inclusiveness, elimination; in the name of diversity, conformity. But the apparent contradiction is an illusion. In opposing college recognition for the Christian-ness of the Christian Fellowship—and, in so doing, provoking no discernible outrage on or off campus—the students were only applying the familiar lessons of multiculturalism. These lessons taught them, simultaneously, to embrace "diversity," since we are all different, and to deny distinction, since we are all the same. In embracing diversity and denying distinction, then, the students set out to stop a Christian group from being led by believing Christians—and it all made perfect multicultural sense. That is, there's no contradiction when the "diversity" being embraced is non-Western, and the distinction being denied is Western.

The result? This multiculti bear hug has left society in a state of moral, cultural, and political paralysis, which the following report should illustrate. It comes from Steven Vincent, the American journalist who in 2005 was kidnapped and murdered in Iraq. In his final Internet post, this one on corruption in Basra, he interviewed a Gary Cooperesque U.S. Air Force captain in charge of handing out contracting jobs worth up to $1 million to the locals. The captain explained his modus operandi.

> "I want to have a positive effect on this country's future," the Captain averred. "For example, whenever I learn of a contracting firm run by women, I put it at the top of my list for businesses I want to consider for future projects." I [Steven Vincent] felt proud of my countryman; you couldn't ask for a more sincere guy.
>
> Layla [Vincent's translator], however, flashed a tight, cynical smile. "How do you know," she began, "that the religious parties haven't put a woman's name on a company letterhead to win a bid? Maybe you are just funneling money to extremists posing as contractors." Pause. The Captain looked confused. "Religious parties? Extremists?" . . .

Layla and I gave him a quick tutorial about the militant Shiites who have transformed once free-wheeling Basra into something resembling Savanorola's Florence.

The Captain seemed taken aback. . . . "I'll have to take this into consideration . . . I certainly *hope* none of these contracts are going to the wrong people." . . . Collecting himself, "But should we really get involved in choosing one political group over another?" the Captain countered. "I mean, I've always believed that we shouldn't project American values onto other cultures—that we should let them be. *Who is to say we are right and they are wrong?*" [Emphasis added.][33]

Et tu, Captain America?

As Vincent observed, "And there it was, the familiar Cultural-Values-Are-Relative argument, suprising though it was to hear it from a military man." "Surprising" isn't the word. It's one thing to get this mindless mantra from a Maryland public school teacher with rings on his toes and multiculturalism on his agenda, quite another to hear it from a twenty-first-century Gary Cooper–type. But there it was: wings on his chest and nonjudgmentalism in his heart. Layla, for one, "would have none of it," Vincent continued, describing a scene of pathos reminiscent of Cervantes via Broadway, as when in *Man of La Mancha,* Dulcinea and Sancho Panza desperately try to make Don Quixote remember his quest.

"No, believe me!" she exclaimed sitting forward on her stool. "These religious parties are wrong! Look at them, their corruption, their incompetence, their stupidity! Look at the way they treat women! How can you say you cannot judge them? Why shouldn't you apply your own cultural values?"[34]

The question is excellent, the answer depressing. It's not that our "cultural values" are fungible, exactly; in the case of the Air Force officer in Basra, such values came down to equal rights before the law, and maybe just "law" generally—as distinct from the law of the jungle (desert). Such precepts should be easy to stick to. But, as the Air Force officer said, "Who is to say we are right and they are wrong?" It is as widely believed now as gospel once was that Western civilization has contributed to the world just one set of cultural values among many sets of cultural values—even in the eyes of those who fight to preserve them; and even in comparison, in this case, to the lawless Basra barbarism born of totalitarian Islam. *That's not gross; that's their culture.* If such sets of values are truly interchangeable, there is no compelling reason why Captain America should prize, apply, or even prefer, his own. What the American journalist and his Iraqi friend were looking at was the end of the multicultural line; the saturation point. "I want to have a positive effect on this country," the captain said. It is difficult to have a positive effect when Captain America is a liberator who brings nothing but liberty.

There is a hollowness to the whole enterprise that is embodied by the captain's relativism, a barren chamber where the empty slogan "war on terror" echoes on without meaning. That is, terror is a tactic. You don't make war on a tactic; you make war on the people who use it. Imagine if FDR had declared "the war on sneak attack" or the "war on blitzkrieg." It doesn't make sense and neither does "war on terror." And not only does it not make sense, it also uncovers our biggest handicap going in: that perilous lack of cultural confidence, that empty core at our heart. Where an empty core has nothing with which to refute the absurdity of Bush = Hitler, an empty core has nothing with which to define "a war on terror." Who are we to say . . . who we are fighting . . . and why?

This is not a flippant tag. In this war for survival, we don't know who we are; little wonder the identity of the enemy—his history, his teachings, his goals—has remained in many ways anonymous. This identity crisis is profound. But maybe such a phase is inevitable in the life of an adolescent culture like ours. Coined by Erik Erikson in 1970, the now-familiar term "identity crisis" describes that stretch of adolescence, usually marked by "a loss of the sense of sameness and historical continuity of one's self." Culturally, we see that loss in spades. Also, by definition, there may be "confusion over values"—such confusion is universal—or "an inability to accept the role the individual perceives as being expected of him by society." This last symptom is also familiar, given our split personality as both world policeman and world villain. Lacking parental guidance, this adolescent culture of ours may be doomed not only to perpetual adolescence, but also perpetual identity crisis. The glib pop terminology doesn't begin to conjure up the ravages of a culture that has lost its core. Lawrence Auster has written extensively on this condition.

Under the reign of multiculturalism, Americans have been undergoing for decades, as if in slow motion, what the historian Thomas Molnar once described as "the collapse of the old order, the sudden realization that the universe of a given community has lost its center." Molnar, a refugee from Communist Hungary, calls this phenomenon "verbal terror." The actual terrorist, by blowing up actual human beings, makes the members of a society feel that every assumption that has constituted their world, the very ability to walk down a street or ride in a bus, is vanishing, and thus weakens their will to resist the terrorists' political demands. The *verbal* terrorist, by smearing everything great and ordinary about a people and their institutions, makes them feel that nothing about themselves is legitimate.[35]

Put into such terms, our renunciation of cultural paternity begins to make sense; it's a natural consequence of believing in our own illegitimacy. No wonder, then, that when we *do* say something to define or defend all those many "great and ordinary" things about ourselves and our institutions, it invariably comes up short and mumbling, the crucial point missing, withheld by a reticence born of shame. In the debates of the day, we (who are so inclined) rail against hanging obscene art in the museums—Mapplethorpe's bullwhip-bottom studies, for instance, or Serrano's *Piss Christ*—only because such art is helped along by taxpayer dollars, never because it menaces the public life of our culture. We (who are so inclined) rail against teen promiscuity because it's a health risk, never because it's an affront to the probity of our culture. We (who are so inclined) rail against the explosion in illegal immigration because it breaks the law (changeable, after all), never because it's killing our culture. These are off-kilter arguments, timidly oblique, half-hearted—and so very common. Which suggests the total victory the war of "verbal" terror has won. By chastened consensus, Western culture, the expression of Western peoples, is deemed narrow, bigoted, and scrap-heap ready. Only the "inclusion" of non-Western cultures, so the accepted thinking goes, can endow it with the legitimacy of "diversity."

Hence, the cacophony of voices, lumping together sublime William Shakespeare with ridiculous Rigoberta Menchú, that passes for new-and-improved academia; hence, the hodgepodge of cultures that passes for the new and improved nation state. But to what end? The decision by the city of London to erect a statue to Nelson Mandela in Trafalgar Square translates the answer into simple, stone symbols anyone can understand.

Spearheaded by the radical mayor of London, Ken Livingstone, this decision of symbolism and statuary constitutes an "inclusive" act. That's because, in multicultural patois, "inclusive" means introducing a non-Western element (South Africa's antiapartheid hero) into a Western milieu (London's most famous square). Dedicated to the 1805 naval battle that ended Napoleon's plans to invade England but killed its victorious commander, Horatio, Lord Nelson, Trafalgar Square might seem to have been adequately, even admirably adorned by Nelson's towering stone image topping a 185-foot column anchored by a brass capital made from captured French guns. But not according to multiculti theory. Lo, these many decades, it seems, the square has only managed to express a noninclusive monoculture. Introducing a bronze sculpture of Nelson Mandela fixes everything because it introduces a vital "diversity" into the oppressive Britishness of it all.

This is really nothing new in London, where in 1998, for example, Westminster Abbey—storied British site of coronations, royal weddings, and state funerals with monuments and plaques to famed British monarchs, famed British

writers, and famed British political leaders galore—spruced up its façade by fill-
ing the ten empty statuary niches over its massive main entrance with ten Christian martyrs. Notably enough, they were all foreigners—and the first foreigners to
be so honored. Whatever good these worthies may have done—from American
civil rights leader Martin Luther King, Jr., to the liberal Salvadoran Archbishop
Óscar Arnulfo Romero, with lesser known martyrs from Poland, South Africa,
Uganda, Russia, Germany, India, China, and Papua New Guinea in between—
they were neither British, nor were they acting in British interests.[36] What they
represented, besides Christian goodness, was "diversity."

What goes unnoticed is that such "diversity" actually brings more-of-the-
sameness: every place becomes like any other. Or, rather, every Western place becomes like any other; i.e., every Westminster Abbey becomes a mini–United
Nations. The example of the city schoolroom offers a good illustration: When 43
percent of New York City schoolchildren speak one of nearly 170 languages
other than English at home,[37] and between a quarter to more than half of London schoolchildren speak one of three hundred languages other than English at
home,[38] both cities have achieved an indistinguishable "diversity." No longer singularly American or singularly British, they are interchangeably global. Group-
ing Nelson Mandela with Lord Nelson and the several other British war heroes in
Trafalgar Square has the same, if symbolic, effect. No longer will Trafalgar
Square evoke the quintessence of British culture. It will be, as London's Mayor
Ken Livingstone puts it, a "world square."[39]

And that is the point: a world square, not a British one; a global identity, not
a Western one. It is surely a paradox that the rest of the world—meaning the nations of the non-Western world about which the Western world is so assiduously
"inclusive"—remains strikingly, immovably, and unapologetically nondiverse,
uniform even, in every way: ethnically, religiously, and culturally. For example,
students may speak Urdu, Arabic, Pashtun, and Turkish in British, French,
Dutch, and German schools; they don't, however, speak English, French, Dutch,
and German in Pakistani, Arab, Afghani, and Turkish schools. Mosque construction breaks ground all over Europe and the United States, but churches and
synagogues do not rise in the Islamic world. The president of the United States
adds a Koran to the White House library for Ramadan; Bibles are confiscated
and destroyed by the Saudi Arabian government. Born in Benin, Achille Acakpo
teaches traditional African dance and percussion in Vienna; who born in Vienna
is teaching Strauss waltzes in Benin?

In some way, these dramatic acts of inclusiveness—unrequited elsewhere in
the world—may be an extension of the intellectual inquisitiveness that, as Ibn
Warraq writes, "is one of the hallmarks of Western civilization." That is, maybe
the same curiosity that has driven exploration—global, scientific, and artistic—is

a factor in our acceptance of cultural novelty. Warraq quotes J. M. Roberts on the subject of Western curiosity.

> The massive indifference of some civilizations and their lack of curiosity about other worlds is a vast subject. Why, until very recently, did Islamic scholars show no wish to translate Latin or western European texts into Arabic? Why, when the English poet Dryden could confidently write a play focused on the succession in Delhi after the death of the Mogul emperor Aurungzebe, is it a safe guess that no Indian writer ever thought of a play about the equally dramatic politics of the English seventeenth-century court? It is clear that an explanation of European inquisitiveness and adventurousness must lie deeper than economics, important though they may have been. It was not just greed which made Europeans feel they could go out and take the world. The love of gain is confined to no particular people or culture. It was shared in the fifteenth century by many an Arab, Gujarati, or Chinese merchant. Some Europeans wanted more. They wanted to explore.[40]

Having explored the world, having colonized huge swaths of it, having returned again to their little homelands, the West, not the world it conquered, has been transformed. That is, it is the West that has become "inclusive" and "multicultural"; not the "rest." Mayor Livingstone can declare that erecting a Mandela statue in Trafalgar Square signifies "the peaceful transition" from British empire as symbolized by Lord Nelson "to a multiracial and multicultural world," but what he's really talking about is the British transition to a multiracial and multicultural *London*—a fait accompli—where no one can tell Nelson from Nelson. Opposition to the mayor's plan was largely aesthetic, limited to bickering over placement of the statue, not over whether a bronze likeness of Nelson Mandela—the long-suffering South African apartheid-buster with a distressing fondness for despots from Castro to Mugabe to Arafat to Qadafi—constitutes a singular expression of British identity. Indeed, it became apparent that there were no British cultural or historical imperatives at issue here because there were no British cultural or historical imperatives, period. The only cultural objection was an oblique outburst saying the statue represented a "major and awkward change in the narrative of the square."[41] Exactly why it was major or awkward, or what the narrative of the square was to begin with, went undefined, and thus undefended under Admiral Nelson's distant, one-eyed gaze of carved Scottish stone.

It's the story of our civilization—undefined and undefended. As we learn to get along, eyes closed to our own identity, we also turn a blind eye toward everyone else's. Often literally. In the summer of 2005, in the jittery wake of jihadist attacks on the London Underground (notable for being the first Islamic terrorist attacks on a Western country by homegrown Islamic terrorists), *The New York Times* editorialized on the timely topic of commuter safety. The aspect under consideration was searching buses and subways for bombs, something we do in post-identity America.

> The police officers must be careful not to give the impression that every rider who looks Arab or South Asian is automatically a subject of suspicion. . . . Those who are selected simply because they are carrying packages should be chosen in a way that does not raise fears of racial profiling—by, for example, searching every fifth or twelfth person, with the exact sequence chosen at random.[42]

What is most scary about public safety à la *The New York Times*—its absurdity, or the purpose of its absurdity? The point here, according to *The Times,* was not to avoid death by murder-bomber (melted flesh and mangled steel) at the potential cost of racial profiling (hurt feelings); but rather to avoid raising "fears of racial profiling" (hurt feelings) at the potential cost of death by murder-bomber (melted flesh and mangled steel). And mark the creed the enlightened ones urged all good citizens to follow: In the Exact Sequence Chosen at Random We Trust. It makes perfect sense. Since we have denied our own identity so long, the Other—even the Other who may at any moment explode, driving nuts and bolts into the burning flesh of unarmed innocents—has also ceased to matter. Which may or may not seem to amount to much when it comes to the adventures of Mary Poppins, but is it any way to fight a war?

8. THE REAL CULTURE WAR

In my study of communist societies, I came to the conclusion that the purpose of communist propaganda was not to persuade or convince, nor to inform, but to humiliate; and therefore, the less it corresponded to reality the better. When people are forced to remain silent when they are being told the most obvious lies, or even worse when they are forced to repeat the lies themselves, they lose once and for all their sense of probity. To assent to obvious lies is to co-operate with evil, and in some small way to become evil oneself. One's standing to resist anything is thus eroded, and even destroyed. A society of emasculated liars is easy to control. I think if you examine political correctness, it has the same effect and is intended to.

—THEODORE DALRYMPLE[1]

The civilization of dhimmitude* does not develop all at once. It is a long process that involves many elements and a specific mental conditioning. It happens when people replace history by myths, when they fight to uphold these destructive myths more than their own values because they are confused by having transformed lies into truth. . . . They replace history with childish tales, thus living in amnesia, inventing moral justification for their own self-destruction.

—BAT YE'OR[2]

During times of universal deceit,
telling the truth becomes a revolutionary act.
—GEORGE ORWELL (ATTRIBUTED)

Let me ask that question again: Is it any way to fight a war? Which war is that?

Before 9/11, the war for identity was well known as the "culture war." Even at its bloodiest and most wounding, though, this was a fight embodied not by troop movements across hostile terrain, but by syllabus changes in lecture halls. That's not to say that lecture halls weren't hostile terrain, but everyone lived, more or less, to "fight" another day.

---

*"Dhimmitude," which will be discussed at length, is the term historian Bat Ye'or has introduced to the lexicon to describe a mode of behavior or state of mind fostered by sharia-sanctioned religious inferiority.

Or not. To make a long story short, in the battle between the multiculturalists on the Left and the culture warriors on the Right, it was a resounding multiculturalist victory. "Hey, hey, ho, ho, Western culture's got to go!" may once have sounded as shocking as throwing Leonardo da Vinci, Louis Pasteur, Robert Browning, and Clark Gable overboard for being "dead white males," but Western culture went, and DWMs are hangers-on in a new, multicultural pantheon. The Western canon, cultural citadel of Judeo-Christian civilization, was—to extend the war metaphor—breached and overrun by "the rest." In this post-culture-war period, then, what Americans are taught about themselves and their past is no longer identifiably Western but self-consciously multicultural; what Americans expect of their future is no longer minimally Western but increasingly multicultural. This is the result of the education revolution, from preschool to grad school, that became entrenched particularly since 1988 when Stanford junked its Western culture requirement for a multicultural sequence of courses.

Whatever controversy raged at that time is by now cold and scattered ash. Case in point: Nearly twenty years later, having just flipped through a seventh grade reader[3] from a traditional Catholic school, I see a well-balanced, indeed, finely calibrated selection of stories—well-balanced and finely calibrated, that is, with regard to race, color, and creed. The table of contents is, by author, a perfectly planned menu of identity politics, which is not at all the same as a nourishing dish of the cultural best that has been thought and said: Isaac Bashevis Singer (male but okay by virtue of being Jewish), Amy Tan, Nadya Labi, Walt Whitman (male but okay by virtue of being thought to have been homosexual), Emily Dickinson, Walter de la Mare (French), Alex Haley, Bill Cosby, Gary Soto, Johnette Howard, Alice Walker, oh, and William T. Shakespeare ("T" is for token). End of story? Hardly. More like a beginning, and one that doesn't have an ending. Yet.

That became clearest on 9/11, of all days, when the Multicultural States of America, a nation that had taught itself to believe that the complete works of Alice Walker and William Shakespeare were interchangeable—offering equal enlightenment and meriting equal study (giving Shakespeare the benefit of the doubt)—came under cataclysmic attack. Thousands dead in a burning hole in Manhattan; the Pentagon ripped open; a battle in the skies that went smash in the woods of Pennsylvania. It was a real war, this time, not a culture war . . . or was it a real culture war?

As the Twin Towers rained down fire and flesh, a country that had been taught to equate *The Federalist Papers* with the Seneca Falls Declaration; to see in Western capitalism a shade of gray indistinguishable from gulag communism (think John le Carré); to value Tolmec culture as it valued Ancient Greece; to accept that standard English was no more "valid" than so-called black English; to emphasize self-esteem over self-respect; to believe, or at least to pretend to believe, all these things; this same country found itself in the unthinkable position of having to ward off attack, of having to fight off someone or something to protect what soon became officially if somewhat awkwardly known as "the homeland." Suddenly, as we all remember, our streets and shops, cars and lapels, porches and plazas, bristled with flags, that stirring symbol of unity and fight. What is harder to recall is exactly when the flags came down. They did, of course, most of them, even as the war that started on that day goes on.

And to what end? I ask that not as a rhetorical endorsement of the futility of war, to which I don't ascribe; war, fought with just purpose, is never futile. But what do we fight for, and—no less important—what do we fight *against*? These are skull-cracking questions for the post-grown-up, multiculturalist society that now makes up the Western world. It's not just the mystery identity of "we" that's problematic. When a civilization defines itself by an eternally youthful pliance and infinite openness—just as its citizens define their personal lives, not at all coincidentally—it's difficult to determine what, if anything, that same civilization can be definitively closed to.

A snapshot depicting the resulting limbo comes from the Netherlands, land of windmills, tulips, and, in recent decades, mosques. There, what is considered the most boundary-free, tolerant society in the world (gay marriage, legalized drugs and prostitution, euthanasia) struggles to coexist with a walled-off and intolerant Islamic population in the wake of nation-shaking acts of specifically Islamic violence.

To recap: In 2002, Pim Fortuyn, a rocketing political star campaigning against the Islamization of Dutch society, was shot dead. In 2003, his Dutch assassin confessed to killing him in order to, as *The Telegraph* put it, "defend Dutch Muslims from persecution."[4] In 2004, Theo van Gogh was shot off his bicycle, stabbed, and nearly beheaded on an Amsterdam street by Mohammed Bouyeri, a Dutch-born Muslim. The assassin said van Gogh had "insulted" Islam with his film, *Submission,* which critiques the plight of Islamic women, and, as Bouyeri put it while on trial in 2005, "the law [the Koran] compels me to chop off the head of anyone who insults Allah and the prophet."[5]

This, er, "point of view" is prevalent in the Netherlands to the extent that the Dutch Interior Ministry has established a special unit to assess death threats from Islamic groups and provide security for the "soaring number of Dutch academics, lawmakers and other public figures [who have been] forced to accept 24-hour protection or go into hiding." Among those living under Holland's protective lock and key are parliamentarians Geert Wilders and, at least until she emigrated to the United States in 2006, van Gogh's collaborator, Ayaan Hirsi Ali, as well as Amsterdam mayor Jacob Cohen and Afshin Ellian, an Islamic, reform-minded, Iranian-born university professor of—irony of ironies—"social cohesion."[6]

Some social cohesion: Also in 2004, the Dutch government uncovered plans for an Islamic group's attack on the Dutch parliament, Schiphol Airport in Amsterdam, the Borssele nuclear reactor, the defense ministry, and the Leidschendam office of the AIVD, the country's secret service.[7] In 2005, on the first anniversary of van Gogh's death, a shot was fired into the office of the Dutch interior minister, Rita Verdonk, a proponent of Muslim-restrictive immigration policies. She is now said to serve her country in a bulletproof vest.[8] A scholarly conference on Islam in Europe at the Hague in 2006 required a level of security, *The Times* of London reported, "just one level below 'national emergency.' "[9] Given that the Netherlands hasn't seen such currents of violence since the seventeenth century—and then it was a matter of one political assassination—the Amsterdam city council recently pondered what it could do to "moderate" the "extremism" of the city's burgeoning Muslim population. What was needed, the council decided, was an "alternative" media message of "moderate" Islam. This strategy, alas, was about as likely to neutralize the jihadist hatespeak poisoning Dutch society as putting up balloons at a Nazi rally. That's because in urging moderation (balloons), the city council refused to ban any examples of extremism (Nazi rally). This meant that while the council would sponsor messages to Muslims to make nice with infidels, it would do nothing to ban messages, for example, urging Muslims to hurl homosexuals to their death from tall buildings headfirst—as advocated in the Dutch book *De weg van de Moslem,* or *The Way of the Muslim.* (If victims don't die on impact, the book instructs, the faithful should stone the wounded to death.) Book banning, the council said, would limit "the freedom to express opinions," and that, it believed, would be "counterproductive."[10]

But how productive, to use the good Dutch burghers' word, is tolerance without limits? The British philosopher Karl R. Popper formulated his answer more than a half century ago.

> Unlimited tolerance must lead to the disappearance of tolerance. If we extend unlimited tolerance even to those who are intolerant, if we are not prepared to defend a tolerant society against the onslaught of the intolerant, then the tolerant will be destroyed and tolerance with them. . . . *We should therefore claim, in the name of tolerance, the right not to tolerate the intolerant.* We should claim that any movement preaching intolerance places itself outside the law, and we should consider incitement to intolerance and persecution as criminal, in the same way we should consider incitement to murder, or to kidnapping, or to the revival of the slave trade, as criminal. [Emphasis added.][11]

As the situation in Holland reveals, the West is now at the point where enforcing "openness" trumps preserving "tolerance." In other words, better to be "open" to intolerance than "closed" to anything—including intolerance. There must be some rich, ripe irony in the fact, according to this mind-set, that tolerating the intolerant becomes the ultimate act of openness—literally "ultimate," as Popper tells us, since tolerance of the intolerant leads to the destruction of the tolerant. Call it terminal tolerance.

In the meantime—our own era—such terminal tolerance is positively praised as an act of "inclusion"; thus, it never draws multiculti catcalls of "mean-spritedness" or "racism," the two terms of opprobrium the terminally tolerant will do absolutely anything to avoid, to the point of committing cultural suicide. By contrast, any act of closing ranks as a Western culture—banning publications calling for homosexual defenestration, maybe?—is a necessarily limiting, and, therefore, negative act of *ex*clusion, and, as such, autobranded as an act of mean-spiritedness and racism.

Or it would be so branded if any boundary-seeking, line-drawing society actually existed in the West. There isn't one, not in real life, not even in theory— maybe especially not in theory. This is due to the freezing effect multiculturalism has had on the Western logic of making distinctions among cultures, particularly between "the West" and "the rest." *Give me cultural equivalence, or give me death by media feeding frenzy:* This will be the battle cry old-timers of the future will recall from the bad old days of the war on "terror." Already, who can forget the storm of censure that rained down on former Italian Prime Minister Silvio Berlusconi for illuminating the differences between Western and Islamic culture, and for finding—for stating out loud—that Western culture was superior. It was less than two weeks after the attacks of September 11, 2001, which Berlusconi called an attack on "our civilization," when he spoke out, in Italian, about the superiority of Western civilization due to its principles of liberty. The BBC translated his remarks this way:

> We have to be conscious of the strength of our civilization. We cannot put the two civilizations on the same level. All of the achievements of our civilization: free institutions, the love of liberty itself—which represents our greatest asset—the liberty of the individual and the liberty of the peoples. These certainly are not the inheritance of other civilizations such as Islamic civilization.[12]

And the Associated Press wrote:

> We must be aware of the superiority of our civilization, a system that has guaranteed well-being, respect for human rights and—in contrast with Islamic countries— respect for religious and political rights, a system that has as its values understandings of diversity and tolerance. [Western civilization is superior

because it] has at its core, as its greatest value, freedom, which is not the heritage of Islamic culture.[13]

Versions vary somewhat, but the gist is clear. Maybe the billionaire media-mogul-turned-politician was an unlikely champion of the virtues of Western civ—or anything else for that matter. After all, the almost operatically buffoonish and scandal-ridden Berlusconi was in the public eye practically as much for his outrageous financial maneuvers as for his political programs. Nonetheless, this Italian prime minister was the lone ranger on the international horizon to seize on and uphold the essence of Western civilization—liberty, prosperity, human rights—and point out the obvious: Liberty, prosperity, and human rights are not part of Islamic civilization. *We have to be conscious, we must be aware* of this distinction. It was something worth fighting for, Berlusconi presumed, against Islamic terrorists and the Islamic nations and networks that openly, secretly, tactically, financially, or religiously support them. Some reports included Berlusconi's additional point—strangely overlooked—that just as Western liberty had defeated communism, so, too, would it vanquish Islam.

In a pre-PC time, such remarks would have been regarded as boilerplate bromides, the platitudes of a politician trying out new applause lines at the outbreak of war. But back to real life. According to the "international community" circa September 2001, Berlusconi couldn't have said anything more horrifying. First, there was the outcry from the EU outposts of Berlusconi's beloved Western civilization:

"I can hardly believe Mr. Berlusconi made such remarks because the EU is based on values such as multiculturalism and the meeting of different civilizations. . . ."[14]

"These remarks could, in a dangerous way, have consequences. . . ."[15]

"All I can say is that the values of Europe do not allow us to consider that our civilization is superior to another."[16]

"It is clear that Mr. Berlusconi's remarks were offensive and offense has been taken . . . and they were culturally inaccurate."[17]

"We certainly don't share the views expressed by Mr. Berlusconi. . . ."[18]

Not surprisingly, "Islamic civilization" was even more put out. Jordan denounced the remarks as "chauvinistic, fascist and repugnant,"[19] while the Organization of the Islamic Conference (OIC) called them "an act of aggression unbecoming of a civilized nation."[20] The Arab League said it was "waiting for either a denial or an apology," which I guess left Berlusconi the option to deny or apologize for the fact that Western-style freedom isn't a hallmark of Islam.[21] Egypt more subtly demanded "clarifications"—which, in diplospeak, means tracks-covering obfuscation, and which, in fact, is what Berlusconi ultimately ex-pressed.[22] Amidst all the sputtering, though, no one seemed to notice that West and East had found common ground, unity even, a place to vent their shared contempt for these bumptious declarations of the singularity of Western liberty and human rights.

Which again begs the question: Is this any way to fight a war? Berlusconi hadn't said anything even remotely false. Liberty, prosperity, and human rights *are* hallmarks of Western civilization; liberty, prosperity, and human rights *are not* hallmarks of Islamic civilization. End of story. They are not only worth fight-ing for, but also what comes under attack every time an Islamic terror network successfully detonates, beheads, bombs, and burns a Western or Western-allied target—thus stealing the liberty, destroying the prosperity, and revoking the hu-man rights of us all, not to mention those of its victims. So why, then, did the prime minister of Italy, land of Leonardo and La Scala, the Bridge of Sighs and the Vatican, apologize?

The late Oriana Fallaci answered this way in *The Rage and the Pride,* a book she wrote immediately after 9/11, when "I did not eat, I did not sleep, I fed on cof-fee, I kept awake with cigarettes, and the words fell on the paper like a waterfall."[23]

> I have just read that, albeit grossly and inadequately, you [Mr. Berlusconi] pre-ceded me in the defense of the Western Culture. But, as soon as the cicadas yelled racist-racist, you retracted at the speed of light. You spoke of unfortunate blunder, involuntary mistake, you promptly presented your apologies to the sons of Allah, then you swallowed the affront of their refusal and meekly accepted the hypocriti-cal reprimands of your European colleagues plus the scolding by Blair. In short, you got scared.[24]

Fallaci was right; Berlusconi got scared. But why? Certainly, there was the fact that he had zero support for his remarks from his PC colleagues, and going out on a limb is hardly second nature to most politicians. But it may also be ar-gued that he didn't have sufficient *confidence* in his remarks to weather a naysay-ing storm. This, to my way of thinking, is like saying he wasn't grown-up enough. If the confidence that comes of maturity is a casualty of the death of the grown-up, the cultural confidence of the West is a casualty of the destruction of cultural hierarchy that disappeared in the multicultural ascendance—a twenty-first-century institution Berlusconi seemed to have temporarily forgotten in the adre-nal rush of the 9/11 aftermath. When Berlusconi's Euro-confreres juxtaposed their horror at the virtues that define Western civilization with their avowal of the European Union "values" of "multiculturalism," they were expressing not just a bureacratic consensus, but a fervent orthodoxy. In this new secular religion, notions of the superiority of Western culture are heretical, an imminent threat to the leveling arrangement that makes the EU's so-called meeting of different civilizations possible. As the Eurocrats put it, "the values of Europe do not allow us to consider that our civilization is superior to another." Berlusconi's apostasy, however short-lived, threatened to upend those "values," and with them the postmodern "meeting of different civilizations," thus threatening to restore the traditional hierarchy that put Western civilization, for having enshrined liberty and human rights, at the pinnacle.

This would never do—and, of course, it didn't. It couldn't. Let Berlusconi's remarks stand and someone might declare that Shakespeare amounts to more than Alice Walker, or that ancient Greece surpasses Tolmec culture. The next thing you know, the multicultural world order has toppled. Naturally, Berlusconi apologized, and no world leader has made the same "blunder" since. And this is why what we're hearing out there—despite the catchiness of Samuel Huntington's buzz phrase—is not "the *clash* of civilizations" at all. After all, "clash" conjures up the vibrating smash of brass cymbals. There can be no Clash when one cymbal has muffled itself (the West) even as it tries to mute the sound—the attributes—of the other (Islam). What comes across, then, is a lot of shushing.

And sometimes, it sounds like Condoleezza Rice. "We in America know the benevolence that is at the heart of Islam," the secretary of state declared in 2005, addressing assembled Muslim dignitaries at the annual Ramadan dinner at the State Department.[25] The secretary of state's annual Ramadan dinner, by the way, is not to be confused with the president's annual Ramadan dinner, although it's easy to get them mixed up. The legacy of 9/11 has left us with an open-ended war abroad; the introduction of homeland hyperinsecurity; and the open-ended introduction of Ramadan celebrations all over official Washington. The latter is worth a question or two on its own, beginning with: Why? Why has it become the post-9/11 function of the United States government to celebrate Ramadan? The term "Muslim outreach" comes to mind, but, as the Judeo-Christian culture hit by Islamikazes on 9/11, haven't we got it exactly backward? That is, wouldn't Muslims better outreach themselves if the Saudi embassy, for example, celebrated Christmas and Hanukkah?

But I digress. "We in America know the benevolence that is at the heart of Islam," Rice said. Really? Is that what we know? Is that what history tells us? Is that what current events tell us? Rice's speechifying, which included a personal riff on Ramadan as being a time "characterized by sacrifice and abiding faith, by prayer and self-reflection and by compassion and profound joy," made a wicked contrast to real live Ramadan '05 headlines. Not the big ones about Scooter and Judy (remember them?), or bird flu, or Charles and Camilla, or even the substantial ones about a new Supreme Court nominee, Samuel Alito.

I'm thinking of the Muslim suicide bombing in Hadera that killed six Israelis that same Ramadan month,[26] and the Hitlerite promise of Iran's Muslim president that "the stain of disgrace"—Israel—will be "purged from the center of the Islamic world."[27] I'm thinking of the weeks of Muslim rioting in Paris, and the news that a London Underground suicide bomber was buried in Pakistan (his exploded remains, anyway) at *the shrine of an Islamic saint.*[28] In New Delhi, Muslims were suspected of killing sixty in three powerful blasts,[29] while actor Omar Sharif received a death threat on a Web site linked to al-Qaeda for playing St. Peter in an Italian television movie.[30] And I have never forgotten the three Christian girls who were beheaded in Indonesia en route to their Christian high school. Their Muslim killers carried off one of the severed heads to a newly built church, where they left it.[31]

I could go on about the magazine editor in liberated Afghanistan, himself a Muslim, who, just about the time Rice was tucking in to her Ramadan meal, had been sentenced to two years in jail for "blasphemy"—that is, criticizing sharia. Then there's *Jyllands-Posten,* the newspaper in Denmark that, as of October 2005, had already received bomb threats, become a potential terror target on an al-Qaeda Internet list, sparked street violence in Denmark and Kashmir, and drawn protests from eleven Muslim ambassadors, the Organization of the Islamic Conference, the Council of Europe, and the United Nations human rights commissioner for having published twelve cartoons of Muhammad. (Cartoon Rage 2006 would come later.) Depictions of the Islamic prophet may be a no-no under Islamic law, but redoubtable Denmark and its free (nonapologizing) newspaper was trying to demonstrate that *it* was not under Islamic law.

Condoleezza Rice isn't, either. But her soft-soap "benevolence" routine sounds more like supplication than statecraft, particularly in the context of a standard stump speech she delivers comparing the Iraqi and U.S. constitutions—with the "miracle at Philadelphia" coming up way short. "We should note that unlike in our constitutional convention, the Iraqis have not made a compromise as bad as the one that made my ancestors three-fifths of a man," she has said.[32] Yes, in 1787, slaves were indeed counted as a fractional person in pre-abolition censuses that determined how many representatives a state would send to the House of Representatives. (Slaveholders, not slavery opponents, wanted a slave to count as one person to augment that state's political power.) But it is the miracle of that eighteenth-century document that it contained the blueprint for abolition. By contrast, the 2005 Iraqi constitution (also the 2003 Palestinian Authority constitution and the 2004 Afghanistan constitution) contains provisions for a sharia state under which all men are not created equal, and freedom of conscience is denied.[33]

Failing to acknowledge the distinction, Rice engages in cultural equivalence, the Mush of Civilizations which Berlusconi reverted to so quickly back in 2001: *We're not that great; they're not that bad; we're pretty bad; they're pretty great.* There is a point to all this: Cultural equivalence, the universal mantra of the multicultural world, effectively preempts cultural confrontation. There can be no cultural confrontation—no culture clash—if we are all, roughly, the same; if we are all, roughly, no better than the other; and particularly if we (the West) are roughly worse. Such a doctrine is the geopolitical expression of political correctness, and it is informed by the same drive, the same terminal tolerance, to do whatever it takes to supress those nasty catcalls of "racism" and "mean-spiritedness." But to what end?

A few years back, just after the 2002 arrests of the so-called D.C. snipers, John Allen Muhammad and Lee Boyd Malvo, I was listening to a talk radio discussion of the case when a listener called in with a request: Would the media please refrain from identifying John Muhammad as "John Muhammad"? Identifying Muhammad as "Muhammad"—the surname the serial killer took when he converted to Islam—might reflect badly on Islam, which, as the caller explained, is a religion of peace, not violence, and whose prophet, of course, also happened to be named Muhammad. And no, this wasn't a put-on. The caller sounded only sincere, and the hosts treated him accordingly. While they gurgled over the ramifications of the Muhammad mix-up, I realized that what was most disturbing about this "logic"—the urge to repress a truth that undercuts a belief—was not its absurd extremism, but rather its mind-numbing prevalence. The caller may have taken things to its satirical limit, but we're just as likely to hear the same willful line of supression from a newspaper of record, or a head of state setting national policy. There is too much that is considered unmentionable—too much that reflects badly on Islam, not to mention its prophet, Muhammad. If, for example, our leaders spoke up about the primacy of jihad (holy war) as a uniquely Islamic institution established by Muhammad that has almost continuously convulsed large parts of the world in violence for thirteen centuries, how could they also call Islam a "religion of peace"? If our leaders broke the historic silence on the massive tragedy of non-Muslim peoples—dhimmis—subjugated by Islam according to Muhammad's example across those same thirteen centuries, how could they also tell us that Islam is "one of the world's three great religions"? Quite simply they couldn't. So, in the name of cultural equivalence that avoids cultural confrontation, the Mush of Civilizations, they keep their silence—the same sort of silence that the radio-listener, in his absurdist way, hoped to impose on the talk radio hosts.

Similar shushing, for example, characterized the coverage and anaylsis of the 2005 riots in France. In fact, you might say such shushing *was* the coverage and analysis of the 2005 riots in France. It was the Berlusconi brouhaha in reverse:

Where the Italian prime minister was muzzled as the lone voice extolling the virtues of the West (good) next to the lack thereof in Islam (bad), the Muslim riots were trumpeted across the board as being about the evils of the West (bad), and having nothing to do with Islam (good). According to an insta-consensus that emerged from Left to Right, the fault was to all one side: France. No question about it—*please, no question about it.* The rioters were nonaccountable victims, practically bystanders, whose Muslim identity was officially ignored and journalistically renounced, even as heterodox reports surfaced from time to time. One such report came from Amir Taheri, writing in the *New York Post.*

> With cries of "God is great," bands of youths armed with whatever they could get hold of went on a rampage and forced the police to flee. . . . Within hours, the original cause of the incidents was forgotten and the issue jelled around a demand by the representatives of the rioters that the French police leave the "occupied territories." . . . Some are even calling for the areas where Muslims form a majority of the population to be reorganized on the basis of the "millet" system of the Ottoman Empire: each religious community (millet) would enjoy the right to organize its social, cultural and educational life in accordance with its religious beliefs. In parts of France, a de facto millet system is already in place. . . . "All we demand is to be left alone," said Mouloud Dahmani, one of the local "emirs" engaged in negotiations to persuade the French to withdraw the police and allow a committee of sheiks, mostly from the Muslim Brotherhood, to negotiate an end to the hostilities.[34]

Such bombshells sent not even a ripple across the calm and glassy narrative of an impervious elite. And when they did (as when French intellectual Alain Finkielkraut noted the Muslim identity of the rioters in a newspaper interview), they were repressed (he publicly recanted) and smoothed over.[35] Here, as in the Berlusconi incident, Islam was taken neatly and completely off the hook. "Clash" was thus squelched, and a kind of PC peace and quiet—silence—returned to the international arena. To invoke the terminology of the death of the grown-up, the international arena was *pacified.*

This word is apt because in this de facto conspiracy of omission there is more than an element of soothing, calming fantasy; there is a load of political pabulum that fills, or tries to, the gaping void opened by the simply question, Why? Why did these riots occur? *Here, said the intelligentsia, suck on this: Like the terrorism that engraved the blood-drenched anniversaries of 9/11, 3/11, and 7/7 into collective memory, and transformed Amman, Amsterdam, Baghdad, Bali, Beslan, Davao, Hadera, Haifa, Jakarta, Jerusalem, Nairobi, New Delhi, Sharm al-Sheik, Tel Aviv, and Tunisia into hallowed outposts of mass murder, the rioting that convulsed France had nothing to do with Islam.*

Shhhh, shh: There's nothing here that one or two billion Euros won't take care of. So what if twelve French churches were destroyed and/or desecrated during the rioting?[36] So what if French intelligence has determined that 40 percent of French imams not only have no religious training but download their homilies from pro-al-Qaeda Web sites?[37] So what if Jacques Chirac, president of the French Republic, had to deploy more than two thousand police to secure his route down the Champs-Élysées for an Armistice Day ceremony at the Arc de Triomphe as though Paris were not the heart of la République, *but a war zone?[38] So what? Thank goodness none of it had anything to do with Islam and its non-assimilable legions in Europe.*

That was the narrative from the start. It was Our Story, the subtext, the thread to which we cling. The problem driving "youths" to incinerate lines of parked buses or immolate the occasional *grand-mère* on crutches was French racism, neglect, a failure to integrate—or, better, a failure to be integrated due to French racist neglect. Don't forget the snobbery of French waiters and don't forget George W. Bush. Well before the riot's last French fires were kindled, let alone cooled, *The Washington Post* editorial page, for example, said—no, it insisted: "Islamic ideology and leaders have played no part in the disturbances and many of those who are participating are not Muslim."[39] From *The New York Times* to the *National Review,* writers ruled out the role of religion. Writing in *The New York Times,* French Islamic expert Olivier Roy ruled Islam out with equally categorical and doctrinal confidence.[40]

How did they *know*? Yes, the thugs we saw depicted through the smoke of burning civilization weren't dressed for the part by Central Casting—either in the beards and robes of the mosque, or the mask and scimitar of the jihad. They looked like urban punks, "riffraff," as French Interior Minister Nicolas Sarkozy called them before diving under the covers with the rest of the Gallic government. They were, we heard, unemployed toughs and secular criminals, devoted not to Allah so much as to what you might call, loosely and very grimly, French "culture"—French pop culture, that is.

Writing in *The Weekly Standard* some weeks before the riots broke out, Olivier Guitta offered a shocking insight into one expression of that culture—rap music as we in the U.S. have never quite heard it, even at its "cop-killing" worst.[41] As Guitta explained, some of the most successful bands in France are made up "mostly of French citizens of Arab or African descent"—like our pals in the French projects, or "cités." But where so-called gangsta rap, American style, glorifies senseless violence and sexual bestiality, Muslim rap, French style, fuses that same violence and sexuality to attack the State.

Guitta translated some choice examples. There is the rap band Sniper (nice), which, not incidentally, was unsuccessfully sued in 2004 by Nicolas Sarkozy for violence and incitement in the song "La France." Sniper sings: "We're all hot for

a mission to exterminate the government and the fascists. . . . France is a b———
and we've been betrayed. . . . We f——— France, we don't care about the Republic and freedom of speech. We should change the laws so we can see Arabs
and Blacks in power in the Élysée Palace. Things have to explode."

Well, of course, things did. But not, our elites reflexively instructed us, because
of Islamic attitudes toward a non-Islamic country, but because of establishment attitudes toward a downtrodden minority. Integration, we heard, or the lack thereof,
was the problem, so integration was also the answer. But how will France—or
"FranSSe," as rapper Mr. R has titled this song—integrate this? "France is a bitch,
don't forget to f—— her to exhaustion. You have to treat her like a whore, man! . . .
France is one of the b—— who gave birth to you . . . I am not at home and I don't
give a d——, and besides the state can go f——— itself. I pee on Napoleon and
General de Gaulle . . . F—— cops, sons of whores. . . ." It went on, lashing out in
a similarly poisonous vein. Not that this stopped Fnac, the largest chain of French
music stores, from praising the popular Mr. R as "a revelation."

And so he and his rap brethren are. But a revelation of what—urban barbarism or ghetto jihad? Or some new cultural permutation of both? Such press-
ing, pertinent questions went unasked and ignored, just as Muslim rap imagery
went unexamined and unmentioned. But the vicious contempt in these lyrics, the
exhortation to humiliation, the vindictive rape imagery: These are the motifs, at
least, of brutal conquest, patterns and expressions familiar to students of Islamic
jihad for having repeated themselves over the centuries as non-Muslim lands—
Dar al Harb (Land of War)—were conquered and subjugated as Dar al Islam
(Land of Islam). Was that what was going on in France? Without doubt, such
music prefigures a state of war, although no one but the rioters was listening.

More important, no one but the rioters wanted to listen. Who in the West
wants to fight Clash when you can eat Mush? In psychology, they call this act of
mental digging-in "denial." It's familiar to anyone who didn't want to stop believing in Santa Claus even after the gross illogic of the proposition—chimneys, reindeer, ho-ho—became all too clear. Better to keep your eyes closed and *believe*;
better to wear ear plugs and hear what you want: The moderates are coming, the
moderates are coming. Similarly, in Paris, they shut their eyes and ears to the
smoke and sound of jihad, and woke up, if not to Muslim moderates, then to a
peaceable solution: mea culpa. Far less stressful than *J'accuse,* the "mea culpa" solution is part of the Western basis of cultural equivalence. *J'accuse* rings the gong
of "clash," shifting blame to the Muslim community (and demanding confronta-
tional French action). But "mea culpa" allows France to assume responsibility and
write a check. What, the French might ask, are Euros for? Better to pacify. Better
to be pacified. It isn't grown-up, but it's survival.

Only it's not. What gets by in a sheltered childhood doesn't work in the real world. Take Berlusconi again. The enraged heir to ancient Rome defending his civiliation against barbarians in 2001, briefly, became the self-effacing host of Italy's first official fast-breaking Ramadan dinner for Muslim diplomats in 2005. "Italy," he began in a speech guaranteed to mollify every Euro-Arab colleague who ever attacked him, "has a long tradition of fruitful exchanges with Islam. . . ." All the rhetoric of superiority was gone, along with all the pride in human rights and liberty.

Inclusively, he went on from there.

> Our country has always been, is now, and *will always be open to all forms* of spirituality and respectful of all cultures and all religions. . . .
>
> In particular, it is important that Italians learn to understand better the foundations of the Islamic religion because, after the tragedy of 11 September, *it must be clear to everyone that terrorists who kill do not have anything to do with it [Islam]. . . .*
>
> After the defeat of the totalitarianisms of the 20th century, *the new great enemy for many suffering peoples is terrorism, which wants to lure us into the trap of the "clash of civilisations."* This pitfall must be avoided: we must make sure that a new "Iron Curtain" does not divide the West and the Muslim world. . . .
>
> For this reason, we stress the importance of dialogue between our civilisations, that *for all our differences, we are united by the same values of humanity.* [Emphasis added.][42]

If I seem to be picking on Berlusconi, it's only because the voluble former prime minister is never one to let discretion cloud his enthusiasms *di giorno*. Once upon a time, Berlusconi articulated the Clash of Civilizations—the distinction between the West (liberty and human rights) and Islam (the lack thereof). Now, he gums the Mush of Civilizations, which, not incidentally, echoes the canned declarations of every successful beauty pageant contestant: *For all our differences, we are united by the same values of humanity.* The Italian leader is by no means alone in this; indeed, he speaks off the same page as every other world leader, up to and including George W. Bush. It is easy to tell which worldview, Clash or Mush, is politically correct; but which of them is just plain correct? And which offers a strategy for the survival of the world that is Western?

Five days after the 9/11 atrocities, President Bush described the war America was then mobilizing to fight. He counciled patience in the new cause, telling Americans, "This crusade, this war on terrorism, is going to take a while."[43]

Crusade? Did he say *crusade*? Prefiguring the wrath to descend upon Berlusconi the following week, the multicultural grandees and guardians of PC declared the president to be in error—major error. So what if Manhattan was still burning?

The word itself, they said, was inflammatory. So what if al-Qaeda squads of Muslim hijackers had just transformed four U.S. passenger planes filled with men, women, and children into ballistic weapons against American office buildings? Characterizing the response to Islamic terrorism as a "crusade" was just as offensive, according to multicultural logic, and would make Muslims, *including Muslim "moderates,"* go ballistic. But "moderates" don't go ballistic, unless, that is, they really aren't so moderate to begin with—which is the tip-off so hard to pick up on in a multicultural world. The question is, If a more or less literary allusion to "crusade" catapults Muslim "moderates" into the arms of "extremists," either metaphorically or literally to training camp, how "moderate" were they in the first place?[44] No answer. This is another one of those urgent questions that goes unasked. What we are left with in the absence of rational discussion is the phenomenon of the Hair-Trigger Moderate: *Anything* sets him off, from the word "crusade" to Islamic profiling (to catch Islamic terrorists), from Muhammad cartoons to opposition to the proposed operational transfer of six major U.S. ports to a country that has coddled al-Qaeda and helped Hamas. Like codependent family members, we cater to this tick-tick-tick pathology by tying on a gag of self-censorship and playing along with a fantasy of victimhood: Did the president say *crusade*?

Here's how an unnamed White House codependent, I mean, *correspondent* put it to the president's press secretary, Ari Fleischer, exactly one week after the 9/11 atrocities:

Q: The other question was, the President used the word "crusade" last Sunday, which has caused some consternation in a lot of Muslim countries. Can you explain his usage of that word, given the connotation to Muslims?

MR. FLEISCHER: I think what the President was saying was—had no intended consequences for anybody, Muslim or otherwise, other than to say that this is a broad cause that he is calling on America and the nations around the world to join. That was the point—purpose of what he said.

Q: Does he regret having used that word, Ari, and will he not use it again in the context of talking about this effort?

MR. FLEISCHER: I think to the degree that that word has any connotations that would upset any of our partners, or anybody else in the world, the President would regret if anything like that was conveyed. But the purpose of his conveying it is in the traditional English sense of the word. It's a broad cause.[45]

I just love that question—*Does he regret having used that word, Ari, and will he not use it again in the context of talking about this effort?* Thousands are dead,

America is reeling, and a White House correspondent is playing preschool teacher, coaching an erring toddler—the president of the United States—about a naughty word. Too bad Fleischer played along, conceding that the president "would regret" anything to anyone.

Why too bad? Let me count the ways. First, let's examine the word "crusade." It harkens back, obviously, to the brutal wars launched by the armies of European Christendom against the Seljuk Turks and other Muslim armies about nine centuries ago. Why did they crusade—just for sadistic grins? Hardly. Muslims, having waged holy war, or jihad, across the Middle East for the previous five hundred years, had conquered lands from Corsica to India, from Iran to Egypt, from Jerusalem to Syria, from North Africa to Cyprus to Spain to Sicily to Sardinia, brutalizing native Jewish and Christian populations, destroying churches and preying on Christian pilgrims journeying from Europe to the Holy Land. In this historic context of jihad and domination—a clear historical record covered up by PC dogma—the crusades to reclaim the previously Christian (pre-Islam) Holy Land for Christianity may be definitively understood as defensive conflicts. Calling for the First Crusade at the very end of the eleventh century, Pope Urban II outlined a defensive, eminently reasonable rationale for war: "They [Muslim forces] have killed and captured many, and have destroyed the churches and devastated the [Greek Christian] empire. If you permit them to continue thus for awhile with impunity, the faithful of God will be much more widely attacked by them."[46]

Almost a millennium later, the rationale for war against al-Qaeda and other Islamic terror networks, along with the Islamic states that sponsor them, isn't much different, except insofar as "the faithful of God" aren't so faithful anymore. We, roughly their twenty-first-century heirs (if not in all cases their descendants), have created increasingly secular societies that have long and deliberately separated themselves from Christianity as a public creed or government policy. Such detachment from religion marks not only a contrast with our own past, but also with the Islamic present, which to this day is predicated on the perfect union of mosque and state. (Furiously reading V. S. Naipaul in those first days after 9/11, it took me about three hundred pages to get to this eureka revelation: In Islam, there is no separation between mosque and state, religion and politics.) Today, as for the past thirteen centuries, Islam upholds sharia as the ideal public creed and government policy. I suspect it is partly the separation of church and state in the West that has inclined us, erroneously, to regard the religion of Islam as being separate from the inspiration and rationale of both Islamic revolutions (Iran) and Islamic terrorism (almost everywhere).

Another dissimilarity between then and now—at least I hope it's a dissimilarity—is the crusades' ultimate outcome: After eight crusades in roughly

175 years, the Christians were basically driven out of the Middle East for more than five hundred years. In other words, "the faithful of God" (Christian) lost. But in another sense, they won; that is, they won time—time to evolve as defensible societies back home that would ultimately drive Islam from Western Europe at the non-proverbial gates of Vienna in 1683. Islamic expert Robert Spencer has explained the ramifications of this hard-won grace period in his bestselling primer, *The Politically Incorrect Guide to Islam and the Crusades*— a book shut out by the mainstream media (no reviews), even as it found a home on the *New York Times* bestseller list for fifteen weeks. Although the crusaders were ultimately repulsed, Spencer explains, "the level of Islamic adventurism into Europe dropped off significantly during the era of the Crusades." He continues:

> The [Muslim] conquest of Spain, the Middle East, and North Africa, as well as the first siege of Constantinople, all took place well before the First Crusade. The battles of Kosovo and Varna [Bulgaria], which heralded a resurgent Islamic expansionism in Eastern Europe, took place after the collapse of the last Crusader holdings in the Middle East.
>
> So what did the Crusades accomplish? They bought Europe time—time that might have meant the difference between her demise and dhimmitude and her rise and return to glory. If Godrey of Bouillon, Richard the Lionhearted, and countless others hadn't risked their lives to uphold the honor of Christ and His Church thousands of miles from home, the jihadists would almost certainly have swept across Europe much sooner. Not only did the Crusader armies keep them tied down at a crucial period, fighting for Antioch [Turkey] and Ascalon [Palestine] instead of Varna and Vienna, they also brought together armies that would not have existed otherwise. Pope Urban's call united men around a cause; had that cause not existed or been publicized throughout Europe, many of these men would not have been warriors at all. They would have been ill-equipped to repel a Muslim invasion of their homeland.
>
> The Crusades, then, were the ultimate reason why Edward Gibbon's vision of "the interpretation of the Koran" being "taught in the schools of Oxford" did not come true.[47]

I would bet that neither George W. Bush—nor a single one of his advisers— has an inkling of the historic import of "crusade" beyond its politically correct, if historically incorrect, reputation as an early example of chauvinistic Western aggression against peaceable, non-Western utopians. Not that the president was very likely alluding to the literal origins of the word. The Crusades are a historic interlude that doesn't resonate in U.S. prehistory. For Americans, the word is more familiarly and more significantly a metaphoric fixture that potently describes any moral fight for right: "crusade" against ignorance (Thomas Jefferson); women's temperance "crusade" (Susan B. Anthony); equal rights "crusade" (Colin Powell);[48] breast cancer "crusade" (Avon Foundation). In 1948, Dwight D. Eisenhower, supreme allied commander in Europe, wrote his colossal war memoir about the struggle against Nazi Germany and called it, *Crusade in Europe.*

Declared in the burning wake of 9/11, the "war on terror" is a crusade if ever there was one; but this is not to PC-be. Indeed, it is impossible; it is an axiom of PC that Western history and Western point of view are always superceded by non-Western history and non-Western point of view. In other words, when a Western tradition butts up against a non-Western grievance (Christmas, cowboys, Columbus, crusade) in the modern-day mainstream, it is the Western tradition that yields to the non-Western grievance every time. And there is a penalty: For the maximum crime of "giving offense," the sentence on the West is renunciation and apology in perpetuity.

"This crusade, this war on terrorism, is going to take a while," said the president of the United States, warning the nation to gird itself for the long haul with the language of Jefferson, Eisenhower, Powell, and Avon. *Crusade?* Like the journalista said in 2001, the word "caused some consternation in a lot of Muslim countries." Hmm. Would that be consternation in Saudi Arabia (financial engine of international jihad and homeland of fifteen out of the nineteen hijackers and Osama bin Laden himself)? Consternation in Iran (monster sponsor of Hezbollah, Islamic nukes, and "death to Israel")? Maybe consternation in Taliban Afghanistan (home of the Taliban-destroyed Buddhas of Bamiyan, a brutalized female population, and home away from home of al-Qaeda)? Or was there consternation among the Hair-Trigger Moderates (tick, tick, tick . . .)? Frankly, I hope there was consternation; I hope there was fear that the U.S. of A. was about to hit back and hard, contrary to my confreres in the fourth estate. *Does he regret having used that word, Ari, and will he not use it again in the context of talking about this effort?* Yes, said Ari, he surely does, and no, said Ari, he surely won't. Like an offending lesion, the word "crusade" was cut out of the body politic, and regretted. Crusade rage averted.

But here's the point: There was no dipping into the thesaurus for a replacement. In acceding to the multicultural understanding of "crusade" as indefensibly bad and therefore verboten, the president also acceded to a discernible diminishment of the West, trading a facet of our history and language—and our understanding of our history through language—in exchange for . . . what? In accepting the skewed, demonstrably ahistorical "crusade" interpretation of the Other, the president allowed that interpretation to overwrite our own. In bowing to the Muslim world's centuries-old sense of aggrievement—inexplicable, frankly, since the Crusades were an Islamic military triumph—he acknowledged it as the multicultural Word.

It wasn't the last time. After the about-face on "crusade," there was another quick semantic retreat, this one from the highfalutin name given to the military campaign against the Taliban: Operation Infinite Justice. Having gotten word that only Allah dispenses "infinite justice," the Pentagon went into tizzy mode and rechristened (is that okay to say?) the assault Operation Enduring Freedom.[49] This seemed to please everyone—or, rather, every culture. Chalk another one up for self-abnegation. (Five years later, the multiculti beat went on: On the subject of the Bush administration's National Strategy for Combating Terrorism, *U.S. News* reported infighting authors of the plan could agree on one point: "Worried that they will offend Muslims, they've replaced the word 'jihadist' with 'extremist.' "[50])

This may seem like a lot of cultural baggage to load onto a few words, but the crusade against "crusade" and the rest follows a set pattern for culture clash, or, rather, the widely determined lack thereof: an ever contrite West versus an always aggrieved Islam. In the reflexive frenzy to avoid giving offense, we surrender not just words or phrases—whether "human rights," "superiority," or "infinite justice"—but also the legitimacy of the inspiration we derive from them. In so doing, we surrender something of ourselves, our guiding ideals, our storied past. No longer do we confidently depict civilizations that enshrine human rights as being superior to civilizations that don't, we discuss "fruitful exchanges"; no longer do we husband our forces for the long, costly "crusade" against Islamic jihad; we tilt at "extremism." Sure, the moniker Infinite Justice was a little—okay, a lot—on the bombastic side (me, I like "Operation Sledgehammer"), but the fact remains that Allah's law isn't the law of this land. So, why, then, do we enforce it?

Why, indeed. Before broaching the explanation, which also considers the point at which postmodern "sensitivity" becomes old-fashioned appeasement, it's important to make clear that the Bush administration's semantic retreat was neither unique nor exceptional. Indeed, such self-censorship is common to our time, an essential feature of the Mush of Civilizations, which, by definition, gets lost among the shushing. Examples abound, from the official silence on the core Islamic element—jihad—of the ongoing "war on terror" (remember when the president talked only about "evildoers"?), to the de facto media blackout on the Islamic aspect of sundry acts of jihad violence (from Chechnya to Israel to Paris to Sydney), to the blind eye turned to thirteen centuries of jihad waged on the non-Muslim world ("a permanent historic force," Clement Huart summed up in 1907[51]). Anything to avert Clash. Which is not at all the same as doing what it takes to preserve civilization—at least, to preserve *Western* civilization.

There's a difference, the understanding of which may be the fundamental political incorrectness, the taboo to end all. That's because we are at a point in the multiculturing of the West at which the single unifying theme is a fervent, indeed, zealous belief in "universal"—not Western—values. These, of course, come down to your basic life, liberty, and the pursuit of happiness as translated into the modern vernacular of human rights lingo. As a civilization, the West regards these values as "universal" because, as a civilization, the West also believes in their *universalism*: The idea is, such values are not only the *right* of every human being, they are also the *ideal* of every human being. As Berlusconi says, "For all our differences, we are united by the same values of humanity." Great Britain's Tony Blair, in addressing the U.S. Congress in 2003, made the same point still more emphatically. It is a "myth" that "our attachment to freedom is a product of our culture," he said, adding: "Ours are not Western values, they are the universal values of the human spirit."[52]

Whether that *spirit* is universal is never called into question, but some serious reflection on the answer just might lead us to conclude that Blair's straw myth is a hard reality: namely, that our attachment to freedom—Western-style freedom— is very much a product of our culture. To be sure, "universal values" embody the guiding ethos of the Universal Declaration of Human Rights (UDHR), the 1948 code adopted by the United Nations, which begins, rousingly enough, by positing that "all human beings are born free and equal in dignity and rights." The document goes on from there to enumerate a grab bag of dignity and rights already to be found in largely Western societies, the universal hope being that they will somehow, someday, some way, be found in *all* societies, making them thus quite literally "universal." In the imperfect here and now, however, it is not just for rhetorical purposes that they are treated as if they are already a universalist fait accompli. As President Bush has put it,

> The twentieth century ended with a single surviving model of human progress, based on non-negotiable demands of human dignity, the rule of law, limits on the power of the state, respect for women and private property and free speech and equal justice and religious tolerance. . . . When it comes to the common rights and needs of men and women, there is no clash of civilizations.[53]

This is universalist gospel.

But what if these leaders of the Western world—or, better, these leaders of the universal world—are wrong? That is, what if their universal values and common rights are, after all, uniquely Western values and rights? What if it is not a myth that the attachment to freedom is a product of Western culture? "We" may well be the world, like the song says, but what if "we" are *not* united by the "same values" of humanity? Universalists assume all peoples prefer freedom to its absence, which is probably true; but are they correct to believe all peoples define "freedom" in the same way? And if our definitions of "freedom" are different, can there be, as the president believes, only one "single surviving model for human progress"—or is there, instead, one single surviving model for *Western* progress? We in the West believe in freedom from tyranny; that's both evident and, as the Founders said, self-evident. But what if the Other—in this case, the Islamic *umma* (community)—believes in freedom all right, but in *freedom from unbelief*?

In a thought-provoking 1985 essay called "Jihad and the Ideology of Enslavement," Princeton's John Ralph Willis focuses on this particular understanding of Islamic freedom as a motivation of jihad—the holy war that "seeks to ennoble the spirit in Islam—to release the spirit from the bondage of unbelief." Think about that for a moment: *the bondage of unbelief.* If bondage is unbelief in Islam, then it follows that belief in Islam leads to "freedom," yes? In his analysis of the enslavement of non-Muslims that historically followed jihad campaigns, Willis lays out the following brain-twister for Westerners: "the apparent paradox that the *jihad,* in its effort to free men from unbelief, should become a device to deprive men of freedom."[54]

If we even begin to understand the Islamic definition of "freedom," however, this is no paradox. The entry on freedom, or *hurriyya,* in the *Encyclopaedia of Islam* describes a state of divine enthrallment that bears little resemblance to any Western understanding of freedom as being predicated in the workings of the individual conscience. According to the encyclopedia, Islamic freedom is "the recognition of the essential relationship between God the master and His human slaves who are completely dependent on Him." Ibn Arabi, a Sufi scholar of note, is cited for having defined freedom as "being perfect slavery" to Allah.

Written by Franz Rosenthal, a great American scholar of Islam of the mid-twentieth century, the entry continues, describing how such "freedom" fails to engender political free will:

> *Hurriyya,* although much discussed, did not achieve the status of a fundamental political concept that could have served as a rallying cry for great causes. . . . The individual Muslim was expected to consider subordination of his own freedom to the beliefs, morality and customs of the group as the only proper course of behavior. . . . Politically, the individual was not expected to exercise any free choice as to how he wished to be governed. . . . In general, . . . governmental authority admitted of no participation of the individual as such, who therefore did not possess any real freedom [i.e., freedom in the Western sense] vis-à-vis it. On the metaphysical level, the question of how much freedom could be vouchsafed to

human beings in view of the omnipotence of God has occupied the Muslim mind from the very beginnings of Islam. Whatever concessions were made, however, were not made in the name of any kind of individual freedom, but in order to assure a better regulated society.[55]

Worth mentioning, too, is the second section in the freedom (*hurriyya*) entry by Bernard Lewis, the noted historian of Islam. In recent times, Lewis may be the most eminent expert to champion the Bush administration's chimerical notions of transforming the Muslim Middle East via democracy, but he did not see fit, apparently, to infuse his encyclopedia entry with similar optimism. In discussing *hurriyya* in modern times, from "the Ottoman Empire and after," Lewis writes:

> . . . there is still no idea that the subjects have any right to share in the formation or conduct of government—to political freedom, or citizenship, in the sense which underlies the development of political thought in the West. While conservative reformers talked of freedom under law, and some Muslim rulers even experimented with councils and assemblies, government was in fact becoming more and not less arbitrary.[56]

Lewis went on to conclude that Western colonialism had actually improved the situation:

> During the period of British and French domination, individual freedom was never much of an issue. Though often limited and sometimes suspended, it was on the whole more extensive and better protected than either before or after. In the final revulsion against the West, Western democracy too was rejected as a fraud and a delusion, of no value to Muslims.[57]

Would that Lewis and other Islamic "experts" had bothered to consult the encyclopedia to remind themselves of the incompatibility of the Islamic definition of "freedom" (freedom from unbelief, or freedom as slavery to God) and the Western ideal of freedom (freedom from man-made tyranny with a hearty emphasis on freedom of conscience).

For the average infidel, whose personal reflections on universal values may be summed up by a peace-on-earth "holiday" card, such an exotic notion will induce a headache, one that can only be relieved by the comforting prattle of universalism. But failing to examine and evaluate Western freedom vis-à-vis Islamic freedom has got to be a new height of Western arrogance, a lazy kind of neo-chauvinism that is willfully blind to the crux of the issue: Where freedom from unbelief (Islam) is the ideal, freedom from tyranny (Western values) is anathema. As predicated on freedom of conscience, equality of rights, equality of religions, and equality of sexes, the Western concept of "freedom from tyranny" isn't just an obstacle to Islam's "freedom from unbelief," it's a threat. Such freedom in the West, based in secular institutions, necessarily undermines "freedom from unbelief" as predicated on Islamic religious supremacy, inequality of rights and inequality of sexes. "East is East and West is West and never the twain shall meet," said Kipling. No doubt President Bush and his supporters would dismiss such a line as so much churlishness from one of those "skeptics of democracy." The president's statement from the 2004 State of the Union address is a likely rejoinder. "It is mistaken and condescending to assume that whole cultures and great religions are incompatible with liberty and self-government. I believe God has planted in every human heart the desire to live in freedom."[58] Such an assertion relies more on wishful thinking than on the historical or theological record. "Whole cultures and religions"—Islam, for instance—have been by design and history not just incompatible with, but deeply hostile to such liberty and self-government, driven as they have been by the desire to create or impose a very different kind of "freedom"—one inspired by Allah through his prophet Muhammad. Grasping this fundamental concept helps us understand how, for example, the Web site of Saudi Arabia's embassy in London, in a document titled, "Saudi Arabia—Questions of Human Rights" could answer a question as to whether Saudi Arabia accepts "universally accepted human rights" by stating: "No, Saudi Arabia doesn't accept that. Some human rights are controversial, and yet others are anathema to a large portion of humanity."[59]

Sayyid Qutb, one of the signal Islamic scholars of the twentieth century, has written extensively on what might, in this context, be thought of as the nonuniversalism of Islam. Known as "the father of modern [Islamic] fundamentalism," Qutb may be dismissed by some for also being "the father of the tiny band of extremists"—that Islam-hijacking terrorist minority we read about. But Qutb's influence is by no means marginal given the prevalence of such "modern fundamentalism"—as revealed, for example, in a 2006 poll showing that 40 percent of British Muslims support the establishment of sharia in Great Britain.[60] Qutb wrote, "Islam is a comprehensive philosophy and a homogenous unity, and to introduce into it any foreign element would mean ruining it. It is like a delicate and perfect piece of machinery that may be completely ruined by the presence of an alien component."[61]

Commenting on this passage, Robert Spencer explains:

The chief "alien component" was secularism. Qutb regarded Western secularism not as the solution to the problems of the Islamic world (as many have proposed) but as the chief source of the problem: It destroyed the fundamental unity of Islam by separating the religious sphere from that of daily life.[62]

Understanding that "fundamental unity" helps explain why the ideal Islamic government is based upon sharia, and not the Judeo-Christian-derived, now secularly established precepts of "liberty and self-government" compatible with George W. Bush's idea of both God and the human heart, not to mention the Universal Declaration of Human Rights. It is neither "mistaken" nor "condescending," as President Bush suggests, to point this out. On the contrary, it is vitally important to understand also, for example, that Sayyid Qutb's idea of universal values—something for everybody—is to guarantee "a basic human right to be addressed with the message of Islam."[63] Boning up on such theory helps explain why sharia is not just incompatible with, but also inimical to such secularly grounded "universal" rights. And vice versa.

The resulting disconnect—ignored by the universalist West—has a lot to do with what the two-year-old revolutionary Islamic Republic of Iran was trying to tell the world in 1981 when it declared to the United Nations General Assembly that the Universal Declaration of Human Rights wasn't really so "universal" after all. As historian David G. Littman put it, the Iranians said that the UN human rights decaration "represented a secular interpretation of the Judeo-Christian tradition, which could not be implemented by Muslims." Ever since, as Littman has cataloged in a series of statements and essays drawn from his work and observations as a NGO representative of the Association for World Education to the United Nations in Geneva, Iran has been at the forefront of global Islamic efforts to modify the Universal Declaration of Human Rights to better accommodate sharia-observant states. Littman summed up this first Iranian declaration this way: "If a choice had to be made between [the stipulations of the human rights declaration] and 'the divine law of the country,' Iran [said it] would always choose Islamic law."[64]

Iran's declaration of independence from the recognized norms of settled human rights law was by no means the ravings of a lone revolutionary state on the fringe of Islam. On the contrary, the Islamic world as a diplomatic whole ended up codifying the distinctions between Islam and the West that George W. Bush and Tony Blair so assiduously deny. Also in 1981, the Islamic Council of Europe dropped the explosive Universal Islamic Declaration of Human Rights (UIDHR) into the cozy nest of universalism; in 1990, foreign ministers of the OIC trumpeted the Cairo Declaration of Human Rights in Islam (CDHRI). Both Islamic human rights documents are unadulterated endorsements of sharia, with the latter, for example, establishing sharia as "the only source of reference" for the protection of human rights in specifically Islamic countries. Not only are both

Islamic documents by definition nonuniversal, they claim to supercede the Universal Declaration of Human Rights (UDHR)—a supremacy, Littman reminds us, "based on divine revelation."[65] He continues:

> The aim of those who drafted and approved of the UDHR was precisely to affirm [a] universal human identity, separating it from particular and religious contexts, which introduce and sanctify differences and discriminations. Any attempt to bring in cultural and religious particularisms would simply remove the specifically universal character of the [universal rights document.]
>
> Neither the UIDHR nor the Cairo Declaration of Human Rights in Islam is universal, because both are conditional on Islamic law, which non-Muslims do not accept. The UDHR places social and political norms in a secular framework, separating the political from the religious.
>
> In contrast, *both the UIDHR and the [Cairo Declaration] introduce into the political sphere an Islamic religious criterion, which imposes an absolute decisive and divine primacy over the political and legal spheres.* [Emphasis added.][66]

Universal human rights versus Islamic human rights: Despite the seamlessly conciliatory rhetoric of the three "B"s (Bush, Blair, and Berlusconi), a real matchup would make for a resounding bang of civilizations—if, that is, the "universalist" side ever dared to mention the fact that sharia, the body of law derived from the Koran and other Islamic writings, and enshrined in the conception of Islamic human rights, is precisely the kind of theocratic legal code that secular Western democracies reject—*as a matter of universal human rights*—because it both sanctifies and institutionalizes the inequality of man.

Ruling more or less absolutely in Iran, Saudi Arabia, Pakistan, and Sudan, sharia and its principles govern to varying degrees throughout the rest of the Islamic world. Even in American-liberated Afghanistan and Iraq, the democratic process has yielded constitutional provisions to ensure that no law may violate sharia. As an early result, for example, Ali Mohaqeq Nasab, the Muslim editor of *Women's Rights* magazine in Afghanistan was sentenced in 2005 to two years hard labor for "blasphemy" against Islam. His "blasphemy" consisted of publishing "un-Islamic" articles criticizing the sharia penalties for adultery, theft, and apostasy (leaving Islam) of stoning, amputation, and death.

"Sometimes the whole religion and the rules of Islam were attacked," explained Mohammed Aref Rahmani, who sits on Afghanistan's council of Islamic scholars, referring to Nasab's "crimes." Attacked? "For instance," Rahamani told the *Chicago Tribune,* "he [Nasab] says one woman should be equal to one man, as a witness in a case, which is completely against our religion."[67]

Yes—those seismic vibrations rolling across your eardrums are the sound of culture clash. Under Islamic law, a woman's court testimony is worth half as much as a man's—another rank inequality Nasab's magazine had oppposed—so I guess you could say that the Islamic scholar has an *Islamic* point. At the same time, such Islamic "crimes" equal Western virtues, a fact that left Aghan officials unimpressed: Kabul's chief prosecutor went back to court, seeking the death penalty for Nasab. At this point, Nasab lost his fiery defiance. He publicly recanted his "apostasy," apologized for it, and went free. Or did he go "free"?

Not long after Nasab dropped from world radar, another Afghan, Abdul Rahman, appeared on the Western media's screen. Rahman, it seemed, had committed what counted for a felony in U.S.-liberated Afghanistan. He had not just criticized Islam, he had left it. In other words, Rahman had converted to Christianity, and an "apostate" living under Islamic law was subject to the death penalty. "Prosecutors say he should die," reported the *Chicago Tribune*. (Indeed, the lead prosecutor called him "a microbe in society" who should "be cut off and removed from the rest of Muslim society and should be killed.") The newspaper continued: "So do his family, his jailers, even the judge." When the prosecutor offered Rahman a deal—he would drop his charges if Rahman would drop his Christianity—Rahman refused. When the case was dismissed on the grounds that Rahman was mentally unfit (only a fruitcake would convert to Christianity, right?), Rahman's troubles were hardly over: With so many Muslim clerics still calling for his death, the Afghans at large seemed ready to do what the court would not and punish Rahman's apostasy. (" 'We will cut him in little pieces,' said Hosnia Wafaysofi, who works at the jail, as she made a cutting motion with her hands.") And when the Parliament demanded that Rahman not be allowed to leave the country, it looked like the end. The next thing anyone knew, he turned up in Italy, where then-Prime Minister Silvio Berlusconi had offered him asylum.*[68]

So much for post-Taliban—and, come to think of it, post-Operation Enduring Freedom—life in Afghanistan. Maybe the more useful exercise here is not to wonder how the United States of America became midwife to a theocratic police state, but to see what may be learned from it. One thing is clear: wherever Islam is protected from so-called blasphemy, Western freedoms (freedom of conscience, freedom of speech, let alone women's rights) are not. In "extreme" Saudi Arabia, it is illegal for non-Muslims to practice their religion;[69] indeed, it is illegal for a Jew to travel to Saudi territory,[70] and illegal for any non-Muslim to venture into Mecca or Medina, Islam's holiest sites.[71] But in "moderate" Egypt, Coptic Christians suffer harassment and discrimination that includes imprisonment and

---

*Rahman's ordeal wasn't over on his arrival in Italy. In October 2006, when Italian photojournalist Gabriele Torsello was kidnapped in Afghanistan, kidnappers offered to free Torsello in exchange for Abdul Rahman. Italy made no such deal. Three weeks later, Torsello (a Muslim convert, by the way) was released.

reports of forced conversions.[72] In "extreme" Iran, girls may be married at age nine[73] (nine was the age of Muhammad's favorite wife[74]). In "moderate" Jordan, Jews may not become citizens,[75] and so-called honor killings—the murder of women deemed unchaste—are often prosecuted on a par with misdemeanors.[76]

These injustices of the Sharia States are, of course, wholly irreconcilable with the provisions of "universal" human rights—which, in effect, is just what the Iranians tried to bring to the free world's attention back in 1981, when it fired its salvo against the concept of universalism itself. Only by ducking has the West preserved its devotion to, indeed, its faith in universalism. Such evasive maneuvering, however, doesn't change the fact that there is as gaping a gulf between Islamic and universal conceptions of human rights as there is between the Sharia States and the Free World. Now that there has been a massive influx of peoples from Sharia States into the Free World—migrations that became significant only shortly before the 1979 Islamic revolution in Iran—the question becomes: What happens when Islamic human rights meet universal human rights *in the West*?

We received our first inkling in February 1989, when Ayatollah Khomeini in Iran pronounced a death fatwa, or death sentence, on British writer Salman Rushdie for his critique of Islam in the novel, *The Satanic Verses.* The fatwa sent Muslims rioting over the book in Sharia States like Iran and Pakistan, but also in merry olde England itself. Few among us realized the significance at the time. I certainly didn't; I couldn't make sense of it. It didn't help that I found Rushdie's book unreadable. Undecipherable, really; the Islamic allegory is all but unintelligible to your basic infidel. Then there was the fact that the roiling protests, crazed rhetoric, book burnings, and bomb threats (and actual bombs) were somehow preposterously barbaric; Khomeini himself was a cartoon of evil. How could such crude exotica matter to the modern world?

Looking back, it seems clear that the Rushdie case was, as some have noted, the greatest freedom of speech case of our time. It was certainly the seminal case that set the formula for subsequent post–Cold War culture clash, pitting an aggrieved Islam against a contrite West. As author Ibn Warraq reminds us, the cruel and unusual death penalty against Rushdie—technically, a *hukm,* which doesn't expire with the death of the issuing imam as does a fatwa—was greeted with a flurry of statements and articles "by Western intellectuals, Arabists, and Islamologists *blaming Rushdie* [emphasis added] for bringing the barbarous sentence onto himself by writing *The Satanic Verses.*"[77] Rushdie himself apologized and went into hiding courtesy of British security—an ironic sidelight as the anti-Establishment writer became the ward of the Establishment. Some publishers postponed or scrapped the book's publication. As Daniel Pipes has chronicled in his book *The Rushdie Affair,* most of the leaders of the Western world sounded, or, rather, mumbled retreat.

British prime minister Margaret Thatcher and the leader of the opposition, Neil Kinnock, "kept silent about the ayatollah's threat for a full week," Pipes wrote.

The newly installed secretary of state, James A. Baker III, limply character-ized the death threat as "regrettable."

Germany parsed the fatwa as "a strain on German-Iranian relations."

Japan's response was a haiku of surrender: "Encouraging murder is not some-thing to be praised."

Pipes continues: "International organizations wanted nothing to do with *The Satanic Verses* issue, for it polarized emotions and *challenged the comfortable as-sumptions of a single order* which underlie such institutions [emphasis added]."[78] This is an apt summation: Without the "comfortable assumptions of a single order"—Universal Mush—international organizations would have had to face a genuine casus belli—Clash. At the United Nations, the silence on the Rushdie matter lasted *for four years,* and then was broken with only the most oblique ref-erence.[79] Meanwhile, the Europeans opted for Huff, recalling their top diplo-mats from Tehran in one. Significantly, no European country broke diplomatic relations with Iran. As Pipes tells it, there remained a general expectation that the Iranians would ultimately rescind the Rushdie death sentence.

Didn't happen. On the contrary, the Iranian parliament followed the diplo-vacuation with "a bill that stipulated a complete break [in relations] unless the British government declared 'its opposition to the unprincipled stands against the world of Islam, the Islamic Republic of Iran, and the contents of the anti-Islamic book, *The Satanic Verses.*'" Pipes wrote:

> Prodded by feelers from "pragmatists" in Tehran, British leaders did what they could to satisfy Tehran. On March 2, Foreign Secretary Sir Geoffrey Howe went on the BBC World Service to show foreign listeners that the government wished to distance itself from Rushdie. "We understand that the book itself has been found deeply offensive by people of the Muslim faith. It is a book that is offensive in many other ways as well. We can understand why it could be criticized. The British Government, the British people, do not have any affection for the book. The book is extremely critical, rude about us. It compares Britain with Hitler's Germany. We do not like that any more than the people of the Muslim faith like the attacks on their faith contained in the book. So we are not cosponsoring the book. What we are sponsoring is the right of people to speak freely, to publish freely."
>
> Two days later, Prime Minister Margaret Thatcher made similar remarks.[80]

Hate to say it, but it sounds as if the Iron Lady herself went wobbly. In this power struggle between the reliably contrite and the perpetually aggrieved, the

West was all struggle, ceding power to Islam. As maniacally bloodthirsty as the statements out of Tehran were, the leaders of the United Kingdom delivered unsettlingly good impersonations of show trial defendants recanting the Rights of Man. Tehran broke diplomatic relations anyhow because Rushdie remained alive and well—as alive and well as a man can be under an Islamic death sentence— and his books remained on sale, even if very often under the counter. Meanwhile, trade relations between the UK and Iran, Pipes noted, never missed a beat—or, better, shipment; the British, however, shut down a consulate, expelled a few Iranians, and managed to call the Iranian regime "deplorable."

British Islamic scholar Mervyn Hiskett framed the impasse as coming down to the conflict "between Western, secular, man-made legal systems and the Islamic system, which is transcendental, based on [divine] revelation." It is that transcendental nature of the Islamic system that Westerners overlook, even though it explains Islamic behaviors that lie beyond Western reason. Hiskett, an ardent admirer of Islam—only not in Great Britain—saw a problem in "the Muslims' own often intransigent demand that Islam must be accepted uncritically as divine revelation *by non-Muslims as well as well as by Muslims* [emphasis added]." Muslims, he wrote, believe this uncritical acceptance "must be reflected in the structure and conduct of the state, and of society." In other words, as far as Muslims everywhere were concerned, "democratic processes cannot be permitted to diminish the absolute authority of revelation."[81] No Mush here.

When it came to the right to life (Rushdie) and the right to call for death (Islam), this presented a problem. There was a bona fide divine rationale—if you were Muslim, that is—that made it an infringement on the Islam religion to oppose the Rushdie fatwa. And there was the law of Britain, if you were a loyal subject of the queen, that made it a crime to incite murder, religion my eye. Question for universalists: Is incitement to murder, or recourse to censorship, ever a religious right? The West has never so much as acknowledged this question, let alone answered it. Actually, that's not quite right: in the Actions Speak Louder than Words Department, Great Britain ended up charging no one in connection with the Rushide fatwa with the crime of incitement to murder. Clash was averted, but that doesn't count as a victory—at least not for the West.

When the foreign ministers of the Organization of the Islamic Conference met in Riyadh to discuss the Rushdie affair, they condemned not Iran, of course, for its barbaric call for the death of a British writer, but *The Satanic Verses,* concurring that the author was "a heretic." (The OIC didn't specifically endorse Iran's death sentence, but it condemned Rushdie's "apostasy"—a "crime" punishable by death under sharia.) The Islamic conference also appealed "to all members of society to impose a ban on the book and to take the necessary legislation to insure the protection of the religious beliefs of others"—other Muslims,

that is, given the "religious beliefs of others" don't require such protective measures as book banning. Saliently, the Islamic conference also declared that "blasphemy cannot be justified on the basis of freedom of expression and opinion."[82]

This is a key concept, perhaps the crucial difference between Islam and the
West: In Islamic society, "blasphemy"—a concept thoroughly outmoded in modern democracies—cannot be justified as a matter of freedom of speech or conscience. Period. This means that in Islamic society, freedom of speech, freedom
of conscience, cannot be justified, either (likely as they are to lead to "blasphemy"). Period again. In their Rushdie statement, the OIC ministers specifically
declared that "religious belief"—Islam—requires legislative "protection" from
"blasphemy." This may help explain the existence of "blasphemy laws" across
the Islamic world, from Pakistan to Indonesia, from Saudi Arabia to Turkey. It
may also explain, taken with Hiskett's point, the pressures exerted by Muslim
populations in the West on the West to enact, or enforce, the spirit of such laws.
But it doesn't explain the de facto acceptance of such laws by the West. It
doesn't explain why a British prime minister dignified an ayatollah's fatwa; why,
twelve years later, an American president retracted his just "crusade"; why
Burger King, UK, canceled an ice cream dessert in whose wrapper, Rorschach-
like, may be seen the name Allah;[83] why a recent West End revival of Christopher
Marlowe's 1580 play *Tamburlaine the Great* changed a climactic Koran-burning
scene into an ecumenical book bonfire;[84] why Fox television altered a *24* plotline
about a domestic Muslim terror cell and cobbled onto the show public service
announcements praising Islam;[85] why an Australian hospital eliminated ham
from its Christmas menu;[86] why a once-proud Western free press self-censored a
handful of Danish cartoons of Muhammad. And why, even as I write in 2006,
both the EU and the UN are receptively considering an OIC drive to outlaw religious defamation, legislation that can only diminish the right to religious dissent
and freedom of conscience.[87]

All these actions fall into line with sharia. They are even in accord with
sundry declarations of "Islamic human rights." They are anathema, however, to
free societies. So far, free societies fail to notice, preferring to fall back on the
cushy bromides of universalism. To return to Pipes's rendition of the model
Rushdie affair, this seminal scandal ended with a whimper.

A British official responded by attempting, not to explain that freedom of
speech did indeed encompass blasphemy, but "to disassociate his government
from Rushdie."

Foreign Office Minister William Waldegrave went on the BBC's Arabic Service to
explain: "I would like to put on record that the British Government well recognizes the hurt and distress that this book has caused, and we want to emphasize

that because it was published in Britain, the British Government had nothing to do with and is not associated with it in any way. . . . What is surely the best way forward is to say that the book is offensive to Islam, that Islam is far stronger than a book by a writer of this kind."[88]

Exactly one month after the decision to withdraw top European diplomats from Iran, the foreign ministers met again and decided, under only British objection, to send them back.

Pipes writes: "The Iranian foreign minister greeted the decision as a 'return to realism' and 'a realization of the importance of Islam; Khomeini took enormous satisfaction from this about-face. He described the Europeans' returning 'humiliated, disgraced, and shame-faced, regretful of what they did.' " Lamely, the French Foreign Ministry called this an "exaggeration."[89]

The controversy disappeared from sight by the middle of March 1989.

And maybe from mind. But not from the unseen engines driving the culture. For the first time, the secular West and Islam had come head-to-head in a conflict at the heart of the West, changing not Islam, but the heart of the West. No longer could freedom of expression be taken for granted; no longer could freedom of expression be guaranteed. Henceforth, bookstores might become bomb craters, and publishers assassins' targets. And not because the democracies had fallen to a dictator, but rather because a new, antidemocratic force had entered Western society, one intolerant of freedom of expression and conscience to a point familiar to Hitler, Stalin, and Mao—but with a crucial difference. The intolerance of this new, antidemocratic force was itself tolerated, quite paradoxically, as the exercise of another democratic freedom—freedom of religion. Indeed, attacks on the intolerance of this new (to the West) antidemocratic force were themselves labeled intolerant, bigoted even, forcing what little debate that occurred to a frustrated impasse—or worse.

In Geneva, David G. Littman was watching as the flaccid Western response to the assault on the freedom of speech and conscience in the West gave rise to what he has called the "Rushdie Rules," or, alternately, "creeping Islamism," at the UN—home, of course, of the Universal Declaration of Human Rights. "Emboldened" Islamic states, Littman wrote, "sympathetic to the enhancement of the Sharia, proceeded to try to introduce Khomeini-style restrictions on freedom of speech about certain political aspects of Islam to the United Nations itself. Thus did the 'Rushdie Rules' begin affecting UN bodies, and especially the Commission on Human Rights, eating away at international norms."[90] (Note: Littman's "certain political aspects" is a tactful catchall covering human rights violations inside Islamic society—slavery, forced conversions, etc.—and outside Islamic society, including Islamic terrorism against the West.)

The degree to which the Islamic states have been successful is no rarified story of parliamentary maneuverings among the diplomatic niceties in simulcast translation. Rather, this is the story of the insidiously dangerous methods used by some international diplomats to erode, and others to accept the erosion of, freedom of speech and conscience in the name of freedom of religion—in this case, freedom of Islam. The strategy goes like this: Mention the adjective "Islamic" and the noun "terrorism" in the same phrase (as in "Islamic terrorism") and trigger cries of "sacrilege" in the international arena—at least according to Pakistan's ambassador to the UN in Geneva, speaking on behalf of the OIC in 2005.[91]

Or, try reading the words of Muhammad—as taken from the 1988 Hamas Charter—into the record at the UN human rights commission in Geneva, also in 2005, and rouse Morocco, Cuba, and Pakistan to cries of "defamation," also in 2005. ("I am quoting from the Charter of Hamas. I am not attacking Islam," said Littman.[92])

Or simply enter, as Littman did in 2004, into the UN record a lesson describing Muhammad's teachings on the decapitation of infidels from a grade-eleven religious textbook (prepared under the supervision of the Al-Azhar Religious Institute and published by the Egyptian government), and drive Sudan to calls of blasphemy, and Pakistan to lecture "Islam was a religion of peace . . . and it was unacceptable that this religion be thus despised."[93]

Or compile, at the behest of the human rights commission, a record of human rights atrocities in Sudan (killings, rape, slavery, forced conversions to Islam, death penalty for apostasy . . .), and point out the giant discrepancies between Sudan's sharia-guided criminal code and sundry "universal" human rights convenants to which Sudan is a signatory. That's what Gaspar Biro, UN special rapporteur on Sudan, did in 1994 only to be accused by Sudan of launching "a vicious attack on the religion of Islam."[94]

Three years later, there was a similar case—this time involving the UN's special rapporteur on racism. In his independent report for the human rights commission on racism—"against Blacks, Arabs, and Muslims, xenophobia, negrophobia, anti-Semitism and related intolerance"—Maurice Glèlè-Ahanhanzo, the rapporteur, included a section on anti-Semitism. In this section was a subheading titled, "Islamist and Arab Anti-Semitism," which included the following quotation taken from an annual survey, *Anti-Semitism Worldwide*: "The use of Christian and secular European anti-Semitism motifs in Muslim publications is on the rise, yet at the same time Muslim extremists are turning increasingly to their own religious sources, first and foremost the Qur'an, as a primary anti-Jewish source."

"Blasphemy." That's what representatives from Turkey, Egypt, Pakistan, and Algeria called this passage. Indonesia, speaking on behalf of the OIC, elaborated.

> This [passage] amounts to the defamation of our religion, Islam, and blasphemy against its Holy book, Qur'an. We are infuriated that such a statement has been included in the report of the Special Rapporteur. The Commission on Human Rights cannot become a silent spectator to this defamation against one of the great religions of the world. We, therefore, call on the Commission to express censure for this defamatory statement against Islam and the Holy Qur'an and ask you, Mr, Chairman, to express this censure on behalf of the Commission.[95]

Notice the Indonesian ambassador didn't call the offending passage phony or even selectively misleading. How could he, with the words of the Koran, to take just one example, recounting Allah's transformation of Jews into "apes and swine"[96]—a recurring motif in mosque sermons.[97] And how could he, to take just one more example, when the hadith collections, the putative words and deeds of Muhammad, as transmitted by Islamic religious authorities centuries ago, provide Muslims with endless religious justification for anti-Semitism to this day—as may be seen in Article 7 of the Hamas Charter, which concludes with the words of a canonical hadith:

> The Last Hour would not come unless the Muslims will fight the Jews and the Muslims would kill them until the Jews would hide themselves behind a stone or a tree and a stone or a tree would say: "Muslim, or the servant of Allah, there is a Jew behind me; come and kill him."[98]

For the Muslim representatives, simply noting the existence of Islamic religious sources of anti-Semitism in the UN report was itself "blasphemy" and "defamation."

By definition, "blasphemy" includes irreverence, which the special rapporteur's findings did not; and by definition, "defamation" includes a false statement, which the special rapporteur's findings did not. But the words themselves—"blasphemy" and "defamation"—seemed to cast a spell, paralyzing the rest of the commission. No country rebutted or even investigated the OIC's charges; on the contrary, all fifty-three members of the human rights commission, including the United States and several other Western countries *agreed with the OIC*. Talk about the enabling behaviors of codependency. Yes, the world's human rights representatives said in unison, by all means we must censure this blasphemy, this defamatory statement against Islam (*just don't say anything to set them off, tick-*

tick-tick . . .). Citing Islamic religious sources of anti-Jewish invective—even Muhammad's own words as recorded in the hadiths—was, indeed, blasphemy and defamation, they agreed. As the world human rights body, they decided:

1. . . . Without a vote to express its indignation and protest at the content of such an offensive reference to Islam and the Holy Qur'an;
2. Affirmed that this offensive reference should have been excluded from the report;
3. Requested the Chairman to ask the special rapporteur to take corrective action in response to the present decision.[99]

Please. "Corrective action" meant suppressing the truth. The "offensive reference" was ripped out of the report, leaving in its place a dangerous precedent for censorship. This precedent for censorship has brought about an even more dangerous rise in self-censorship. As Littman observed, for the next seven years, UN special reports on racism omitted any and all references to anti-Semitism in Arab countries, Iran, and elsewhere in the Muslim world, including in the Palestinian media, where it is well known to be rampant.

"There is a proper sensitivity to the belief systems of government representatives that is part of diplomatic culture," Littman writes, "but sensitivity should not induce blindness."[100] Nor, of course, should "sensitivity" impose censorship. Nor should "sensitivity" excuse genocide. But that's what's happening. When the OIC set out in 1999 to pass a resolution at the UN human rights commission condemning the "defamation of Islam," the resolution that ultimately passed was called "Combating the Defamation of Religions"; Islam, however, as Littman has pointed out, was the only religion mentioned. The operative paragraph of the resolution expresses "deep concern that Islam is frequently and wrongly associated with human rights violations and with terrorism."[101] And this was two years before 9/11.

Is Islam really "frequently" or "wrongly" associated with terrorism? Having gagged and blindfolded itself, the international community (notwithstanding the occasional Berlusconi outburst) has done everything possible to avoid the question, functioning in a strange state of "sensitivity" that has, paradoxically, deadened the senses and blunted logic—a condition resembling not just appeasement but surrender. As "defamation" and "blasphemy" have become, like Pavlovian gongs, instant conversation-enders, Islam has become increasingly insulated not just from criticism (real or imagined), but also from the poking and prodding of analysis—from reality itself. This may be precisely the kind of "protection" from secular blasphemy (read: criticism) that Islam has long maintained it requires—remember the OIC statement on Rushdie—but the $64,000-question is, why are non-Muslims so obsessively doing everything they can to provide it?

The answer, promised many pages ago, is a complicated affair, closely linked to the confidence crisis of the West, the identity crisis of the perpetual adolescent, and to something else as well. That something else is the age-old relationship not between the West and the rest, but between *Islam* and the rest: namely, the relationship between Islam and the dhimmi, the millions of non-Muslims through the centuries who have lived in Islamized societies. To live as a dhimmi is to have an inferior legal status under sharia, a codified condition as old as the Islamic conquests of non-Islamic peoples. The Muslim-dhimmi relationship is, at best, a master-servant relationship, pitting an identifiable authority figure against an identifiable supplicant. This was often literally the case since, in many historical contexts, dhimmis were required by sharia to be recognizable by their clothes, the size and color of their homes, their modes of transportation (donkeys). The relationship's "core element," explains Bat Ye'or, the leading modern scholar of the dhimmis, "pertains to the premise of Muslim superiority over all other religious groups."[102]

Bat Ye'or has introduced a term to the lexicon to describe a mode of behavior or state of mind fostered by sharia-sanctioned religious inferiority: "dhimmitude." Forbidden to possess arms, own land, criticize sharia, or defend themselves either in a fight or in court against a Muslim (among many, many other prohibitions), dhimmis developed cross-cultural, cross-continental survival strategies that worked not for the fittest, but rather for the most deferential—self-abasement as self-preservation. A good example: Since criticism of sharia was severely punished, dhimmis "adopted a servile language and obsequious demeanor for fear of retaliation and for their self-preservation," Bat Ye'or writes.[103] In this struggle to survive were lost precious markers of the self: history and identity, truth and tradition. What was left were self-censoring societies, stunted by fear, compromised by fearfulness. Writing in 1918, Jovan Cvijic, a Serbian sociologist and geographer, described Christian society in Macedonia, which had long been subject to such fear.

> There are regions where the Christian population has lived under a reign of fear from birth until death. In certain parts of Macedonia, they don't tell you how they fought against the Turks or against the Albanians, but rather about the way that they managed to flee from them, or the ruse that they used to escape them. In Macedonia I heard people say: "Even in our dreams we flee from the Turks and the Albanians." It is true that for about twenty years a certain number of them

have regained their composure, but the deep-seated feeling has not changed among the masses of people. *Even after the liberation in 1912 one could tell that a large number of Christians had not yet become aware of their new status: fear could still be read on their faces.* [Emphasis added.][104]

I don't think we, at this point, can read fear on our faces. But I do think there are alarming similarities between dhimmi life under Islam and PC life in a multi-cultural world.

We have long lived in a self-censoring society, stunted by a kind of fear of po-litical correctness—of opprobrium, ostracism, or professional failure—and have certainly been long compromised by fearfulness. Traditionally—because multi-culturalism has been with us long enough to be characterized as a tradition—this has had nothing to do with Islam or the dhimmi. But that doesn't negate the comparison. Indeed, it helps explain a seamless compatibility between dhimmi-tude and the multicultural mind-set that flourishes in a post-grown-up world.

Quite intriguingly, Bat Ye'or has demonstrated that dhimmi status under sharia in Islamic societies is by no means a prerequisite of dhimmitude. Indeed, definite patterns of dhimmi behavior exist not only in the Sharia States, but throughout the Free World. (Western dhimmitude is discussed at greater length in chapter 9.) For death-of-the-grown-up purposes, one aspect has particular res-onance, or nonresonance: the silence of dhimmitude regarding Islam. It is the si-lence of the insecure society. Or maybe it is the silent insecurity of the post-adult, identity-less society, the one that never quite grows up into itself.

Maybe this hush of dhimmitude fell over the West during the Rushdie case, when the notion of "protected" Islam—"protected" from criticism on pain of death—was first communicated to a wide Western audience. And now? It's part of our society. Roughly a decade and a half after Rushdie, a British broadcast watchdog group notes that "Islam was accorded far more respect on television and radio than other religions." (Said Lord Dubs, chairman of the Broadcasting Standards Commission in 2003: "In portraying Muslims [writers] have held back, they have censored themselves, they are timid. I have seen them pour scorn on Christianity . . . followed, to a lesser extent, by Jews and Hindus."[105]) Roughly a decade and a half after Rushdie, the EU racism watchdog shelves a report on anti-Semitism in Europe because it concluded Muslims and Palestinian groups were responible for most of the incidents.[106] Roughly a decade and a half after Rushdie, a British Foreign Office minister apologizes repeatedly for a line in a speech that called on British Muslims to choose between political dialogue and "the way of the terrorists."[107] Roughly a decade and a half after Rushdie, an American president ends his crusade before it begins and declares Islam a reli-gion of peace.

Not only does such dhimmitude protect Islam from truths about itself, it also protects Islam from the "offensive"—that is, non-Islamic—aspects of the world outside Islam. Norwegian authorities prohibit Jewish symbols—stars of David, Israeli flags—at an Oslo anniversary comemmoration of Kristallnacht to prevent "trouble" (this in a city that regularly hosts pro-Palestinian events).[108] France's chief rabbi warns French Jews against wearing yarmulkes in public to prevent violence.[109] The British Red, um, Cross bans Christian content in store Christmas displays for fear of giving "offense."[110] The University of the Incarnate Word in Texas exchanges its crusader mascot for a cardinal (the bird, not the prelate), also for fear of giving offense.[111] Swiss tourist brochures in Arabic omit scenic snaps of Tyrolean churches and replace a picture of a pork salami speciality with some local cheese.[112] To be sure, churches are not mosques, and pork is not eaten by Muslims; but why does Switzerland, a country of churches and pork salami, want to pretend otherwise?

It's easy to see why dhimmi populations in Islamic lands would collude in "protecting" Islam from such "offense" or criticism; they fear the sharia consequences. But why do Westerners, in the media, the White House, the United Nations, or the tourist board collude in these same "protections"? Why the reluctance to acknowledge patent differences between Islam and the West? Why the refusal to examine whether Islam plays a central role in the so-called war on terror? Why the failure to study whether the "war on terror" is a defensive response to the latest manifestation of thirteen centuries of Islamic jihad? Why the cold-sweating fear over even asking the questions?

Bat Ye'or has described Western silence on Islam—today's gruesome human rights violations, yesterday's bloody conquests—as "the politics of dhimmitude."[113] The term is provocative, describing a framework of concessions to Islam that goes far beyond multicultural theorizing in a lecture hall, or PC politesse in the public arena. Indeed, the whole concept of dhimmitude—predicated on the historic abasement of non-Muslims in Islamic society—envisions a new conception of world affairs. Gone are the old paradigms of the great powers and Cold War rivalries; in their place, a complex power struggle between the West and Islam that plays out on a deeply psychological level that may make Cold War machinations look something more like a game of Red Light, Green Light.

Whether characterized as a courtesy, a favor, or appeasement, every Western wince, from Lady Thatcher's concessions to the ayatollah to George W. Bush's retreat on "crusade," may be seen as a form of dhimmitude because they are clear manifestations of sharia's influence on the West. So, too, the self-censorship of the media when it came to Cartoon Rage 2006 over twelve Danish cartoons of Muhammad. Such behavior indicates, as Bat Ye'or writes, an "implicit submission to the shari'a prohibitions of blasphemy." This is seriously troubling. Islam must not be "disrespected," says Islamic law; Islam is not "disrespected," according to Western practice. There is more than etiquette at work when there is no criticism of Muslim oppression of Christians from Sudan to Nigeria to Pakistan to the Palestinian Authority to Indonesia; when there is no discussion of where religious tolerance of religious *in*tolerance might end. There is fear. And where there is fear, there is silence. Of this silence—this tacit, noncomprehended acceptance of Islam's dictates—Bat Ye'or writes: It "puts the Western public sphere in the position of conforming to one of the basic rules of dhimmitude: the express prohibition of Christians and Jews to criticize Islamic history and doctrine."[114]

It fits. From the multicultural teachings of the politically correct classroom, we as a culture have learned to censor "incorrect" thoughts. In the absence of adults, we have found ways to sidestep taxing reponsibilities. As no-confidence codependents, we have conspired to rationalize away unpleasant realities. By chance or not by chance, dhimmitude is compatible with all of these destructive impulses. This is why the culture war is now so "real." More than a syllabus is at stake; more than the ethnic makeup of college graduates is at issue; more than the feminization of the hard sciences is under consideration. Looking back, it becomes clear that there was a great luxury in fighting a culture war in a classroom or boardroom. But if the settings were somehow artificial, the hits taken were very real, disabling faculties of judgment and discernment, and undermining confidence and authority—traits, of course, associated with our lost maturity.

This has left the West ill-equipped to survive the real culture war. And who is public enemy number one, anyway? Jihadist terrorists or fanatical multiculturalists? It may be that the only faith on Earth more messianic than Islam is multiculturalism. Maybe that's because its irrational faith in the chimera of universalism relies on a perpetual suspension of disbelief that contradicts inescapably Western traditions of logic and analysis. If distinctions between the West and Islam were articulated, if the "meeting of cultures" were recast as a conflict of cultures, if the incompatibility of Western secular logic and Islamic divine revelation were evaluated, if Islamization were perceived as a threat to the West—if, in other words, Clash were allowed to ring out—Islam itself would remain unchanged, very likely energized by the resulting breach. The whole multicultural project, however, would come tumbling down. And, to the multiculti priesthood, that would be apostasy, Western-style.

The penalty of such apostasy is not death (as under Islam), but the resulting abyss is an existential crisis that the multiculturalists will avoid at any cost. Better to put faith in "fruitful exchanges"; better to preach "universal values." Better to tolerate the intolerant. Better to pretend. Better to lie. Better to barricade the public square, and station guards at synagogues and churches. Better to dispense bulletproof vests to civil servants. Better to guard public buildings with gauntlets of metal detectors and Jersey walls. Better to search granny's purse. Better to search granny. There is an Orwellian logic to it all.

Down with Clash. Mush rules.

We are, after all, the world.

Because if we aren't the world, who are we?

9. MEN, WOMEN . . . OR CHILDREN?
OR: THE FATE OF THE WESTERN WORLD

The predicament of Western civilization
is that it has ceased to be aware
of the values which it is in peril of losing.
—ARTHUR KOESTLER

Draw your chair up close
to the edge of the precipice
and I'll tell you a story.
—F. SCOTT FITZGERALD

One thing I do as a columnist perusing the morning Internet is read the military obituaries in the British press, usually *The Daily Telegraph.*
Almost invariably, these write-ups mark the passing of a veteran of World War II in the kind of scope, as critic James Bowman has noted, never found in an American newspaper. The battles of sixty-plus years ago are recounted as though the outcomes still matter, as though the wi-fi, sat-linked, iPod-plugged reader is well-served by a reminder of the obscure men from disbanded armies that vanquished evil for a forgetful world. Sometimes, I print these biographical essays and save them in a file, as though the paper record retains some essence of these indomitable spirits, preventing them from slipping away altogether into the cyber-obscurity of yesterday's news, not to mention yesterday. A couple of summers ago, there was Wing Commander David Penman, eighty-five, one of five Lancaster bomber pilots (out of twelve who began the mission) to return from a daring, low-flying, daylight raid on a German engine plant in 1942; a while before that, there was Capt. Philip "Pip" Gardner, a Victoria Cross–winning tank commander captured at the 1942 fall of Tobruk. His death at age eighty-eight left only fifteen surviving VC-holders. Now there are twelve. More recently, there was eighty-four-year-old Petty Officer Norman Walton, who, after the British cruiser *Neptune* was sunk in a minefield off Libya in 1941, endured three days in the sea and two on a raft to become the sole survivor out of 765

crew members. A boxer of some note after the war, Petty Officer Walton let fly a left hook and a head butt to thwart two muggers at age eighty-two.

But there is more to these tales than derring-do. There is usually a line, maybe two, that offers the twenty-first-century reader an almost shocking glimpse of behavior that is not just old-fashioned—as a lacy cravat is old-fashioned next to a necktie—but wholly outmoded, sundered from any contemporary social logic. Just as "men's clubs" or "polite company" have lost a logical connection to today's society (after *Sex in the City,* what's "polite company"?), the state of mind behind the actions that made these lives noteworthy seems to have been subtracted from today's human calculus, indicating that a behavioral transformation has taken place. It shouldn't be shocking, really. In daily life, for example, anyone over forty may mark the transformation every time a grown man doesn't surrender his bus seat to a standing woman, even a very old woman or even a very pregnant woman *because the thought doesn't occur to him.* This reprogramming of the brain waves may seem superficial, but it's not. It is evidence of the cultural eradication of the communally protective impulse of the adult male that once governed public etiquette, and the ramifications are profound.

Digging into the obituary evidence, like strata of sedimentary rock, we may see how an earlier civilization, one not yet under the influence of a youth culture of licentious boys (sex, drugs, and rock 'n' roll) and petulant girls (women's lib), shaped that most basic human instinct—survival. Elevated by a maturing belief in duty, honor, loyalty, and forbearance, the instinct to survive wasn't just a self-concern; it was, it turned out, the saving grace of civilization. This realization may help explain the shock value of these obits. It always comes as a shock to recognize that, in their most vigorous youth, these men—now lost to us as "dead, white males"—exemplified something beyond the cultural ken of the post-grown-up mainstream: hip, edgy, and out to "get mine" against "the system."

Set by fate into the midst of world war, the deceased acquitted themselves admirably, to use the precise parlance of their military service. To be sure, theirs was a way of life untouched by hipness or edginess—nicely exemplified by eighty-five-year-old Maj. Basil Tarrant, a Military Cross–winner, who, after surviving Dunkirk, fighting onto Juno Beach on D-day, and battling retreating Panzer units deep into Germany, resumed a successful career manufacturing decorative, hinged biscuit tins. It was also a life unconstrained by irony's strictures—as poignantly expressed in the account of the final moments of the *Neptune* when Petty Officer Walton described clinging to the side of a life raft in cold, heavy seas thick with engine oil and lost sailors. "We saw the ship capsize and sink," he recalled, "and gave her a cheer as she went down."

Was it a huzzah? Or did they shout hip, hip, hooray? In their struggle for survival, these doomed men mustered a salute that would save not their lives, but their gallantry. They could have railed at the gods, cursed the boat, and shrieked in extremis, but instead they evinced a courage and fortitude that ennobled both their fight and their fate. But can't you just see it now: Jon Stewart, say, "interviewing" this sole survivor on *The Daily Show,* deconstructing a beau geste of the past into jagged bits of present pointlessness. Severed by a cutting derisiveness from the gravity of life and death—and severed from that civilization of grownups—such virtues as courage and fortitude do appear to shrink and wither. This diminishment may seem to compensate for the stunted stature of post-grown-up culture, but it also has the unmistakable effect of leaving that culture in a state best described as unmanned.

It's easy to imagine Lt. Col. Duncan Campbell, ninety-one, who, as his obituary noted, was awarded two Military Crosses in the East Africa Campaign, getting the same sarcastic smack down. Walking ahead of the two infantry companies he was leading on a well-defended Italian position in 1940, *The Telegraph* reported, "he ensured that his C.O. did not lose sight of him in the rough terrain by singing the theme song from the film 'Sanders of the River' at the top of his voice amid the crack of rifle bullets and the noise of shell explosions." (I gather *Sanders of the River* is a cinematic ode to empire along the lines of the 1939 version of *The Four Feathers.*) It's hard to look back on such a bravura display of selfless determination without also picturing a Monty Python–esque parody popping up like a jack-in-the-box, replacing the officer's daring leadership in the cause of victory with a knee-jerk mockery in pursuit of guffaws. This is not to call for a ban on laughs, but take Danny Kaye in *The Secret Life of Walter Mitty* (1947), daydreaming his way into the impersonation of a British officer heroic to a point of comedic absurdity, and compare it to the *Strangelove*-ian spoof of the warrior that took hold in the 1960s and never let go. Kaye's comedy makes puckish fun of the henpecked dreamer who is *not* the hero; *Strangelove* satire utterly destroys the heroic ideal itself, not to mention any and all violent notions of self-defense. It's a big difference, one worth marking if only to establish that once upon a time, the cultural mainstream actually regarded stuff like duty and honor as dependable anchors rather than balls and chains.

That, of course, was more than a half century ago. In the interim, the sensibility that prizes such manly virtues has died a death for which there has been no obituary. This is not to say that such virtues no longer exist; just visit Centcom online and read up on manly virtues in action in Afghanistan and Iraq. But these virtues are no longer the object of emulation, admiration, or even consideration among elites and their acolytes who dominate the cultural mainstream. Even after 9/11, that cultural mainstream just keeps rolling along as though such virtues were obsolete and forgotten. This explains why, on 9/11, the heroism of the young and not-so-young men who climbed out of forgotten obsolescence and into the burning towers was so shocking—and, as current events, more shocking than any obituaries—particularly to those same elites who interpret the news of the day.

More than a war was revealed to us that September morning. A throwback world was uncovered, a fireman culture more exotic than that of aborigines in the rain forest—which, after all, is a vacation destination not unfamiliar to trend-conscious ecotourists. In the wilds of Queens and Staten Island, it seemed, there were men who married their high school sweethearts, followed their fathers and uncles into the force, and died to save their fellow man. As stricken office work-ers fled down the stairways of the burning towers, these same fearless men kept climbing upward, shouldering their fateful responsibilities as purposefully as their one-hundred-pound packs. To the mainstream culture, it was a staggering revelation—all 343 of them who perished, not to mention thirty-seven Port Au-thority police and twenty-three New York City police.

What was this remarkable new species, many wondered; the American male, you say? But wasn't he long ago consigned to the ash heap of whatever? His comeback was much discussed. In a 2003 essay in *The Nation* called "Neo-Macho Man," Richard Goldstein pointed out, "Not so long ago, you couldn't say 'macho man' without thinking of the Village People. Hypermasculinity was so thoroughly discredited that it seemed fit for camp. Now, it's back, in earnest."[1] Brooding on this development from the Left, Goldstein wasn't happy, conflating what he called the "dominant male" with "bitch-slapping" examples of the most infantile brutishness—à la Eminem, gangsta rap, even the "authoritarianism" he decided was personified in Rudy Giuliani. He did manage to squeeze out a single line of praise, sort of, for the "heroes of 9/11"—adding, however, that they pre-sented a "benign image [that] allows us to forget that the dark side of macho has also been unleashed." Over on the Right, meanwhile, Peggy Noonan heralded the return of traditional "manliness" in "Welcome Back, Duke," a *Wall Street Journal* essay appearing shortly after 9/11.[2] The way she explained it, "We are ex-periencing a new respect for their old-fashioned masculinity, a new respect for physical courage, for strength and for the willingness to use both for the good of others." And, she added, "none too soon."

Whether it was condemned as "hypermasculinity" or lauded as "manliness," something lost and forgotten was new and in the public eye again—and, as Noo-nan wrote, it had to do with the adult males who take care of things, who save lives, who do unpleasant work that must be done. Soon, many of them would be at war, fighting in Afghanistan and Iraq. But if 9/11 revealed the restorative pow-ers of brawny men in a high-tech world under fiery attack, it was the manly virtues—courage, loyalty, duty—inspiring their brawny actions that gave these men stature in the reopened eyes of society. It's not that these men were supposed to be saints their whole lives through. Under cataclysmic duress, however, in a time of national crisis, they were able to draw from a reservoir of goodness—I can't think of a better word—that lies apart from the toxic waters of the cultural mainstream, which, from *Easy Rider* to *M*A*S*H* to *Born on the Fourth of July,* from Woodstock to Summer of Love to gangsta rap, from *Naked Lunch* to *Catch-22,* from cartoonists Conrad to Ted Rall, has long depicted such "courage" and "loyalty" as a chump's game or a commodity, and duty as a grind. (The mass, save-yourself desertions of the New Orleans Police Department during Hurricane Katrina in 2005 may offer a more au courant take on "duty."[3]) On 9/11, American society was awestruck by the same manly virtues—read: *adult* virtues—that our youth culture, our rock culture, our MSM culture had long ago derided as uncool, unhip, inauthentic, corny, out-of-touch, old-fashioned, schmaltzy, dry, dead, and totally over.

Given the long-standing entrenchment of these overlapping youth, rock, and MSM cultures, the retro-virtues of the adult weren't going to prevail as cultural norms without a fight. And they haven't, so far. No culture war is being waged against them, exactly, but maybe a form of not-so-benign neglect. Capt. Roger Lee Crossland of the U.S. Naval Reserve picked up on this aspect of the stalemate when he wrote in 2004 about the glaring absence of bona fide war heroes—not in the prosecution of what we persist in calling "the war on terror," but in its all-important narrative.

> Everyone knows the name Jessica Lynch. She wore her country's uniform, went willingly to her duty in Iraq, and suffered grievous injuries, but does she qualify to be known first among those who served in this war? We have brushed aside battlefield resolution and action—which should be foremost—and allowed the image of victimization and suffering to take its place.[4]

Soon, we would also get to know the name of Lynndie England, the victim*izer*, whose depredations at Abu Ghraib, of course, make Josef Mengele's experiments at Auschwitz look like the Pillsbury Bake-Off (not). But Crossland makes an excellent point. Describing the origins of what he calls the "victim-hero," Crossland looks back to the Vietnam War, domestically contentious to the point where "battlefield heroes were ignored or actively disparaged." But, as he notes, "the returning prisoners of war (POWs), however, were something different."

> They were unequivocal victims, many of whom had resisted their captors heroically with the little means they had at hand. There were no issues of collateral damage or innocent lives lost in their stories of captivity. . . . These were noncontroversial

stories of great resolve. Contemporaneous stories of battlefield heroism were never accorded the same priority.

Was it at this point that we began our descent on the slippery slope of "safe" heroes, heroes whose conduct was laregly nonviolent, played out off the battlefield? Was it at this point we began to abandon warriors performing warriorlike acts as our models?[5]

Yes, and yes, I'd say. And, given their nonviolent sacrifice on 9/11, New York's Bravest fall into this same "safe" hero category. This is not to take away from their heroism, or that of any other rescue workers on 9/11. But the fact remains, the kind of war hero who makes the Heroes in Action page at the Centcom Web site doesn't show up in the post-grown-up pantheon that showcases Crossland's victim-hero.

And this is key. If, as Crossland indicates, the victim-hero first emerged as a "noncontroversial" manifestation of patriotism that allowed Americans to wave the flag without antagonizing the "youths" of the antiwar movement, this suggests that the victim-hero emerged in response to the influence of the "youths" of the antiwar movement—and thus has a strong connection to the death of the grown-up. Warriors, after all, are adults, mature men whose example can make non-warriors or anti-warriors feel grossly inexperienced and sheltered—very much like children. Next to the real-life experiences of the battlefield hero, the ideal of "forever young" can feel tediously callow; next to the manifestation of maturity's virtues (the same virtues the mainstream culture had deep-sixed by the 1960s), the sex, drugs, and rock 'n' roll ideal can seem downright tawdry. "Victims," as Crossland points out, "are easier to identify and celebrate than heroes," they are "less controversial," and they "inspire sympathy." And there's something else: As Crossland notes, "it is their [victims'] status rather than their acts or intentions that define them."[6] And it is that passive status of the vulnerable victim, not the aggressive acts of the valorous hero, that allows the non-adult, non-warrior to continue to stand tall, and to continue to define himself as head mainstream man. From a microphone on high, he can hand sympathy *down* to the victim: With the hero, he would have to look up. In short, the adolescent culture celebrates the victim because the hero is too big for it.

This explains why, for all intents and purposes, we—our adolescent culture—effectively pretend heroes don't exist, and why the military itself has been effectively diverted from the mainstream, tied off, in a way, by those ubiquitous yellow ribbons. "Support our troops" may be the talisman we stick to our bumpers to ward off a recurrence of the shameful slanders against our fighting men that sullied the Vietnam era with epithets of "baby killers" and the like, but there remains a telling lack of depth to the slogan. "Support our troops," after all, leaves plenty of wiggle room *not* to support our president, a sentiment that may lead to all kinds of actions that don't, in fact, support our troops. In any case, just wearing our red-white-and-blue hearts on our cars hasn't changed the fact that bona fide heroes of the war in Afghanistan and Iraq—a Bronze Star–winner such as Spc. Matthew Wester, a Silver Star–winner such as M. Sgt. Anthony S. Pryor, a Distinguished Service Cross–winner such as Col. James H. Coffman, Jr.—remain heroes to a military-friendly subculture, effectively cordoned off from, and unheralded by, the reflexively military-wary and all-enveloping media culture. For example: Superbowl XL included tributes to the late Rosa Parks and Coretta Scott King; however, from the beginning of pregame programming to the end of postgame programming, there was no mention of our many thousands of troops in harm's way.[7] We embrace the heroic victim to the exclusion of the hero every time.

This mainstream reflex offers a vivid insight into post-grown-up culture—and more evidence of the same flattening force that has steamrollered all traditional hierarchies, leveling intrinsic differences not just between heroes and victims, but also between men and women, maturity and adolescence, communism and capitalism, Islam and the West, Walker and Shakespeare, Schubert and the Beatles, Madonna and Child and "Dung Virgin," terrorists and freedom fighters. But there's an important psychological dimension that becomes evident in the cultural byplay of heroes and victims, one that takes us away from all the hothouse theories and back to the "real" culture war. Heroes fight. Victims suffer. Heroes take action. Victims languish. And victims are precisely what terrorism—flying planes into office buildings, blowing up commuter trains, pizzerias, discos, and the like—is calculated to create. Inflicting widespread fear and scattershot violence on civilian populations won't ever result in a *military* victory; what's achievable, however, is the demoralization of those civilian populations, which can be fatal to civilization itself. Insecurity, vulnerablity, aching loss, numbing shock—these are the poison fruits of terrorism in a world where anyone who submits to an airport body search, or even looks over his shoulder boarding a train, has assumed, however briefly, the status of a victim. Bat Ye'or would likely call such conditioned reflexes a form of dhimmitude: We are taking fearful or invasive precautions because our freedom—freedom from fear, freedom of movement—has been curtailed by threats of violence (I prefer "acts of jihad") that are specifically Islamic, and therefore contribute to a culture of religiously dictated fear and limitation. The threat of such violence became more acute after 9/11, but it has been an unclear if present danger for decades. This helps explain why the condition of dhimmitude has in fact become a veritable Western institution. Bat Ye'or looks back to its origins.

It was in the early 1970s, with the outbreak of Arab Palestinian terrorism world-wide, that dhimmitude erupted on European soil through violence and death deliberately inflicted on one category of persons: the Jews, who were singled out as in the Nazi period by their religion. Security precautions and instructions posted on synagogues and Jewish community buildings implied that being Jewish and practicing the Jewish religion in Europe might again incur the risk of death, and that the freedom of religion and freedom of thought had been restricted.[8]

So, that's how it started. When I first read that passage a few months after 9/11, something clicked. I remembered a visit to Brussels in December 1990, during which I saw armed guards posted outside a city synagogue. Such security precautions in Europe, as Bat Yeo'r writes, were by then routine, but it was the first time I had witnessed them. And it was only after 9/11 that I realized what they really meant: It wasn't that government authorities were preparing to target a specific, limited threat of violence to battle and eliminate it; on the contrary, the authorities were responding to an *ongoing* threat that reflected the permanent fact that Jewish citizens in Belgium (and elsewhere) were no longer able to exercise their religion freely. And why weren't they able to exercise their religion freely? As in the 1970s, the reason in 1990 was Arab Palestinian terrorists. In retrospect—namely, post-9/11—it seems odd that these terrorists have always been called "Arab terrorists," or "Arab Palestinian terrorists," and have never been labeled according to the animating inspiration of their religion as "Muslim" terrorists. Such coyness has buried a relevant part of the story: the Islamic context. Just as a rose by any other name would smell as sweet, it was *Muslim* terrorism that had come to Europe, and, as a result, Jews were worshiping, if they dared, at their own fearsome risk.

And not just Jews. By now, the same fearsome risk extends to whole populations, in houses of worship and the public square alike. After reading Bat Ye'or, I realized that the now-familiar strategies of fearsome risk management—guns around the synagogue, for example—represents a significant capitulation. The security ring around the synagogue—or the airport ticket counter, the house of parliament, or the Winter Olympics—is a line of siege, not a line of counterattack. The threat of violence has become the status quo, and, as such, is incapable of sparking outrage, and is certainly not a casus belli. Guns at the synagogue door—or St. Peter's Basilica, or the Louvre—symbolize a cultural acquiescence to the infringement of freedom caused by the introduction—better, the incursion—of Islam into Western society. Thus, dhimmitude—institutional concessions on the part of non-Muslim populations to Islam—has arrived in the West.

And it's here in the U.S. of A, as well. Brandishing automatic weapons, police and soldiers patrol our cities, our buses, our banks, our institutions, our subways, our trains, our stadiums, our airports to prevent specifically Islamic violence. This, lest we forget, is a situation unparalleled—unimagined—in our history. Official Washington has become an armed camp. No longer does traffic stream down Pennsylvania Avenue past the White House; the historic street is now a cement block–lined "plaza" blocked off by retractable security stumps. The Capitol, meanwhile, sits behind a hamster cage Rube Goldberg might have designed, its grand staircases blocked, and metal posts—called "bollards," I recently learned— bristling down the sidewalks. The fact is, we are living in a state of siege. After 9/11, the United States embarked on an open-ended war against Islamic terror- ism, with varying degrees of foreign cooperation. But even as we fight abroad, we simultaneously assume the status of victims at home, surrendering our bags and purses for security searches, erecting aesthetics-destroying metal detectors, trans- forming our ennobling vistas and public halls into militarized zones under twenty- four-hour surveillance. This is necessary, we understand, for public safety: But is it the new "normal"? Or do we ever get Pennsylvania Avenue back? Do we ever get to make that mad dash down the airport concourse onto a plane just pushing off from the gate again? (This was an odd, if recurring point of pride, for a family friend who used to time his drive from Kennebunkport, Maine, to Logan Airport with perilous precision). Don't hold your breath; these homeland defenses sprouting up across the country look and feel like they're here for good.

In this seemingly permanent climate of fear, then, ignoring genuine heroes— our exemplars of such adult virtues as bravery and sacrifice, honor and duty—is more than a cultural matter of infantile vanity. It is a security risk. "By our focus on victimization," Crossland writes, "we have adopted our enemies' standard of measure, and are handing them a victory."[9] It's a psychological victory, of course, not a strategic one; but this, above all, is a psychological war.

As a people, then, we begin to make choices predicated on our new siege mentality, choices that a free people—free from fear, and, I would add, free from dhimmitude—would never make. Take Cartoon Rage 2006, the cultural nuke set off by an Islamic chain reaction to those twelve cartoons of Muhammad appear- ing in a Danish newspaper. We watched the Muslim meltdown with shocked at- tention, but there was little recognition that its poisonous fallout was fear. Fear in the State Department, which, like Islam, called the cartoons unacceptable. Fear in Whitehall, which did the same. Fear in the Vatican, which did the same. And fear in the media, which failed, with few, few exceptions, to reprint or show the images. With only a small roll of brave journals, mainly in continental Europe, to salute, the proud Western tradition of a free press bowed its head and submitted to an Islamic law against depictions of Muhammad. That's dhimmitude.

Not that we admitted it. Resorting to delusional talk of "tolerance," "respon- sibility," and "sensitivity," we tried to hide the fear that kept the Danish drawings out of the press. We even congratulated ourselves for having the "editorial judgment" to make "pluralism" possible. "Readers were well served by a short story without publishing the cartoons," said a *Wall Street Journal* spokesman. "We didn't want to publish anything that can be perceived as inflammatory to our readers' culture."[10] "CNN has chosen to not show the cartoons in respect for Islam," reported the cable network.[11] On behalf of the BBC, which did show some of the cartoons on the air, a news editor subsequently apologized, adding: "We've taken a decision not to go further . . . in order not to gratuitously offend the significant number" of Muslim viewers, both in Britain and worldwide.[12] Left unmentioned was the understanding (editorial judgment?) that "gratuitous offense" would doubtless lead to gratuitous violence. Hence, the capitulation to fear—not the inspiration of tolerance but of capitulation—and a condition of dhimmitude. In calling these cartoons "unacceptable," in censoring ourselves "in respect" to Islam, we brought ourselves into compliance with a central statute of sharia. As *Jyllands-Posten*'s Flemming Rose noted, that's not respect, that's submission.[13]

There is something weak and underdeveloped in this unprotesting submission—something that strikes me as cultural immaturity. Of course, it would, given my premise about the death of the grown-up. Still, the act of cartoon submission—the quick and easy surrender of a hard-won, core liberty to an implacable religious demand—is not an act to associate with a muscular and robust cultural profile. Revealing infinite give and no take, it is the childlike act of the uncertain minor, not the behavior of the worldly guardian; it is the passive act of the victim, not the take-charge response of the hero. It is the directionless act of the follower who lacks any civilizational orientation—and the follower, here, is following Islam.

This should begin to explain why a world without grown-ups is such a dangerous place. I didn't realize how dangerous it was a decade ago, when I first began thinking through the death-of-the-grown-up theory. At the time, it seemed to culminate in a Bill Clinton, a presidential phenomenon whose tastes and behaviors, from fast food to quicky sex, were flash-frozen in a punky adolescence from which he never evolved. I thought the theory offered a novel, possibly useful take on the cultural shifts that had brought us up to the Clinton years, and a way to understand the era through its defining death-of-the grown-up moment. This, I submit, took place on the very day the former president's lewd liaison with an intern was revealed in some—not yet all—lurid detail. It was the day Bill Clinton thought he was a cooked goose. At least, as anyone who recalls his first filmed reactions to the Lewinsky scandal, he looked as though he thought he was a cooked goose. More important, he acted like one, doing everything he could from that point forward to cover up a scandal for which the American public, it turned out, had no intention of penalizing him. But Clinton didn't know that. He didn't know there would be no collective wrath—despite the best efforts of the "vast, right-wing conspiracy"—and not even a collective frown. The fact is, Bill Clinton, our first adolescent president, thought his country was more grown-up than he was.

It wasn't. The United States slouched its way through the 1990s—the decade Charles Krauthammer dubbed "our holiday from history"—as if to prove the point. Rather than censuring Clinton (as Clinton himself so obviously expected) the electorate acted more like a posse, circling the wagons around a man who had demeaned himself, his family, his office, and his country for all the world to see, including, of course, Osama bin Laden and his jihadist gangs of thugs.

It may have been *our* holiday from history, but it certainly wasn't history's holiday from us. On February 26, 1993, thirty-eight days into the Clinton era, the World Trade Center was bombed (six killed, one thousand injured) by an Islamic network with ties to al-Qaeda and Iraq. In early October 1993, the debacle known as the Battle of Mogadishu took place, in which eighteen American soldiers were killed; it is now believed to have had al-Qaeda participation. (It certainly drew al-Qaeda attention, with Osama bin Laden subsequently citing our retreat as a sign of exploitable weakness.) In 1995, the Clinton administration learned of an interrupted plan by al-Qaeda operative Hamzi Yousef (mastermind of the first WTC attack) to hijack eleven airlines and smash one of them into CIA headquarters in Langley, Virginia. On June 26, 1996, the Khobar Towers Barracks was attacked (nineteen U.S. servicemen killed, 273 wounded) by Iranian-backed Hezbollah, quite possibly aided by al-Qaeda. On August 7, 1998, U.S. embassies in Kenya and Tanzania were bombed (220 killed, four thousand injured) by al-Qaeda. On October 12, 2000, the USS *Cole* was attacked by al-Qaeda (seventeen sailors killed, thirty-nine injured). Holiday from history? Looking back now on just some of the bloody milestones to jihad against the West, it's becomes apparent that we, as a people, navigated the Clinton years in blinkers along an alternate route—a deep, dark tunnel marked, indeed, made by tawdry domestic scandal.

Byron York has highlighted the unmistakable Clinton-era pattern that pit scandal management against fighting terrorism. Nannygate, which brought down Clinton's nominees for attorney general Kimba Wood and Zoe Baird, served as a distraction from the first WTC bombing; significantly, Janet Reno's subsequent confirmation hearings to become attorney general never once mentioned the attack. When the Khobar Towers were blown up by Iranian terrorists, we were deep into Whitewater and Filegate. At the time of the twin embassy attacks in Africa, the focus was on Monica Lewinsky and the blue Gap dress she didn't take to the cleaners. Even as the administration was winding down at the end of 2000, when it came to the October suicide bombing of the USS *Cole,* negotiations between Israelis and Palestinians, ultimately futile, "took the edge in preoccupying senior administration officials," reported *The Washington Post,* because "it presented a broader threat to Clinton's foreign policy aims," that is, the Legacy. As York summed up, "Whenever a serious terrorist attack occurred, it seemed Bill Clinton was always busy with something else."[14]

From this perspective, the post-grown-up president was a dangerous man. And from this perspective, the post-grown-up world was a perilous place. No one, least of all the political class charged with national security, bothered to notice we were living in a period of resurgent Islam, an imperial faith now into a phase of jihadist expansionism for the first time since before the rise of European colonial empires in the eighteenth and nineteenth centuries. As the Europeans returned home from their empires in the twentieth century, they were followed—or, rather they invited—their former subjects, many of whom were Muslim, into Europe. The resulting demographic shifts of Muslims into Europe in the last several decades were actually part of a strategic policy engineered by Euro-Mediterranean elites—oil for immigration, political power through political alignment—to compete with Superpower America by creating what Bat Ye'or has identified as "Eurabia." The policy has led not to the Westernization of Islam in Europe, but rather to the Islamization of Europe—a process, Bernard Lewis told the German publication *Die Welt* in 2004, that will turn the continent Islamic by the end of this century. If true, this represents a tectonic shift in world history.

Even now, has post-grown-up America noticed? What will it do about this? What should it do? What can it do to stop it? Or does it even want to? Does America need to take precautions against Islamization at home? (Yes.) Such questions may expose a widespread, sleepy ignorance, even impotence, but they are the questions of the century, and they must be addressed now. But who will address them? Once it seemed the death of the grown-up took us to the tawdry pass of the Clinton scandals—a smutty low, but survivable. Now it becomes apparent that the post-grown-up freefall extends beyond any one person or presidency. Huge forces are in flux. What is at risk is civilization—and yes, as we know it.

Standing around Logan Airport last summer with some time to kill, I watched crowds of travelers winnow down to single file in order to pass through a phalanx of metal detectors, dutifully unstrapping wristwatches, dropping off keychains, and removing their shoes. They were, of course, cooperating with airport screeners charged with determining whether any of them had secretly bought a ticket to paradise—not the pearly gates one, but the seventy-two virgins kind—and not some earthbound destination. I wondered whether these low-level indignities would get passengers home safe and sound, or whether they would require body bags, burn masks, and prosthetics to reach their final destination. It was shortly after the London Underground bombings, and it seemed like an open question. As this final line of defense against murder-in-the-skies deployed, I wondered when the arsenal would also include those high-tech scopes and scanners we read about that are designed to identify retinas and fingerprints; and I thought how strange it was that even as we devise new ways to see inside ourselves to our most elemental components, we also prevent ourselves from looking full face at the danger to our way of life posed by Islam.

Notice I wrote "Islam." I didn't say "Islamists." Or "Islamofascists." Or "fundamentalist extremists." Or "Wahhabism." Except for Wahhabism—an overly narrow term for the jihadism that permeates all schools of Islam, not just this infamous Saudi one—I think I've tried out all the other terms in various columns since 9/11, but I've come to find them artificial and confusing, and maybe purposefully so. In their amorphous imprecision, they allow us to give a wide berth to a great problem: The gross incompatibility of Islam—the religious force that shrinks freedom even as it "moderately" tolerates, or "extremistly" advances jihad—with the West. Worse than its imprecision, however, is the evident childishness that inspires this lexicon, as though padding "Islam" with extraneous syllables ("-ism," "-ist" "-ofascist") is a shield against PC scorn of "judgmentalism"; or that exempting plain "Islam" by criticizing fanciful "Islamism" or "Islamofascism" puts a safety lock on Muslim rage—which, as per the Danish cartoon experience, we know explodes at any critique. Such mongrel terms, however, keep our understanding of Islam at bay. To take just one example: In writing about Cartoon Rage 2006, Charles Krauthammer clearly identified why the Western press failed to republish the Danish Muhammad cartoons. "What is at issue is fear. The unspoken reason many newspapers do not want to republish is not sensitivity but simple fear." Clear as a bell, but then he went all mushy on us: "They know what happened to Theo van Gogh, who made a film about the Islamic treatment of women and got a knife through the chest with an Islamist manifesto attached."[15]

What's mushy about that? Well, Krauthammer has written that Theo van Gogh made a film about the "*Islamic* treatment of women" and was killed by a knife "with an *Islamist* manifesto" attached. Given that both Theo's film and the murder manifesto were directly and explicitly inspired by the verses of the Koran, what's Islamic about the treatment of women that's not also Islamic about the manifesto? The "-ist" is a dodge, a nicety, a semantic wedge between the religion of Islam and the ritual murder of van Gogh. But why, oh why, is it up to Charles Krauthammer, or any other infidel, to save face when the face is Muhammad's—the certifiable religious inspiration of jihad murder and dhimmi subjugation, not to mention the oppression of women? If the "-ist" is undeserved here, it is also misplaced—a fig leaf where there should be no shame in understanding.

Am I right? Who's to say? Both the topic of Islam and, more pertinent to a Westerner, the topic of Islamization—for that is what is at hand, and very soon in Europe—are verboten. And maybe they're not even verboten; for a topic to be forbidden implies that it's also on the tip of everyone's tongue, even if they do keep their mouths shut. Islam as a whole, as a historical continuum, as the theology of what we know as terrorism, as a rationale for dhimmi repression, is off the charts; out of bounds, really, and way beyond acceptable discourse. The issues central to Islam's incompatibility with modernity—which, where the West is concerned, come down to jihad and dhimmitude, those Islamic institutions on which relations between Muslims and non-Muslims turn—are ignored according to an unspoken consensus and, thus, never appear on the public agenda. What is left is a black hole.

Why did this happen?

We can look to the thick, blanketing fog of political correctness that hangs over the political landscape, shrouding difference, obscuring significance, and clouding debate. But something besides what we know as "PC" plays into the resulting hush. The uniformity of the silence, from Left to Right, from academia to politics to journalism, tells us we have moved beyond PC to a more profound, more enveloping level of orthodoxy. After all, what we know as political correctness implies the existence of a flip side: namely, a school of political *in*correctness that supplies the counter-narrative to contradict or subvert the PC orthodoxy. Such a school of thought—at least in what passes for the political mainstream where ideas are publicly debated—has not come into existence regarding the role of Islam in the so-called war on terror, or, worse, the Islamization of the West.

Example: When, in the shell-shocked wake of 9/11, President Bush began his historically inaccurate and theologically absurd "Islam is peace" offensive—which to this day relies on a willful ignorance of the jihad ideology that has driven Islamic history for thirteen centuries—no voices of correction, no attempts at historical analysis coalesced into a school of thought that was admitted into the political mainstream, not even among pro-war, anti-PC conservatives. Ultimately, I came to understand this as a post-adult moment because it felt as if no *grown-ups* were speaking up; indeed, it became alarmingly clear that there were no . . . grown-ups . . . to speak up—at least, in voices heeded and debated in the post-grown-up culture.

But there exists a formidable body of contemporary scholarship that bravely explicates the history of jihad and its modern-day applications—a bibliography I was relieved to find after 9/11 when the happy talk of a Karen Armstrong or a John Esposito sounded out of sync with what was actually being heard on the news. Some of these authors I have cited in previous chapters: Over four decades, Egyptian-born Bat Ye'or has pioneered the study of dhimmitude, the non-Muslim experience under Islam that follows jihad. The Pakistani-born scholar Ibn Warraq has, since the Rushdie affair, compiled a wrenching record of "apostasy," the fearfully dangerous Muslim experience of leaving Islam. Daniel Pipes has long cataloged the progress of jihad and Islamization in the West. In the years since 9/11, Robert Spencer has produced several clear-eyed studies of Islam for both laymen and experts, also establishing a Web site that tracks current events called jihadwatch.org. Andrew G. Bostom, also since 9/11, has compiled a scholarly compendium of writings on jihad that offers many key texts and studies in English for the first time, including those of Islamic commentators on the Koran (al-Baydawi, al-Tabari, Suyuti), the Sufi mystic al-Ghazali's surprisingly bellicose pronouncements on jihad war, and those of overlooked historians (C. E. Dufourcq, Clement Huart, Dmitar Angelov, Maria Mathilde Alexandrescu-Dersca Bulgaru). But such research has been largely relegated to the the sidelines, scholarship all but ignored by elites for purposes of public discussion and debate.

It's enough to engender nostalgia for the Cold War, mushroom clouds and all. From that epic struggle emerged an indomitable anticommunist movement, Cold Warriors who perservered and triumphed by following a clear, rational line of academic analysis and astute polemic. They were ideologues who believed in freedom, but they were also realists who sought to defend the West by repelling and defeating a morally bankrupt ideology—Soviet communism bent on world domination. In those days, in that movement, ex-communist intellectuals and refugees from communism, such as Arthur Koestler, Whittaker Chambers, and Aleksandr Solzhenitsyn, were embraced and championed by Cold Warriors.

By glaring contrast, ex-Muslim intellectuals such as Ibn Warraq, Ali Sina, Wafa Sultan, and Ayaan Hirsi Ali, and refugees from Islam such as Bat Ye'or and Brigitte Gabriel, are held at arm's length by the most fervent warriors on terror, members of a post-PC generation that see in their dreams of Islamic "reform" the key to a strategy of avoiding civilizational clash. Thus, they seek to defend the West by repelling or defeating "Islamic extremists," but not the ideology contained within mainstream Islam that seeks to establish a world caliphate ruled by sharia. It's as if yesterday's Cold Warriors had staked the freedom of the Western world on a utopian vision of communist "moderates" who would someday, somehow emerge to "reform" the *Communist Manifesto* into something as compatible with the secular, post-Judeo-Christian West as the Girl Scout creed. Far from realpolitik, this is dreampolitik. Warming to their policies of wishful thinking, today's Terror Warriors keep the apostates and critics of Islam out in the cold, their copious knowledge of the dire perils of jihad and dhimmitude unheeded, unexplored, undebated. This has helped enforce a terrible silence on the urgent questions of our time.

For example: Remember when word came down in 2003 from the Vatican that Pope John Paul II had watched Mel Gibson's *The Passion of the Christ* and liked it? The anonymously sourced story sparked a media firestorm around the globe as reporters sought confirmation of the papal equivalent of two thumbs-up. "It is as it was," the pope supposedly said.[16] This sounded like the perfect biblical movie blurb, but did the pontiff actually utter the words? After some nonclarifying retractions from the Vatican, it was ultimately hard to say for sure—although not for journalistic want of trying. This natural curiosity stands in striking contrast to the media silence, journalists, pundits, and politicians alike, that met a far more significant report of papal opinion: namely, that Pope Benedict XVI was said to believe that Islam is incapable of reform.

This bombshell dropped out of an early 2006 interview conducted by radio host Hugh Hewitt with Father Joseph D. Fessio, S.J., a friend and former student of the pope. Father Fessio recounted the pope's words on the key problem facing Islamic reform this way: "In the Islamic tradition, God has given His word to Mohammed, but it's an eternal word. It's not Mohammed's word. It's there for eternity the way it is. *There's no possibility of adapting it or interpreting it* [emphasis added]." Father Fessio continued, elaborating on the pope's theological assessment of a religion with a billion-plus followers, some notorious number of whom are currently at war with the West. According to his friend's report, the pope believes there's no changing the Koran—that is, no changing Koranic teachings on infidels, women, polygamy, penal codes, and other markers of Islamic law—in such a way as to propel Islam into happy coexistence with modernity.[17]

As I said, a bombshell—at least to Terror Warriors and other Westerners depending on a mythological Islamic reform movement to reengineer the ludicrously nicknamed "religion of peace" into post-Enlightenment compatibility. But this was a bombshell that didn't explode because no one wanted to touch it. Hugh Hewitt posted the extraordinary interview online, a couple of Internet blogs picked it up, and Middle East expert Daniel Pipes wrote a short piece taking exception to it,[18] but, as the *Asia Times Online* columnist Spengler noted (in a column called "When Even the Pope Has to Whisper"), "not a single media outlet has taken notice."[19] Posting the Spengler column at the Corner at *National Review Online*, Rod Dreher wrote: "Spengler is amazed by the silence from the Western media over this remarkable statement attributed to the current pope. . . . and he suggests that we shrink from acknowledging it because the consequences of the pope being right about this are too horrible to contemplate."[20] Indeed,

with one exception, *NRO* Corner regulars failed to comment on the pope's putative words—noteworthy, given the magazine's tradition of a Catholic identity.

Then again, was it really such a bombshell after all? Here is part of a letter I
received from a Muslim reader about a column I wrote on the subject.

> Dear Diana,
>
> I read your article, but I failed to understand where the bombshell is. The
> pope has the right to express his opinion about the impossibility to reform Islam.
> It is just that Islam does not need any reform. We do not as Muslims mess with the
> word of God, we do not fit the religion to our needs [as] Christians have done and
> still do.

In other words, while the pope's reported belief in what amounts to the non-
reformability of Islam was, as Dreher put it, for non-Muslims "too horrible to
contemplate," the same notion struck my Muslim reader as being noncontroversial to the point of being unremarkable—not a bombshell, but a dud. Maybe
Western horror came from Western embarassment: simply acknowledging the
fixity of doctrines so deeply offensive to Western sensibilities struck Westerners
as insulting to Islam, and was thus repressed. Here, however, what is offensive in
the West is a point of Muslim pride, as in: Of course, the Koran is unchangeable;
it is the word of Allah. As my correspondent wrote:

> To us Muslims, [the Koran] is the word of God; therefore, who are we to reform
> the laws He set for his creation? We were given the freedom to either accept them
> or reject them. If we accept them, then we have to do our best to follow all of them
> to the limit of our capabilities. However, it would be a form of arrogance if we
> started fitting the religion to our own desires. . . . He created us, therefore he
> knows what's best for us.

So, accept the Koran, reject the Koran, but don't change the Koran. In describing the persistence of slavery in Islamic societies, K. S. Lal, an Indian me-
dievalist, came up with a vividly pointed metaphor that helps explain the fixity of
the Koran and its teachings.

> Muhammed could not change the revelation; he could only explain and interpret
> it. So do the Muslims do today. There are liberal Muslims and conservative Mus-
> lims, there are Muslims learned in theology and Muslims devoid of learning. They
> discuss, they interpret, they rationalize, but all going round within the closed cir-
> cle of Islam. There is no possibility of getting out of the fundamentals of Islam;
> there is no provision of introducing any innovation.[21]

But please. Let's not be smug: The West inhabits a similarly "closed circle"—not, in our case, of Islam, but of being politically correct in regard to Islam. And, so far, there's no getting out of these fundamentals, either; nor does there seem to be, as Lal might have said, a way of introducing any innovation. Just as we refuse to examine the relationship between Koranic fixity and Islamic reform, we refuse to look at the teachings of jihad as revealed by Muhammad. Indeed, Cartoon Rage 2006 has revealed that we refuse even to look at Muhammad—as a show, some would argue, of good manners. Failing to groove to "artistic" attacks on Christianity such as *Piss Christ* or "Dung Virgin," the Good Mannerists among us understand the consternation of the Cartoon Ragers—at least to some point shy of death threats, arson, and murder—and see self-censorship as a matter of common decency.

Is their comparison valid? And is their politeness deserved? Absolutely not, and here's one big reason why. As I have mentioned before, Christianity and Islam are not interchangeable belief systems of generic divinity and influence. One relevant distinction between them is the way they operate in relation to their societies. As I have also mentioned before, historically, Christianity has abided by the separation of church and state; Islam knows no separation whatsoever. This is key. This unity of mosque and state makes the theological teachings of Islam as revealed by Muhammad, codified in the Islamic law that drives Islamic societies, the basis of the Islamic political sphere. For its political role, then, Islam demands what we might think of political scrutiny—analysis and criticism. But it doesn't get it. And when it does—even in the mildest form of satirical commentary—the Islamic world blows up.

Let's take what are considered the most inflammatory of the Danish Dozen: Bomb-head Muhammad; and Muhammad in the clouds, telling arriving suicide bombers that Islamic paradise is plumb out of virgins. What Denmark's cartoonists did in these caricatures is something few writers have dared to do in words: They made visual reference to the copious historical and contemporary theological underpinnings of jihad and suicide bombings. What is offensive here, then, is not the extremely mild caricature, but rather those theological underpinnings of holy war and suicide bombings. When the widely influential Sheik Yusuf al-Qaradawi can praise Muhammad as "an epitome for religious warriors [mujahideen],"[22] Muhammad, a jihad model, shouldn't be a taboo subject in the West, either in caricature or commentary, and certainly shouldn't be super-sacralized, in effect, by a fearfully polite censorship. The subject should be laid out for all to see, but it isn't.

The valiant Dutch ex-parliamentarian and ex-Muslim Ayaan Hirsi Ali explained why silence is a problem: "You cannot liberalize Islam without criticizing the Prophet and the Koran. . . . You cannot redecorate a house without entering inside."²³ But who among us has even gone up to the door to ask whether jihad in all its modern manifestations—airplane hijackings, skyscraper massacres, bus bombings, train bombings, rioting over novels, rioting over cartoons, car bombs, suicide bombs, pursuit of nuclear bombs—is not the perversion of a noble faith, but rather a core institution? In denial there is defeat.

After addressing the Pim Fortuyn Memorial Conference in the Hague—a scholarly conference on Islam in Europe in February 2006—Robert Spencer posted the following anecdote at his Web site jihadwatch.org.²⁴ It concerned an extraordinary discussion he had had at an American embassy reception with an official of the Dutch Ministry of Integration—a woman, Spencer writes, "who spends her days in dialogue" with Dutch imams and other Muslim leaders. I say their talk was extraordinary because Spencer's summation conveys in almost gruesome detail the acute paralysis of observation and reasoning powers on which multiculturalism, in its practical applications, must rely.

> We began a wide-ranging discussion about the nature of the jihad threat and the proper response to it. In the course of this I asked her how many Muslim leaders she encountered who were ready to lay aside attachment to the sharia, and accept the Dutch governmental and societal structure and the parameters of Dutch plu-ralism, and be willing to live in Dutch society as equals to, not superiors of, non-Muslims indefinitely. She told me that there were only very few, but insisted that we had to work with them, and indeed had to place our faith and hope in them, for otherwise the future was impossibly bleak.

Keep the faith, in other words, or plunge into the abyss. Spencer continued:

> I asked her if she had read the Qur'an. She told me no, she hadn't, and wouldn't because *she didn't want to lose all hope*—and because whatever was in it, she still had to find some accord with the Muslim leaders, *no matter what.* [Emphasis added.]

The unflinching Oriana Fallaci called the Koran the *Mein Kampf* of the jihad movement because it exhorts the annihilation and subjugation of the non-Muslim. While her analogy is shattering to any PC peace, as Spencer has pointed out elsewhere, it is also a statement, through analysis and debate, "that can be verified or disproved." ("And indeed," he writes, "Islamic terrorists such as Osama bin Laden, Zarqawi, and others have never hesitated to quote the Qur'an copiously to justify their actions. It remains for those who identify themselves as moderate Muslims to convince violent Muslims that they are misusing the Qur'an—if indeed they are—and should lay down their arms. They have had

no notable success in this so far."[25]) I introduce the notion for a rhetorical reason. Imagine if Spencer's conversation with the Dutch official had taken place in
1939. It might have gone something like this: *I asked her if she had read* Mein
Kampf. *She told me no, she hadn't, and wouldn't because she didn't want to lose
all hope—and because whatever was in it, she still had to find some accord with the
Nazi leaders, no matter what.*

"No matter what"? Was this the clear-eyed assessment of a rational adult
seeking information and solutions in her engagement with reality? Or was this
reliance on blind faith and studied ignorance a symptom of a fearfully stunted
mentality, childishly hoping to awaken from a bad dream?

There's more.

> I urged her to ask the imams with whom she spoke questions that made their loy-
> alties clear, insofar as they would answer them honestly. I urged her to ask them
> whether they would like to see sharia implemented in the Netherlands at any time
> in the future, and whether they were working toward that end in any way, peaceful
> as well as violent. I asked her to ask them whether they would be content to live as
> equals with non-Muslims indefinitely in a Dutch pluralistic society, or whether
> they would ultimately hope to institute Islamic supremacy and the subjugation of
> non-Muslims.
>
> She said she couldn't ask them those questions. . . . Such questions would im-
> mediately put their relationship on a confrontational plane, when cooperation was
> what they wanted, not confrontation. But, I sputtered, you're not getting coopera-
> tion as it is. The confrontation is already upon us. What is to be gained by pre-
> tending that it isn't happening?[26]

A world of make-believe; a world of "cooperation"; a world of silence. Silence on such crucial questions not only denies us answers, it denies us a fighting
chance. And you know the silence is deafening when Abu Qatada, a notorious
British imam thought to have links to al-Qaeda, has to interrupt his busy jihad to
try to set the record straight: "I am astonished by President Bush when he claims
there is nothing in the Qur'an that justifies jihad or violence in the name of Islam.
Is he some kind of Islamic scholar? Has he ever actually read the Qur'an

Abu Qatada's darkly comic relief aside, the resolute denial of the relationship
between Islam and jihad is perplexing, exhausting all routine exercises of common sense. Indeed, these bizarre loops of logic take us into a psychological realm
of delusional thinking—patterns of thought at odds with reality. While this may
be terrain best navigated by the nineteenth-century Russian novelist, Harvard
psychiatric instructor Kenneth Levin has made a recent study of such patterns in
modern-day Israelis and Jews in history. In his 2005 book *The Oslo Syndrome:*

Delusions of a People Under Siege, Levin focused on both the Israeli experience, in which Israel entered into concessionary negotiations with a "peace partner" openly dedicated to Israel's destruction, and the historical Jewish Diaspora experience, in which Jewish populations typically identified with their tormentors and even echoed their anti-Semitism. According to Levin's diagnosis, these interactions, engendered by a permanent condition of siege mentality, relied on delusional thinking. There are two kinds: One is delusional thinking about the intentions of the aggressor (Arab Muslim or European Christian); the other is delusional thinking regarding the victim's ability to change the aggressor's intentions. Such thinking is common to victims of chronic abuse, particularly children. They fool themselves into thinking that they, the victims, control the abuser by, in their own minds, linking the abuse they suffer to their own behavior. In other words, in their delusional mode of thought, they see their own behavior as the cause of their own abuse. This mind game, Levin says, gives victims a vital sense of control over situations that are expressly beyond their control (an abusive parent, for instance), thus avoiding the devastating alternative: helplessness and despair.

And so the besieged victim pretends: Daddy doesn't really want to hurt me; if I'm a better girl, he'll stop. Israel pretends: Muslims don't really want to destroy us, and so we'll give them land for peace. Jews in pre-Nazi Europe pretended: The anti-Semites are really right; we deserve a pogrom. Intriguingly, Levin writes, "But the book's themes have a still broader relevance. Even ostensibly powerful and secure populations, under conditions that entail ongoing threat and vulnerability, can manifest similar trends."[28]

Ongoing threat and vulnerability, huh? That certainly sounds like the American condition after 9/11. Our superpowerful condition may not compare with tiny Israel's; nonetheless, color-coded terror alerts are practically part of our daily weather report, security procedures have become routine, and open access everywhere has been slammed shut for the duration. This has placed our population effectively under siege. And don't forget the toll of the culture wars. Those raging battles, which have severed, or at least weakened, the connection between "dead, white males" and "liberty and justice for all," among other things, have undermined American confidence and purpose. While similarities between the demonization of Jews in the Diaspora, say, and the demonization of the American white males (dead or alive) are necessarily quite limited, there nonetheless remains a way in which the American male specifically, and the American adult in general, has been subjected to a cultural form of the chronic abuse that Levin pinpoints as a cause of siege mentality. And it is that siege mentality, he writes, that leads to delusional thinking.

Thus, we pretend Islam isn't a threat to Western liberty; it's those awful "extremists." Jihad isn't a historic and theological tradition in Islam; it's those awful "extremists." Sharia isn't a threat to freedom of expression and sexual equality; it's those awful "extremists." This gaping disconnect with reality dovetails nicely with the overall post-grown-up cultural reluctance—dare I say, *childish* reluctance?—to face extremely unpleasant facts. Rather than confront the hard truths of our times, we tell ourselves soothing tales; rather than act on the logic of reality, we deny its implications. Such delusional thinking, which sounds like something Dr. Levin might care to study next, comes naturally to a culture that has perpetuated and enshrined immaturity for more than a half century. But how much longer can a society in denial last?

Imagine: If, as I believe, the "war on terror" is actually a defensive war against modern-day manifestations of jihad—the same jihad by which Islam has traditionally (and, where dhimmi peoples are concerned, tragically) expanded—the implications are dire. There are implications for our immigration policy (do we allow proponents of sharia to settle here?); implications for our conceptions of religious tolerance (do we tolerate the intolerant?); implications for the way in which we fight the war on terror (are Islamic hearts and minds beyond our infidel reach?). Without a thorough, no-PC assessment of Islam—and in particular, its institutions of jihad and dhimmitude—how do we reckon with these vital issues? For too long, a sketchy, politically correct assessment of Islam is all we have had. Writing in 1991, the French intellectual and Protestant theologian Jacques Ellul observed:

> In a major encyclopedia, one reads phrases such as: "Islam expanded in the eighth or ninth centuries . . ."; "This or that country passed into Muslim hands . . ." But care is taken not to say how Islam expanded, how countries passed into [Muslim] hands. . . . Indeed, it would seem as if events happened by themselves, through a miraculous or amicable operation. . . . Regarding this expansion, little is said about *jihad*. And yet it all happened through war![29]

Ellul made this comment in a foreword to Bat Ye'or's *The Decline of Eastern Christianity: From Jihad to Dhimmitude,* a masterful survey of the Islamization of the formerly Christian lands stretching from Anatolia to Afghanistan, from Egypt to Palestine to Syria to Iraq to Armenia to Cyprus. The book is history, yes, but it probably comes as news to many that such "Muslim lands" were once bastions of a varied and vital Christendom, and home to similarly thriving communities of Jews, Zoroastrians, and other religions. As much as anything else, the point of Ellul's foreword was to prepare unsuspecting readers for the cruel and violent nature of the Islamic transformation of these lands, as unearthed from a compendium of historical sources by Bat Ye'or. This transformation, in short, is the story of jihad. And, as Ellul wrote, "In the general current climate of favorable predispositions to Islam, . . . there has been a reluctance to allude to the *jihad*. In Western eyes, it would be a sort of dark stain on the greatness and purity of Islam."[30] Never mind that such a stain is there for all to see; we are just not supposed to notice—not then, not now. Then, perhaps, the exercise was academic; now, it is suicidal.

Ellul was elaborating on a theme begun in an even earlier piece of writing: his 1983 preface to Bat Ye'or's previous work, *The Dhimmi: Jews and Christians Under Islam*. Ellul described that earlier book as being both "important" and "sensitive": important, for dealing with "the reality of Islamic doctrine and practice with regard to non-Muslims"; and sensitive, because of the passions this reality could provoke. He was writing four years after the Islamic revolution in Iran, five years before the Salman Rushdie affair, and twenty-three years before the days of Cartoon Rage 2006. In other words, he was writing at a time when such passions were still something new to the modern scene.

> Half a century ago, the question of the condition of non-Muslims in the Islamic countries would not have excited anyone. It might have been the subject of a historical dissertation of interest to specialists. . . . or the subject of a philosophical and theological discussion, but without passion. That which was related to Islam and the Muslim world was believed to belong to a past that, if not dead, was certainly no more alive than medieval Christianity. The Muslim people had no power; they were extraordinarily divided and many of them were subjected to European colonization. . . . And then, suddenly, since 1950, everything changed completely.[31]

Ellul identifies four stages leading to Islam's reemergence on the world stage. First, there was the general process of decolonization in both Muslim and non-Muslim lands. Next, there was a reemphasis on precolonial identity; in the case of Islamic lands, this identity was religious rather than either ethnic or tribal.[32] The third stage Ellul described was, despite periodic Muslim-on-Muslim conflict, an overarching "awareness of religious unity in opposition to the non-Muslim world." And the final stage was the development of Islamic oil clout. Quite suddenly, it seemed, there was nothing ancient about Islam; nonetheless, critical study remained mired in premedieval taboos. "The moment one broaches a problem related to Islam, one touches a subject where strong feelings are easily aroused," Ellul wrote in 1983. On picking up this thread in 1991, the Islamic hypo-sensitivity he described earlier had intensified, demanding not just care, but silence. "So widespread is the agreement on this silence," he observed, "that it can only be the result of a tacit agreement based on implicit presuppositions"—those presuppositions being the putative "greatness and purity of Islam." Anything undercutting Islam's greatness or marring Islam's purity, he explained, is automatically dismissed as being either "blasphemous" or "polemical."[33]

From then to now, it has been ever thus. Ellul's point is all the more striking today because he was writing in the 9/10 world—that seemingly antediluvian period in which Islam was practically unknown to most Americans. The fact that this same reluctance to discuss Islam—to study its history, dissect its institutions, analyze its impact—is only more rigid after 9/11 is nothing short of incredible. But even twenty-odd years ago, Ellul saw fit to inject a cautionary note: "The Muslim world has not evolved in its manner of considering the non-Muslim, which is a reminder of the fate in store for those who may one day be submerged within it."[34] At this point, "one day" is getting too close for dhimmi comfort.

All the more reason, then, that these Islamic institutions on which relations between Islam and non-Islam turn, jihad and dhimmitude, become *the* hot topics. But no. Our leaders and pundits, our generals and academics, pay repetitive and obsequious obeisance to "noble Islam" (with never a bow, of course, to "noble" anything else). They depict jihad as a mutation of Islam—the "distorted," "hijacked," or "defiled" practice by the "violent fringe" or "tiny band of extremists"—despite jihad's central, driving, animating role throughout the history of imperial Islam.[35] As for dhimmitude, it remains an alien concept, even as non-Muslims in the West are increasingly accommodating themselves to Islamic law and practices. While the president of the United States appears no longer to consider Islam an out-and-out religion of "peace," he's settled into an equally ahistorical formulation by delegitimizing jihad violence as "the perversion by a few of a noble faith into an ideology of terror and death."[36] In other words, Jihad Is From Mars and Islam Is From Venus.

Oslo Syndrome, anyone? Historically and tragically, the Islamic extremism the president reviles has always coursed through the Islamic mainstream. Irshad Manji, the self-proclaimed "Muslim refusenik," has discussed their connection. Asked in an interview to assess the extent to which Islam in Europe could be described as "extremist," she replied,

> It mostly depends on how you define extremism. If you mean "literalism," then it is more than widespread—it is mainstream. If you mean the overt preaching of violence, then it percolates on the margins. The key here is to recognize that because literalism is mainstream in Islam today, the thin minority of Muslims who have any intention of engaging in terror are nonetheless protected by the vast majority of moderate Muslims who don't know how to debate and dissent with that proclivity. . . .

I subscribe to Ayaan Hirsi Ali's point that "Islamic terrorism, both in the Netherlands and abroad, is able to thrive because it is embedded in a wider circle of fellow Muslims." This is a reality that most Western security experts have yet to grasp.[37]

That, of course, is putting it mildly. Not only have Westerners in general "yet to grasp" the connection, we do everything we can to cover our eyes and run away from it.

But why?

Before taking a final fly at explaining this potentially fatal ostrich routine, it's time for a nice, bracing dose of Churchill—Winnie's assessment of Islam following his experiences as a young subaltern in the Sudan. Written over one hundred years ago, the excerpt catalogs many of the same problems that remain endemic to Islamic societies to this day—as noted, as a matter of fact, in a widely reported 2002 study commissioned by the United Nations on human development in the Arab world that blamed religious fanatacism, economic stagnation, repression of women, and social paralysis for a lack of progress. What has changed beyond recognition in the intervening century, however, is the mode of expression. Sharp and direct, Churchill says what he has seen, and what he thinks about what he has seen—sans gag, filter, rose-colored glasses, or net. A high-flying display of the late-nineteenth-century British sensibility, it is enough to take one's breath away in the twenty-first.

How dreadful are the curses which Mohammedanism lays upon its votaries! Besides the fanatical frenzy, which is as dangerous in a man as hydrophobia in a dog, there is this fearful fatalistic apathy. The effects are apparent in many countries. Improvident habits, slovenly systems of agriculture, sluggish methods of commerce, and insecurity of property exist wherever the followers of the Prophet rule or live. A degraded sensualism deprives this life of its grace and refinement; the next of its dignity and sanctity. The fact that in Mohammedan law every woman must belong to some man as his absolute property, either as a child, a wife, or a concubine, must delay the final extinction of slavery until the faith of Islam has ceased to be a power among men. Individual Moslems may show splendid qualities. . . . But the influence of the religion paralyses the social development of those who follow it. No stronger retrograde force exists in the world. Far from being moribund, Mohammedanism is a militant and prosletyzing faith. It has already spread thoughout Central Africa, raising fearless warriors at every step; and were it not that Christianity is sheltered in the strong arms of science, the science against which it had vainly struggled, the civilisation of modern Europe might fall, as fell the civilisation of ancient Rome.[38]

Today, some, many, most—all?—would probably call this "hatespeak." But does Churchill speak hatred? Or is he rather expressing a pre-PC appraisal of Islam that is rooted in a wholly non-Islamic tradition once known as the Western world? There is no answer to such questions, because there is no discussion of such questions. There is only silence—the silence of fear. Fear has become the new reason. We fear more Rushdies, more Cartoon Rage, more protests. We fear more Theo van Goghs, more assassinations, more intimidation. We fear more embargoes, more boycotts. We are afraid of more violence, more burning flags, more gutted embassies. Afraid of more bomb threats. Afraid of more bombs. And so we close our eyes and close our circle, "-ists" and "-isms" going all around, pretending outselves into a status quo of our own making, a condition dependent on our own delusions. Moderate Islam is coming. Democracy is the answer. And don't ask any questions. Because there is something else post-grown-up culture fears more than anything else: We are afraid to *do* anything about our fears—even name them.

The war on terror aside: The growth of Islam in the West augurs the peaceful spread of sharia into the West, this by dint of natural procreation and unchecked immigration. Logic should tell us, then, that the growth of Islam in the West threatens Western-style liberty: threatens freedom of expression, freedom of conscience, and upends religious and sexual equality. But logic doesn't tell us that. Or, if it does, no one will admit it. The logic may be incontrovertible; we are at a point, however, where we are afraid of logic, too. That's because logic leads to discrimination—and by "discrimination," I am going back to *Webster's* "ability to make or perceive distinctions; perception; discernment." If we revive our innate ability to make distinctions, suddenly rub our eyes and see the beliefs of Islam and the beliefs of the West at irreconcilable odds, it's not just Islam's place in the West that becomes an acknowledged threat to the survival of the West. The multicultural mirage of interchangeable diversity and "universal values" necessarily vanishes as well; in its place arises an inevitable hierarchy of discrimination. Not all religions are equally benign; not all religions are equal. Not all cultures have made equal contributions; not all cultures are equal. To our elites, Right and Left, this is a bad thing because it sets into motion a right of passage, a painful, difficult awakening from a dreamworld of sunny universalism and pale indecision into a stark reality of black and white, good and evil, win or lose, do or die.

Our inaction depends on our silence, just as avoiding clash depends on our self-censorship. For example, as a culture, we ignored Ibn Warraq's plea in 2006 for "unashamed, noisy, public solidarity" with the Danish cartoonists as a means of safeguarding freedom of expression; we also ignored his warning that from our silence, "the Islamization of Europe will have begun in earnest." We called our self-censorship the silence of respect; in reality, it was the silence of fear. We called it the silence of tolerance; actually, it was silence of cultural acquiescence. There was no clamor to defend the public square from religious tyranny; there was only shame. In vain, then, Warraq wrote:

> Be proud, do not apologize. Do we have to go on apologizing for the sins of our fathers? Do we still have to apologize, for example, for the British Empire, when, in fact, the British presence in India led to the Indian Renaissance, resulted in famine relief, railways, roads and irrigation schemes, eradication of cholera, the civil service, the establishment of a universal educational system where none existed before, the institution of elected parliamentary democracy and the rule of law? What of the British architecture of Bombay and Calcutta? The British even gave back to the Indians their own past: It was European scholarship, archaeology and research that uncovered the greatness that was India; it was British government that did its best to save and conserve the monuments that were a witness to that past glory. British imperialism preserved where earlier Islamic imperialism destroyed thousands of Hindu temples.
>
> On the world stage, should we really apologize for Dante, Shakespeare, and Goethe? Mozart, Beethoven and Bach? Rembrandt, Vermeer, Van Gogh, Breughel, Ter Borch? Galileo, Huygens, Copernicus, Newton and Darwin? Penicillin and computers? The Olympic Games and football? Human rights and parliamentary democracy? The West is the source of the liberating ideas of individual liberty, political democracy, the rule of law, human rights and cultural freedom. It is the West that has raised the status of women, fought against slavery, defended freedom of inquiry, expression and conscience. No, the West needs no lectures on the superior virtue of societies that keep their women in subjugation, cut off their clitorises, stone them to death for alleged adultery, throw acid on their faces, or deny the human rights of those considered to belong to lower castes.[39]

Ibn Warraq's catalog of Western treasure—onto which I would append an American index represented, say, by the Founding Fathers, Mark Twain, Thomas Edison, Irving Berlin, Ella Fitzgerald, Watson and Crick, Laurel and Hardy, Ted Williams, Jonas Salk, and the 82nd Airborne—is indeed something to be proud of, to derive strength from; guidance, too. It is also more evidence of the crock that is "universal values." Be proud, don't apologize—and don't look now, but the end of jihad in the West also means the end of multiculturalism in the West. And maybe the truth is that, prisoners of our closed circle, we don't want that; can't think that.

All of this makes a new world, all right, but, with apologies to Huxley, anything but brave. And anything but grown-up. Maybe it wouldn't matter if this really were "the end of history," that postcommunist pause in the early 1990s that lasted all of thirty minutes. Maybe then we could chase eternal youth all the way to assisted living; revel in self-loathing at the spa; even support our troops and never meet one. But ours is a time of supreme, even ultimate struggle. The cushioning luxury of affluence; the hard sacrifice of our parents or grandparents; the hookah-pipe dream of world peace are no longer sufficient protections of our liberty, if they ever were. They're gone now, used up, spent on a long and vainglorious youth. What next? Ours is an age marked by a startling confluence of stunted Western models faced with a colossal threat, an almost science-fictional fate of cultural transformation via Islamization. Arrayed against this looming threat stands a veritable gathering of the miniature clans: the perpetual adolescent; the delusional victim; the caving dhimmi whose rush to sharia will surely take us there.

It makes a kind of horrific sense, because it is dhimmitude that is perhaps the ultimate phase of human infantilization: the abject surrender of liberty to implacable authority, the human condition that, by force, is never allowed to attain the maturity of free will. It sounds like a living death. Wasn't it, "Give me liberty or give me death"? And how many American men have chosen their death for our liberty? For our peace. For our prosperity. For our ease. For our convenience. For our inaction. For our laziness. For our fear. For our closed circle. For our silence. For our dhimmitude?

Never. Eternal youth is proving fatal; it is time to find our rebirth in adulthood.

EPILOGUE

Having just defined all of recent history, culture, politics, and war in terms of callow youth and scorned adulthood, I think a final word is in order.

Looking back over these pages, I see that most of the people praised for their adulthood—these not necessarily happy few—are individuals who said no.

No, said the Montgomery County parents to cucumber sex ed; no, said the Scarsdale principal to transcript tampering; no, said the Queensborough College professor to passing her class-flunking revolutionaries; no, said the Batavia Rotary wife to hubby's striptease. So much of adulthood today, such as it exists, is a necessarily negative force, a damper on behaviors unconstrained by lines and boundaries; a hook on impulses unfettered from either fixed morality or esteemed tradition. It puts me in mind of William F. Buckley, Jr.'s, memorable line about "standing athwart history, yelling Stop."

That was in 1955. Writing in that first issue of the *National Review,* Buckley noted that a conservative magazine like his might seem redundant in a nation reknowned for its conservatism. Not so, he said, adding: "If *National Review* is superfluous, it is so for very different reasons: It stands athwart history, yelling Stop, at a time when no one is inclined to do so, or to have much patience with those who so urge it."[1]

Half a century later, I am struck by similarities in the atmosphere he describes. Being a grown-up today—like being a conservative yesterday—usually involves yelling "stop" when no one is inclined to do so, sounding a note that has become discordantly lonely over the years as the chorus of adults has thinned and petered out. (I'll leave it to someone else to argue whether being a grown-up is the same as being a conservative.) There may still be times when just yelling "stop," or "no," is enough, times when a line needs to be drawn fast, or a vanished boundary redefined. After "no"—or, maybe, after enough "no"s—lines and boundaries begin to reappear. But if "no" can function as a restorative, "no" is still not enough.

The instinct behind these "no"s—the moral instinct—is where what might be called our "inner grown-up" still lives, a tentative, marginal, and, I would add, demoralizing existence in the post-grown-up milieu. Historian Gertrude Himmelfarb has written extensively about the *re*moralization of society that occurred in the Victorian era, a period in which human behavior in all its variations was guided by the ideals of virtue and the effects of stigma. Indeed, remoralization requires both. As she put it a decade ago, "Stigmatization is the other side of the coin of virtue. You can't have a set of virtues, a system of values, without having a corresponding system of stigmas." Stigmas, you might say, are what keep virtues or values honest. Not that Himmelfarb uses this terminology interchangeably. She went on to explain the crucial difference between virtues and values.

> The idea of virtue goes back to antiquity, and it varied in the course of time. The ancient virtues were not the Christian virtues, and they were certainly not the Victorian virtues. But what was common to all of these virtues, to the very idea of virtue, was a fixed moral standard—a standard by which all people at all times and under all circumstances would be judged. Today we have abandoned that idea of virtue and have adopted instead what we now call "values". Value is a subjective, relativistic term; any individual, group, or society may choose to value whatever they like. One cannot say of virtues what one can say of values, that anyone's virtues are as good as anyone else's, or that everyone has a right to his own virtues. This shift from virtues to values represents the true moral revolution of our time.[2]

I bring this up in these final pages because it may be that in this conception of virtue as a fixed standard lies the unforgiving but inspirational essence of adulthood. As a means by which society is regulated, as a means by which individuals regulate themselves, a devotion to virtue as "a standard by which all people at all times and under all circumstances would be judged" is a way for post-adult society to reapproach maturity.

And not just the maturity of the individual. Mature individuals make up a mature society. Such a society, it would seem, stabilized by the fixed standards of a remoralized citizenry, would no longer founder in the shifting "values" of multiculturalism. How could it? A clear moral standard would serve to anchor a clear cultural standard as well. This isn't a call to sainthood, or even necessarily to religion, and it doesn't involve what is always derided as "turning back the clock." What is required, rather, is some serious contemplation of the notion that, to put it simply, virtues are for striving grown-ups and values are for perpetual adolescents.

Grown-ups are more likely to recognize the singular nature of Western civilization; perpetual adolescents remain "open" to the relative values of multiculturalism.

Of course, there's more than virtue at work in that restorative "no" mentioned above. There is a clear judgment call being made, a choice expressed through a reflexive faculty of discrimination. Here, I think, is where the future of the grown-up lies: in the cultivation of that very faculty. Such an effort would be nothing less than revolutionary. The resulting confidence, the reemergence of a Western point of view, would be anathema to the cult of indiscriminate nonjudgmentalism as preached and practiced in our PC times; indeed, it would necessarily bust up the multiculti monopoly. This makes me think that the nonjudgmentalism that dominates our PC times is, among other things, one of the leading factors of infantilization. Growing up, then, would not only mark the rebirth of the adult, but the end of multiculturalism as well.

It all sounds so theoretical, but, as I have tried to demonstrate, there are desperately concrete applications. When I started this project a decade ago, the multicultural assault on the West still seemed to be a battle of the books waged by eggheads; after 9/11, it became clear that the "real" culture war had started. Having jettisoned the works of our greatest "dead white males," having leveled the hierachies that they adorned, and having disabled all Western "constructs" of judgment and reason, we were and continue to be totally ill-equipped to defend ourselves—our Western selves, that is—against a *real* multicultural challenge as embodied by Islam—or, rather, by Islamization. The unlimited expansion of Islamic influence in the West—through both violence (terrorism) and peaceful means (demographics)—spells the end of Western civilization. It is a force to be reckoned with, beginning with debate, discussion, and minute analysis by mature men and women who can face all the facts, and not by children who hide from them.

What to do? It's not enough to yell "stop," or even "grow up." It's a start, though, if, in the process, we withstand the likely excruciating growing pains to undertake a serious, candid reexamination of the human condition, circa twenty-first century: as parents who need to guide children to maturity; as individuals who need to reimpose boundaries on personal behavior; and as nation states that need to reassert border control and enforce immigration policies that preserve, rather than transform, this uniquely Western culture. Such an undertaking begins by breaking our silence. And breaking our silence begins by conquering our fears, which is also a part of growing up. We have nothing to lose. It should now be clear that the civilization that forever dodges maturity will never live to a ripe old age.

NOTES

1. RISE OF THE TEEN AGE

1. Eric Hoffer, *Reflections on the Human Condition* (New York: Harper & Row, 1973), 29.
2. Christopher Noxon, "I Don't Want to Grow Up!," *New York Times*, August 31, 2003.
3. Dinitia Smith, "Writing Frankly, Young-Adult Author Pushes Limits," *New York Times*, February 23, 2005.
4. Entertainment Software Association, "Top 10 Industry Facts," 2006, http://www.theesa.com/facts/top_10_facts.php.
5. Marcel Danesi, *Forever Young: The 'Teen-Aging' of Modern Culture* (Toronto: University of Toronto Press, 2003), 104–105.
6. Ibid., 105.
7. Jennie Bristow, "An Anti-independence Culture," *spiked,* March 26, 2002, http://www.spiked-online.com/00000006D864.htm.
8. Philip Willan, "Italian Court Tells Father to Support Stay-at-Home Son, 30," *Guardian,* April 6, 2002.
9. Donald MacLeod, "Italian Mammas Making Offers Their Sons Can't Refuse," *Guardian,* February 3, 2006.
10. Gary Strauss, "Life's Good for SpongeBob," *USA Today,* May 17, 2002.
11. Bruce Orwall, "Cut the Cute Stuff: Kids Flock to Adult Flicks," *Wall Street Journal,* August 29, 1997.
12. William Booth, "Leo and Howard; with 'The Aviator,' DiCaprio Steered Through Eccentric Mogul's Turbulent Air," *Washington Post,* December 19, 2004.
13. Frank Furedi, "The Children Who Won't Grow Up," *spiked,* July 29, 2003, http://www.spiked-online.com/Articles/00000006DE8D.htm.
14. Lionel Trilling, *The Last Decade: Essays and Reviews, 1965–1975* (New York: Harcourt Brace Jovanovich, 1977), 175.
15. Ibid., 175.
16. Furedi, "The Children Who Won't Grow Up."

17. George Orwell, *Essays* (New York: Alfred A. Knopf, 2002), 40–42.

18. Robert H. Bork, *Slouching Towards Gomorrah: Modern Liberalism and American Decline* (New York: HarperCollins, 1996), 21–22.

19. Irving Kristol, *On the Democratic Idea in America* (New York: Harper & Row Publishers, 1973), 28.

20. Thomas Frank, *The Conquest of Cool* (Chicago: University of Chicago Press, 1997), 29.

21. Patricia Jobe Pierce, *The Ultimate Elvis: Elvis Presley Day by Day* (New York: Simon & Schuster, 1994), 245.

22. Egil Krogh, *The Day Elvis Met Nixon* (Bellevue, VA: Pejama Press, 1994), 35–40.

23. U.S. Bureau of the Census, *Demographic Trends in the Twentieth Century,* November 2002, fig. 2-5.

24. Joseph F. Kett, *Rites of Passage: Adolescence in America from 1790 to the Present* (New York: Basic Books, 1977), 38.

25. Dwight MacDonald, "Profiles: A Cast, a Culture, a Market—I," *New Yorker,* November 22, 1958.

26. Grace and Fred M. Hechinger, *Teen-Age Tyranny* (New York: Fawcett Publications, 1963), 143–44.

27. James S. Coleman, *The Adolescent Society* (New York: Free Press, 1961), 3.

28. MacDonald, "Profiles: A Cast, a Culture, a Market—I."

29. Ibid.

30. Dwight MacDonald, "Profiles: A Cast, a Culture, a Market—II," *New Yorker,* November 29, 1958.

31. MacDonald, "Profiles: A Cast, a Culture, a Market—I."

32. Phillip H. Ennis, *The Seventh Stream: The Emergence of Rocknroll in American Popular Music* (Middletown, CT: Wesleyan University Press, 1992), 245.

33. Hechinger, *Teen-Age Tyranny*, 18.

34. Bork, *Slouching Towards Gomorrah*, 5.

35. Hechinger, *Teen-Age Tyranny*, 15–16.

36. Ibid., 23.

37. Maureen Daly, ed., *Profile of Youth* (Philadelphia, PA: J. B. Lipincott Company, 1951), 8.

38. Hechinger, *Teen-Age Tyranny*, 149.

2. THE TWIST

1. Michael Dirda, review of *Huck's Raft: A History of American Childhood* by Steven Mintz, *Washington Post Book World,* December 12, 2004.

2. Michael Dirda, review of *I Am Charlotte Simmons* by Tom Wolfe, *Washington Post Book World,* November 7, 2004.

3. Frederick Lewis Allen, *Only Yesterday: An Informal History of the 1920's* (New York: Harper & Row, 1964), 78–79.

4. Loren Baritz, ed., *The Culture of the Twenties* (Indianapolis, IN: Bobbs Merrill, 1970), 256. The 202–102 vote, tallied by *The Literary Digest* in 1921, breaks down this way: "In round numbers, 55 college student-editors believe that conditions are unusually bad as against 38 who believe that they are not. Of the college presidents

and deans, the proportion stands 52 against 43. The religious press, as might be expected, shows a larger ratio of condemnation. Fifty-three religious editors believe we are having something like an immorality wave, as against six who believe we are not."

5. Ibid., 262.
6. Ibid., 258.
7. Ibid., 255.
8. Allen, *Only Yesterday,* 76.
9. Paul H. Bonner, ed., *The World in Vogue* (New York: Viking Press, 1963), 127.
10. Rosalind S. Helderman, "Loudoun's New Move: The Tussle," *Washington Post,* October 22, 2004.
11. Ibid.
12. Grace Palladino, *Teenagers: An American History* (New York: Basic Books, 1996), 97–115.
13. Eugene Gilbert, "Why Today's Teen-Agers Seem So Different," *Harper's Magazine,* November 1959.
14. Kenneth Clarke, *Civilization* (New York: Harper & Row, 1969), 4.
15. Harvey Mansfield, "The Legacy of the Late Sixties," in *Reassessing the Sixties,* Stephen Macedo, ed. (New York: W. W. Norton, 1997), 37.
16. Jon Pareles, "With McCartney, No Need to TiVo This One," *New York Times,* February 7, 2005.
17. MacDonald, "Profiles: A Cast, a Culture, a Market—I," 62.
18. Hechinger, *Teen-Age Tyranny,* 149.
19. Ian Brailsford, "History Repeating Itself: Were Post-War American Youngsters Ripe for Harvest?" http://www.Kingston.ac.uk/cusp/lectures/Brailsfordpaper.doc.
20. Hechinger, *Teen-Age Tyranny,* 133–134.
21. Russell Sanjek, *American Popular Music and Its Business: The First Four Hundred Years, Volume III: From 1900 to 1984* (New York: Oxford University Press, 1988), 246.
22. Steven Mintz, *Huck's Raft: A History of American Childhood* (Cambridge, MA: Harvard University Press, 2004), 299.
23. Palladino, *Teenagers,* 110.
24. Ibid., 104.
25. "A Last Word," *Esquire,* July 1965, 100.
26. Danesi, *Forever Young,* 13.
27. Mintz, *Huck's Raft,* 282.
28. Hechinger, *Teen-Age Tyranny,* 117.
29. Elia Kazan, *A Life* (New York: Anchor Books, 1989), 538.
30. Seymour Martin Lipset, *Rebellion in the University* (Boston, MA: Little, Brown and Company, 1972), xxi.
31. Sam Kashner, "Dangerous Talents," *Vanity Fair,* March 2005, 441.
32. Gertrude Himmelfarb, *Victorian Minds* (New York: Harper Torchbooks, 1968), 278.
33. Marguerite and Willard Beecher, *Parents on the Run: The Need for Discipline in Parent-Child and Teacher-Child Relationships* (New York: Grosset & Dunlap Edition, 1967), 3.
34. Hechinger, *Teen-Age Tyranny,* ix.

35. Peter Wyden, *Suburbia's Coddled Kids* (New York: Doubleday & Company, Inc., 1962), 76.

36. David Riesman with Nathan Glazer and Reuel Denny, *The Lonely Crowd: A Study of the Changing American Character* (New Haven, CT: Yale University Press, 1961), 97.

37. Noxon, "I Don't Want to Grow Up!"

38. Glenn C. Altschuler, *All Shook Up* (New York: Oxford University Press, 2003), 72–74.

39. Herm Schoenfeld, "Teenagers Like 'Hot Rod' Tempo," *Variety,* January 19, 1955. Grace Palladino's *Teenagers* led me to revisit mid-1950s reviews and editorials on rock 'n' roll in *Variety,* beginning with this one.

40. Palladino, *Teenagers,* 124.

41. Jose. "Dr. Jive's Rhythm & Blues Troupe Hits Swinging Beat at Apollo B.O.," *Variety,* August 24, 1955.

42. Ibid.

43. Abel., "A Warning to the Music Business," *Variety,* February 23, 1955.

44. Paul Whiteman & Mary Margaret McBride, *Jazz* (New York: J. H. Sears & Company, 1926), 137–139.

45. Altschuler, *All Shook Up,* 6.

46. Bruce Handy, "The Time 100," *Time,* June 8, 1998.

47. Dennis Prager, "Judaism's Sexual Revolution: Why Judaism (and then Christianity) Rejected Homosexuality," *Crisis,* September 1993.

48. Sheryl Van der Leun, "Indecent Exposure: When Did Cookware and Fly-Fishing Go X-Rated?," *Washington Post,* November 14, 2004.

49. *Variety,* "A Warning to the Music Business."

50. Altschuler, *All Shook Up,* 74–75.

51. Ibid., 76.

52. A. Scott Berg, *Goldwyn: A Biography* (New York: Alfred A. Knopf, 1989), 107.

53. Subcommittee on Communications of the Committee on Interstate and Foreign Commerce, *Amendment to Communications Act of 1934 (Prohibiting Radio and Television from Engaging in Music Publishing or Recording Business),* 85th Cong., 2nd sess., 1958.

54. Ennis, *The Seventh Stream,* 261.

55. Sanjek, *American Popular Music and Its Business,* 523.

56. Rosemary Clooney, *Girl Singer: An Autobiography* (New York: Doubleday, 1999), 172–173.

57. Ibid., 173.

58. Hechinger, *Teen-Age Tyranny,* 95.

59. Ibid., 96.

60. Ibid., 97.

3. CLASH

1. Christopher Caldwell, "1968: A Revolting Generation Looks Back," *Weekly Standard,* September 7, 1968.

2. Mintz, *Huck's Raft,* 274.

3. Ibid., 278.

4. Ibid., 276.

5. David Horowitz, *Radical Son: A Generational Odyssesy* (New York: Touchstone, 1997), 195.

6. Richard John Neuhaus, "The 'Lessons' of Vietnam," *First Things,* March 1996.

7. Todd Gitlin, *The Sixties: Years of Hope, Days of Rage* (New York: Bantam Books, 1989), 258.

8. Lipset, *Rebellion in the University,* 3.

9. Roger Rosenblatt, *Coming Apart: A Memoir of the Harvard Wars of 1969* (Boston, MA: Little, Brown and Company, 1997), 169.

10. Mansfield, "The Legacy of the Late Sixties."

11. George F. Kennan, *Democracy and the Student Left* (Boston, MA: Atlantic Monthly Press, 1968), 16–17.

12. Rosenblatt, *Coming Apart,* 215–216.

13. Lipset, *Rebellion in the University,* xviii.

14. Roger Kimball, *The Long March: How the Cultural Revolution of the 1960s Changed* (New York: Encounter Books, 2000), 108.

15. Bork, *Slouching Towards Gomorrah,* 42.

16. Peter L. Berger and Richard John Neuhaus, *Movement and Revolution* (New York: Anchor Books, 1970), 31.

17. Horowitz, *Radical Son,* 107.

18. Kimball, *The Long March,* 102.

19. Barnard Electronic Archive and Teaching Laboratory, http://beatl.barnard.columbia .edu/columbia68/time1.htm.

20. Kimball, *The Long March,* 112–118.

21. Bork, *Slouching Towards Gomorrah,* 42, 44.

22. Ronald Radosh, *Commies: A Journey Through the Old Left, the New Left and the Leftover Left* (New York: Encounter Books, 2001), 95–96.

23. Diana Trilling, *We Must March My Darlings: A Critical Decade* (New York: Harvest Books, 1977), 121.

24. Ibid., 135.

25. Henry Kissinger, *Years of Renewal* (New York: Simon & Schuster, 1999), 49–50.

26. Jacques Barzun, *From Dawn to Decadence: 1500 to the Present* (New York: Harper-Collins, 2000), 371.

27. Berger and Neuhaus, *Movement and Revolution,* 34–35.

28. Ibid., 35.

29. Rosenblatt, *Coming Apart,* 44–45.

30. Diana Trilling, *We Must March My Darlings,* 117.

31. Bork, *Slouching Towards Gomorrah,* 47.

32. Henry Kissinger, *White House Years* (Boston, MA: Little, Brown and Company, 1979), 293.

33. Ibid., 307.

34. Horowitz, *Radical Son,* 304.

35. Kissinger, *White House Years,* 300. The Harvard band was satirizing a statement by Vice President Spiro T. Agnew: "A spirit of national masochism prevails encour-

aged by an effete corps of impudent snobs who characterize themselves as intellectuals."

36. Trilling, *The Last Decade,* 173.

37. Barnard Electronic Archive and Teaching Laboratory http://beatl.barnard.columbia
.edu/learn/timelines/columbia.htm.

38. Trilling, *The Last Decade,* 174.

39. Trilling, *We Must March My Darlings,* 112.

40. Ibid., 113–114.

41. Peter Biskind, *Easy Riders, Raging Bulls: How the Sex-Drugs-and-Rock 'n' Roll Generation Saved Hollywood* (New York: Touchstone, 1999), 39–41.

42. Gerald Nachman, *Seriously Funny: The Rebel Comedians of the 1950s and 1960s*
(New York: Pantheon Books, 2003), 413.

43. Biskind, *Easy Riders, Raging Bulls,* 123.

44. Biskind, *Easy Riders, Raging Bulls,* 96.

45. Kimball, *The Long March,* 118. Walter Berns, Allan Bloom, and Allan P. Sindler,
three of Cornell's most distinguished professors, resigned after the moral collapse of
the Cornell faculty and administration.

46. Walter Berns, "The Assault on the Universities: Then and Now," in *Reassessing the
Sixties,* 163.

47. T.A.M., *Esquire,* "A Last Word," July 1965, 100.

48. "Threads, or What the Well-Dressed Teen-Ager Ought to Wear," *Esquire,* July
1965, 96.

49. Ibid., 100.

50. Rachel Goodman, "The Day the King of Swing Met the Beatles," *Esquire,* July
1965, 111.

51. BBC News, "Bragg Attacks Pistols' Royal Views," May 27, 2002, http://news
.bbc.co.uk/2/hi/entertainment/2010060.stm.

52. Mansfield, *Reassessing the Sixties,* 20.

53. Gary Aldrich, *Unlimited Access: An FBI Agent Inside the Clinton White House*
(Washington, D.C.: Regnery Publishing, Inc., 1998), 100–107.

54. Joseph Berger, "Principal's Pregnancy: Sex Education; Baby First, Then Marriage,
But a Rural Area Is Able to Adjust," *New York Times,* September 16, 1998.

55. Adam Nagourney, "Erotica Dresses Up for the Javits Show," *New York Times,* April
16, 1999.

56. Richard Severo, "John Raitt, 88, Star of 'Carousel' and 'Pajama Game,'" *New York
Times,* February 21, 2005.

57. Todd Gitlin, "Afterword," in *Reassessing the Sixties,* 284.

58. Blaine Harden, "The Clintons Show a Taste for the Big Apple: Birthday Visit for
Chelsea Has Eye-Opening Moments," *Washington Post,* March 3, 1997.

59. Kristol, *On the Democratic Idea in America,* 125–126.

4. PARENTS WHO NEED PARENTS

1. Mike Males, "Enabling Adult Immaturity," *Youth Today,* November 2003.

2. Willan, "Italian Court Tells Father . . ."

3. MacLeod, "Italian Mammas Making Offers Their Sons Can't Refuse," citing: "Intergenerational Transfers: Why Do Most Italian Youths Live with Their Parents?," Marco Manacorda and Enrico Moretti, Centre for Economic Performance at the London School of Economics.

4. Willan, "Italian Court Tells Father . . ."

5. Ylan Q. Mui, "Homebound: Strapped Grads Get Financial Lessons on Familiar Turf," *Washington Post,* September 3, 2006.

6. Jamie Dean, "Parents Rule in Sex-Ed Battle," *World Magazine,* May 21, 2005.

7. "Middle Schoolers Handed Condoms at Health Fair," Associated Press, May 11, 2005.

8. "N.C. Parents Angry Over Gay Children's Book," Associated Press, March 18, 2004.

9. Barbara Dafoe Whitehead, "Failure of Sex Education," *Atlantic Monthly,* October 1994.

10. Mona Charen, "Veggie Porn in School," May 9, 2005, http://jewishworldreview .com/cols/charen/050605.asp.

11. Keith Eldridge, "In-Class Meth Demonstration Angers Parents," http://www .Komotv.com/news/archive/4151301.html.

12. Kimball, *The Long March,* 197.

13. Sue Lindsay, "Mother Supplied Drugs, Cops Say," *Rocky Mountain News,* January 21, 2005.

14. David McKay Wilson, "Man Whose Son Died Rented Party Rooms," *Journal News,* January 4, 2003.

15. Brian McNeill, "Parents Hot and Bothered over 'Sex Ed': Under Proposed Curriculum Changes, the Definition of 'Abstinence' Could Include All Sex Acts Except Intercourse," *Connection Newspapers,* April 20, 2005.

16. Suzanne Fields, "Rape as Sport," *Insight on the News,* May 3, 1993.

17. Kay S. Hymowitz, *Ready or Not: Why Treating Children as Small Adults Endangers Their Future—and Ours* (New York: Free Press, 1999), 171.

18. DeNeen L. Brown, "The Mom-ification of Marilyn Manson: Parents Bond While Kids Rock On," *Washington Post,* May 11, 1997.

19. Yoshiaki Nohara, "Freak Dancing Divides School," *HeraldNet,* October 16, 2004, http://www.heraldnet.com/stories/04/10/16/loc-freak001.cfm.

20. Janet Zink, "For All Punks Big and Small," *St. Petersburg Times,* April 18, 2005.

21. Tamara Audi, "Next Stop: Cancun—Dream Vacation for Kids Means Worry for Parents," and "Sun, Sex and Tequila: For High Schoolers in Cancun, Drinking Goes Until Dawn and Dangers of Alchohol Poisoning and Rape Are Not Far Behind," *Detroit Free Press,* April 25–26, 2001.

22. Ibid.

23. Ibid.

24. Ibid.

25. Ibid.

26. Ibid.

27. Jessica Sommar, Erika Martinez, and Rita Delfiner, "Party Animals: Wall St. Couple Busted Over Stripper at His Bash," *New York Post,* September 6, 2001.

28. Jonathan Bandler, "QB's Parents Arrested at Team Party with Stripper," *Journal News,* September 5, 2001.

29. Oliver W. Pritchard, "Judge Castigates Parents Before Sparing Them Jail in Stripper Party," *Journal News,* May 31, 2002.

30. David McKay Wilson, "It Was Like Stripper Party Was 'No Big Deal': Principal Seeks Help of Community in Teaching Teens Ethics," *Journal News,* September 11, 2001.

31. Ibid.

32. Ibid.

33. Sara Davidson, "Murder in Westwood," *O, the Oprah Magazine,* March 2003, 224–227, 239–241.

34. "In MS-13, a Culture of Brutality and Begging; Jamie Stockwell, Gang's Women Panhandle, Men Plot in Motels, Testimony Shows," *Washington Post,* May 2, 2005.

35. Carolyn Sackariason, "Judge Rules Homeowners Not Liable for Teen's Murder," *Santa Monica Daily Press,* October 20, 2003.

36. Davidson, "Murder in Westwood."

37. Chester E. Finn, Jr., "Can Parents Be Trusted?" *Commentary Magazine,* September 1999.

38. Liz Lightfoot, "Parents Must Help Schools Over Discipline, Says Blair," *Daily Telegraph*, May 3, 2004.

39. Julie Henry, "Children to Be Given Classes in How to Be 'Nice,'" *Daily Telegraph,* March 6, 2005.

40. Liz Lightfoot, "Parents 'Not Fit to Be School Governors,'" *Daily Telegraph,* May 3, 2005.

41. Walter Olson, "Judge Throws Out Lawsuit Over Summer Homework," http:// www.overlawyered.com/archives/001232.html.

42. Walter Olson, "Father Sues Over Bad Grade," http://www.overlawyered.com/ 2005/02/father_sues_over_grade.html.

43. "Lawsuits Over Failing Grades," http://www.overlawyered.com/archives/00jan1 .html#0001046.

44. Ted Frank, "Tennessee Schools End Honor Roll Over Privacy Laws," *Over- lawyered,* January 25, 2004, http://www.overlawyered.com/archives/000756.html.

45. Liz Porteus, "Flunking Out of School? Get a Lawyer," *FOXNews.com,* August 2, 2002, http://www.foxnews.com/story/0,2933,59330,00.html.

46. Nancy Gibbs, "Parents Behaving Badly," *Time,* February 21, 2005.

47. Jane Gross, "A Binge by Teenagers Leads a Village to Painful Self-Reflection," *New York Times,* September 27, 2002.

48. Ann E. Marimow, "Waldorf Mother Accused of School Bus Brawling: Woman Fu- rious Over Disciplining of Daughter Wielded Ice Pick, Jumped on Vehicle's Hood, Police Say," *Washington Post,* June 4, 2005.

49. Bill Pennington, "As Stakes Rise, More Parents Are Directing Rage at Coaches," *New York Times,* June 28, 2005.

50. Walter Olson, "But There Was No Rule Against It," *Overlawyered,* September 19, 2003, http://www.overlawyered.com/2003/09/but_there_was_no_rule_against.html.

51. John Stromnes, "Parents Sue Ronan School Over Deaths of Their Sons," *Missoulian,* November 6, 2004, http://www.missoulian.com/articles/2004/11/06/news/mtregional/news03.txt.

52. Brian K. Smith, "Haven Area Expands Authority Over Student Internet Sites, Cars," *Schuylkill.com,* July 21, 2000.

53 Ramon Coronado, "Court for Boy Charged in Murder Plot," *Sacramento Bee,* November 22, 2004.

54. Finn, "Can Parents Be Trusted?," p. 21.

55. Mark Lisheron, "House Approves Ban on 'Sexual' Cheerleading," *Statesman.com,* May 4, 2005.

56. Michael Gerber, "Road Risks,"*Bethesda Magazine,* March/April 2005, 47.

57. Alexis de Tocqueville, *Democracy in America* (New York: HarperPerennial, 1988), 691–692.

5. SOPHISTICATED BABIES

1. Noel Coward, "What's Going to Happen to the Tots," English version, 1927; American version, 1955.

2. Neil Postman, *The Disappearance of Childhood* (New York: Delacorte Press, 1982), 19.

3. Ibid., 36.

4. Ibid., 36.

5. Ibid., 84.

6. Plum Sykes, "Child's Play," *Vogue,* March 1998, 244.

7. Casey Williams, "MTV Smut Peddlers: Targeting Kids with Sex, Drugs and Alcohol," Parents Television Council, http://www.parentstv.org/PTC/publications/reports/mtv2005/main.asp.

8. Postman, *The Disappearance of Childhood,* 15.

9. Clifford J. Levy, "Condom Plan Is Authorized in New Haven," *New York Times,* July 28, 1993. "The board voted 6 to 1 on Monday night to provide condoms at school health clinics to students as early as the fifth grade, apparently making New Haven the first school system in the nation to adopt such a program for children so young. Some board members said they felt they had to act after a student survey found that 27 percent of sixth graders and 49 percent of eighth graders said they were sexually active."

10. Postman, *The Disappearance of Childhood,* 91–92.

11. Mary S. Foote, *Parents League News,* http://www.markstevenson.com/plofny/parenting90.html.

12. Amanda Paulson, "Under 17 Not Admitted Without R-card," *Christian Science Monitor,* May 24, 2004.

13. Jon Ward, "Sex-ed Battles Raging in Region," *Washington Times,* February 10, 2005.

14. Lloyd Grove, *New York Daily News,* "Designer on the Ball?" October 28, 2004.

15. Gretchen Cook, "Buffer the Children? Advocates for Young Actors Fear Impact of Violent, Risque Material," *Washington Post,* June 5, 2005.

16. Liza Mundy, "Do You Know Where Your Children Are?" *Washington Post Magazine,* November 16, 2003.

17. Benoit Denizet-Lewis, "Friends, Friends with Benefits and the Benefits of the Local Mall," *New York Times Magazine,* May 30, 2004.

18. Walter Berns, "Pornography vs. Democracy," *Public Interest,* Winter 1971, 6.

19. Rochelle Gurstein, *The Repeal of Reticence* (New York: Hill and Wang, 1996), 289.

20. Ibid., 289–290.

21. Berns, "Pornography vs. Democracy," 6.

22. Brent Bozell, "Teen Sex-addict Stereotypes," *Townhall.com,* October 29, 2004, http://www.townhall.com/columnists/BrentBozell111/2004.

23. Berns, "Pornography vs. Democracy," 9.

24. Norbert Elias, *The Civilizing Process: The History of Manners* (New York: Urizen Books, 1978), 179.

25. Berns, "Pornography vs. Democracy," 13.

26. Mary Ann Glendon, "The End of Democracy? A Discussion Continued," *First Things,* January 1997, 23.

27. Berns, "Pornography vs. Democracy," 10–11.

28. Gurstein, *The Repeal of Reticence,* 289.

29. Ann Powers, "Kiddie Pop: Raffi It's Not, But Just What Is It?" *New York Times,* August 21, 1999.

30. *Frontline,* "The Lost Children of Rockdale County," PBS, October 19, 1999.

31. Denizet-Lewis, "Friends, Friends with Benefits and the Benefits of the Local Mall."

32. Kristol, *On the Democratic Idea in America,* 37.

33. Bork, *Slouching Towards Gomorrah,* 150.

34. Gurstein, *The Repeal of Reticence,* p. 114.

35. Kristol, *On the Democratic Idea in America,* 45.

36. Ibid., 38–39.

37. Kay S. Hymowitz, "What's Wrong with the Kids?" *City Journal,* Winter 2000.

38. Marianne Garvey and Carl Campanile, "Kids' Cuff Link; Raunchy 'Sex Bracelet' Fad Hits City Schools," *New York Post,* May 23, 2004.

39. Berns, "Pornography vs. Democracy," 5.

40. Ibid.

6. BOUNDARIES

1. Biskind, *Easy Riders, Raging Bulls,* 45.

2. City of Batavia, http://www.batavianewyork.com/about_batavia.html.

3. Home Gain, http://www.homegain.com/local_real_estate/NY/batavia.html.

4. James Barron, "Imagine Them Naked," *New York Times,* November 25, 2004.

5. Elizabeth Weise, "For a Worthy Cause, Men Bare It for the Calendar," *USA Today,* December 13, 2004.

6. "Bridge Club Members Baring Skin to Save Courthouse," Associated Press, May 12, 2005.

7. Obituary of R. J. Sinnott, *New York Times,* May 3, 2003.

8. David Carr and Constance L. Hays, "3 Racy Men's Magazines Are Banned by Wal-Mart," *New York Times,* May 6, 2003.

9. Berns, "Pornography vs. Democracy," 14.

10. Ruth LaFerla, "More Sex, Less Joy," *New York Times,* May 29, 2005.

11. Randy Kennedy, "An Online Artist Challenges Obscenity Law," *New York Times,* July 28, 2005.

12. Richard Lowry, "The Corner," *National Review Online,* April 12, 2005, http://www.nationalreview.com/thecorner/05_04_10_corner-archive.asp#060516.

13. "Nearly 3 in 10 Young Teens 'Sexually Active,'" *MSNBC.com,* January 31, 2005, http://www.msnbc.msn.com/id/6839072.

14. "Porn Industry Pushing Bush GOP Fund-raiser: Company Issues Press Releases Touting Significance of Event to Adult-Film Biz," *Worldnetdaily.com,* June 7, 2005, http://www.worldnetdaily.com/news/article.asp?ARTICLE_ID=44649.

15. Ron Strom, "Bush Event Organizers OK with Porn Star's Attendance," *Worldnetdaily.com,* June 1, 2005, http://www.worldnetdaily.com/news/article.asp?ARTICLE_ID=44540.

16. "Southern Mississippi Library System Bans Jon Stewart's Best-selling Book," Associated Press, January 9, 2005.

17. Patricia Bosworth, "The X-Rated Emperor," *Vanity Fair,* February 2005.

18. Jim Rutenberg, "Hurt by Cable, Networks Spout Expletives," *New York Times,* September 2, 2001.

19. Nachman, *Seriously Funny,* 403.

20. Ibid., 410–411.

21. Ibid., 410.

22. Biskind, *Easy Riders, Raging Bulls,* 96.

23. Chuck Kim, "'South Park' S-Bombs," http://cache-origin.eonline.com/News/Items/0,1,8456,00.html.

24. Tamara Conniff and Jeff Mayfield, "*Billboard*'s Money Makers List for 2005," *Billboard,* January 23, 2006.

25. Edna Gundersen, "Ringtone Sales Up Music Profits," *USA Today,* January 25, 2006.

26. Tracy Jan, "Prom DJs Are Told to Play It Clean," *Boston Globe,* April 28, 2005.

27. Peggy Noonan, "Almost Heaven: A Visit to West Virginia," *Wall Street Journal,* August 4, 2005.

28. Helen Kennedy, "Whoopi Slams GOP," *New York Daily News,* July 16, 2004.

29. "Laura Bush: First Lady of Comedy?," *USA Today,* May 1, 2005, http://www.usatoday.com/life/people/2005-05-01-laura-bush-comments_x.htm.

30. Elizabeth Bumiller, "White House Letter," *New York Times,* May 2, 2005.

31. Berns, "Pornography vs. Democracy."

32. "The Reliable Source," Richard Leiby, *Washington Post,* May 18, 2005.

33. Julie Salamon, "When Group Therapy Means Coming Clean on TV," *New York Times,* June 22, 2004.

34. Helaine Olen, "The New Nanny Diaries Are Online," *New York Times,* July 17, 2005.

35. Roger Kimball, "The Elephant in the Gallery, or the Lessons of 'Sensation,'" *New Criterion,* November 1999, 4.

36. Ibid., 8.

37. Ibid., 8.

38. Shaila K. Dewan, "One Verging on Stardom, One Left Back, with a Gun," *New York Times,* May 4, 2003.

7. IDENTITY

1. Samuel Huntington, *Who Are We? Challenges to America's National Identity* (New York: Simon & Schuster, 2004) 324. Huntington juxtaposed these Roosevelt and Clinton quotations. In noting additional governmental concessions to bilingualism, he commented: "A bifurcated America with two languages and two cultures will be fundamentally different from the America with one language and one core Ango-Saxon Protestant culture that has existed for over three centuries."

2. P. L. Travers, *Mary Poppins,* illustrated by Mary Shepard (New York: Harcourt, Brace & World, Inc., 1962). P. L. Travers, *Mary Poppins: Revised Edition,* illustrated by Mary Shepard (New York: An Odyssey/Harcourt Brace Young Classic, 1981).

3. Samuel Huntington, *The Clash of Civilizations: Remaking the World Order* (New York: Simon & Schuster, 1997), 22–23.

4. Peter Brimelow, *Alien Nation: Common Sense About America's Immigration Disaster* (New York: HarperCollins, 1996), xiv–xv.

5. Bat Ye'or, *Eurabia: The Euro-Arab Axis* (Madison, NJ: Farleigh Dickinson University Press, 2005), 10.

6. "Bob Dylan Tells All (Almost)," Associated Press, October 5, 2004.

7. Roger Kimball, "The Treason of the Intellectuals and 'the Undoing of Thought,'" *New Criterion,* December 1992.

8. Mike Tobin, "Activists Set Sights on Schools Named for Slave-Owning Founding Fathers," *FOXNews.com,* May 11, 2001, http://www.foxnews.com/story/0,2933 ,24488,00.html.

9. Ikimulisa Sockwell-Mason and David Seifman, "Brooklyn Beep Dumps Pic of 'Old White Man' George," *New York Post,* January 16, 2002.

10. Heather MacDonald, "Revisionist Lust: The Smithsonian Today," *New Criterion,* May 1997.

11. Brimelow, *Alien Nation,* xvii.

12. Ibid., 98.

13. Lawrence Auster, "Victor Hanson—Liberal Universalist with a Gun,"*View from the Right,* April 30, 2004, http://www.amnation.com/vfr/archives/002266.html.

14. Victor Davis Hanson, " 'Little Eichmanns' and 'Digital Brownshirts': Deconstructing the Hiterlian Slur," *National Review Online,* March 18, 2005, http://www.nationalreview.com/hanson/hanson200503180754.asp.

15. Ibid.

16. Ibid.

17. Michael Gardner, "Driver's License for Immigrants Hits Legislative Rush Hour," *Copley News Service,* August 25, 2004.

18. News 8 Austin, "Mexican Independence Day Parade Becomes Immigration Protest," September 8, 2005, http://www.news8austin.com/content/headlines/ ?ArID=145715&SecID=2.

19. "The Politics of Immigration," *Washington Post,* October 5, 2005.

20. Daniel Hannan, "Genocide Argument Is the Last Resort of the Euro-Zealots," *Daily Telegraph,* May 15, 2005.

21. Clifford D. May, "They Shoot School-Teachers, Don't They?," Scripps Howard News Service, September 29, 2005.

22. Daniel Pipes, "They're Terrorists—Not Activists," http://www.danielpipes.org/article/2066.

23. "Shamil Basayev Sends Open Letter to Palestinians," *Pravda,* November 24, 2000.

24. Daniel Pipes, "More on They're Terrorists—Not Activists," http://www.danielpipes.org/blog/323.

25. Ibn Warraq, "Edward Said and the Saidists," in *The Myth of Islamic Tolerance: How Islamic Law Treats Non-Muslims,* Robert Spencer, ed. (Amherst, NY: Prometheus Books, 2005), 491.

26. Warraq, "Foreword," in *The Myth of Islamic Tolerance,* 17.

27. Ibid., 19.

28. Ibid., 21.

29. Spencer, *The Myth of Islamic Tolerance,* 33.

30. Warraq, "Foreword," in *The Myth of Islamic Tolerance,* 24–25.

31. "A Discriminatory Clause: Committee on College Life Should Not Have Allowed HRCF to Remain a Recognized Group," *Harvard Crimson,* April 15, 2003.

32. Ibid.

33. Steven Vincent, "The Naive American," July 26, 2005, http://spencepublishing.typepad.com/in_the_red_zone/.

34. Ibid.

35. Lawrence Auster, " 'Anti-Racism': The Mailed Fist of Multiculturalism," *FrontPageMagazine.com,* July 16, 2004, http://www.frontpagemag.com/Articles/ReadArticle.asp?ID=14261.

36. Jenny E. Heller, "Westminster Abbey Elevates 10 Foreigners," *New York Times,* September 22, 1998.

37. Education Resources Information Center, "Language Proficiency and Home Languages of Students in New York City Elementary and Middle Schools," ED474013. The figure (nearly 170) is based on information gathered by the New York City Department of Education in 1999–2000.

38. "Multilingual Capital—London Only," http://www.cilt.org.uk/faqs/langspoken.html.

39. Charles Moore, "Beware, Within the Walls of Our Capital City Lurks the Trojan Newt," *Daily Telegraph,* September 17, 2005.

40. Warraq, "Edward Said and the Saidists," in *The Myth of Islamic Tolerance,* 495.

41. Nigel Reynolds, "Mandela Statue Provokes Another Battle of Trafalgar," *Daily Telegraph,* September 28, 2005.

42. "Terrorism and the Random Search," *New York Times,* July 26, 2005.

8. THE REAL CULTURE WAR

1. Theodore Dalrymple, "Our Culture, What's Left of It," interview by Jamie Glazov, *FrontPageMagazine.com,* August 31, 2005.

2. Spencer, *The Myth of Islamic Tolerance,* 55. Quotation concludes a paper by Bat Ye'or, "The Tolerant Pluralistic Islamic Society: Origin of a Myth," presented at the Lord Byron Foundation for Balkan Studies and International Strategic Studies Association Symposium on the Balkan War, August 31, 1995, http://www.dhimmi tude.org/archive/LectureE1.html.

3. Kate Kinsella, ed., *Timeless Voices, Timeless Themes, Bronze Level* (Upper Saddle River, NJ: Prentice Hall, 2002).

4. Ambrose Evans-Pritchard and Joan Clements, "Fortuyn Killed 'to Protect Muslims,'" *Daily Telegraph,* March 28, 2003.

5. Craig Whitlock, "For Public Figures in Netherlands, Terror Becomes a Personal Concern," *Washington Post,* November 11, 2005.

6. Ibid.

7. "Terrorists 'Planning to Hit Schiphol, Dutch Parliament,'" Expatica News, September 7, 2004, http://www.expatica.com/actual/article.asp?subchannel_id=19&story _id=11596.

8. "PM Won't Speculate on 'Verdonk Attack,'" Expatica News, November 4, 2005, http://www.expatica.com/actual/article.asp?subchannel_id=1&story_id=25050.

9. Douglas Murray, "We Should Fear Holland's Silence," *Times* (London), February 26, 2006.

10. "Amsterdam Fights Jihad with Tolerance," Jihad Watch, May 22, 2005. http:// www.jihadwatch.org/dhimmiwatch/archives/006285.php.

11. Karl R. Popper, *The Open Society and Its Enemies; Volume I: The Spell of Plato* (Princeton: Princeton University Press, 1971) 265.

12. "Blunkett Condemns Berlusconi Comments," BBC News, September 28, 2001. http://www.news.bbc.co.uk/2/hi/uk_news/politics/156893.stm.

13. Candace Hughes, "Berlusconi Comments Cause Stir," Associated Press, September 26, 2001.

14. Andrew Osborn and Rory Carroll, "Scorn Poured on Berlusconi Views," *Guardian,* September 28, 2001.

15. "EU Deplores 'Dangerous' Islam Jibe," BBC News, September 27, 2001.

16. Greg Burke, "Italy: Berlusconi's War of Words," September 28, 2001, http:// www.time.com/europe/eu/article/0,13176,176876,00.html.

17. "Berlusconi Regrets Islam Jibe," BBC News, September 28, 2001, http://news.bbc .co.uk/2/hi/europe/156908.stm.

18. "EU Deplores 'Dangerous' Islam Jibe," BBC News, September 27, 2001, http:// news.bbc.co.uk/2/hi/middle_east/1565664.stm.

19. "Berlusconi Apologizes to Muslims for Islam Slur," *IslamOnline,* September 29, 2001, http://www.islamonline.net/english/news/2001-09/29/article6.shtml.

20. "OIC Parliaments Union denounces Berlusconi's Anti-Islam Statements," *Arabic News.com,* September 29, 2001, http://www.arabicnews.com/ansub/Daily/Day/ 010929/2001092932.html.

21. "Berlusconi Apology Passes Blame," *CNN.com,* September 28, 2001, http:// archives.cnn.com/2001/WORLD/europe/09/28/gen.italy.berlusconi/index.html.

22. "Berlusconi Apologizes to Muslims for Islam Slur," *IslamOnline.*

23. Oriana Fallaci, *The Rage and the Pride* (New York: Rizzoli, 2001), 25.

24. Ibid., 168.
25. Condoleezza Rice, "Remarks at the Annual State Department Iftaar Dinner," October 25, 2005, http://www.state.gov/secretary/rm/2005/55577.htm.
26. Anti-Defamation League, "Major Terrorists Attacks in Israel," http://www.adl.org/Israel/israel_attacks.asp.
27. "Special Dispatch Series No. 1013," Middle East Media Research Institute, October 28, 2005.
28. "London Bomber Buried in Pakistan," *United Press International,* October 28, 2005.
29. "Lashkar Hand Evident," *Deccan Herald,* March 9, 2006.
30. John Hooper, "St. Peter Role Prompts Death Threat," *Guardian,* October 31, 2005.
31. "Indonesia: Muslim Admits Beheading Christian Girls,"Associated Press, November 15, 2006.
32. Condoleezza Rice, "Remarks with United Kingdom Foreign Secretary Jack Straw at the Blackburn Institute's Frank A. Nix Lecture," October 21, 2005, http://www.state.gov/secretary/rm/2005/55423.htm.
33. Iraq Constitution, http://www.washingtonpost.com/wp-dyn/content/article/2005/10/12/AR2005101201450.html. The provisions in question are included in Article 2: "First: Islam is the official religion of the State and it is a fundamental source of legislation: A. No law that contradicts the established provisions of Islam may be established."
34. Amir Taheri, "Why Is Paris Burning?," *New York Post,* November 4, 2005.
35. Daniel Ben-Simon, "French Philosopher Alain Finkielkraut Apologizes After Death Threats," *Haaretz.com,* November 27, 2005, http://www.haaretz.com/hasen/pages/ShArt.jhtml?itemNo=650155.
36. Alex Corvus, http://alexcorvus.blogspot.com/2005_11_01_alexcorvus_archive.html.
37. Arnaud de Borchgrave, "European Disaster Zone," *Washington Times,* November 24, 2005.
38. "Security Is Tightened in Central Paris," Associated Press, November 11, 2005.
39. "Fires in France," *Washington Post,* November 8, 2005.
40. Olivier Roy, "Get French or Die Trying," *New York Times,* November 9, 2005.
41. Olivier Guitta, "Homegrown Gangstas: France Faces a Wave of Domestically Produced Anti-French Rap," *Weekly Standard,* September 23, 2005.
42. Prime Minister Silvio Berlusconi's Eid Address to Muslim Ambassadors, November 3, 2005, reported online by Adukronos International (AKI).
43. Peter Ford, "Europe Cringes at Bush 'Crusade' Against Terrorists," *Christian Science Monitor,* September 19, 2001.
44. Since 9/11, Daniel Pipes has been tracking stories about seemingly law-abiding, reasonable, Western-integrated Muslims who come to notoriety after engaging in violence against non-Muslims. In 2006, there was Mohammed Reza Taheri-azar, the University of North Carolina at Chapel Hill graduate who stands accused of driving an SUV through a crowd of pedestrians reportedly to "avenge the deaths of Muslims around the world"; in 2005, there were the British-born, seemingly well-adjusted London Underground bombers; in 2004, there was Mohammed Ali Alayed, a son of a Saudi millionaire living in Houston who pled guilty to murdering his one-time Jewish

friend; in 2003, there was Maher Hawash, a prosperous and respected engineer who was arrested in Oregon and later pled guilty to a federal charge of conspiracy to supply services to the Taliban. Pipes calls the phenomenon "Sudden Jihad Syndrome."

45. Ari Fleischer, press briefing September 18, 2001, http://www.whitehouse.gov/news/releases/2001/09/20010918-5.html.

46. Robert Spencer, *The Politically Correct Guide to Islam (and the Crusades)* (Washington, D.C.: Regnery Publishing, Inc., 2005), 126.

47. Ibid. 160–161.

48. Colin Powell, *My American Journey* (New York: Ballantine Books, 1995), 388.

49. "Infinite Justice, Out—Enduring Freedom, In," BBC News, September 25, 2001, http://news.bbc.co/uk/2/hi/americas/1563722.stm.

50. "White House Week," *US News & World Report,* March 6, 2006.

51. Clement Huart, "The Law of War," in *The Legacy of Jihad: Islamic Holy War and the Fate of Non-Muslims,* Andrew G. Bostom, M.D., ed. (Amherst, NY: Prometheus Books, 2005), 283.

52. Tony Blair, CNN, July 17, 2003, http://www.cnn.com/2003/US/07/17/blair.transcript/.

53. The White House, "President Bush Delivers Graduation Speech at West Point," June 2002, http://www.whitehouse.gov/news/releases/2002/06/20020601-3.html.

54. John Ralph Willis, "Jihad and the Ideology of Enslavement," in *The Legacy of Jihad,* 343.

55. Rosenthal, Franz, Lewis, B., "Hurriyya," *Encyclopaedia of Islam,* edited by P. Bearman, Th. Bianquis, C. E. Bosworth, E. van Donzel, and W. P. Heinrichs. (Leiden/Boston: Brill, 2006). Franz Rosenthal's *Encyclopaedia of Islam,* CD-ROM version, (Leiden/Boston: Brill, 1999).

56. Ibid.

57. Ibid.

58. George W. Bush, "State of the Union Address," January 20, 2004, http://www.whitehouse.gov/news/releases/2004/01/20040120-7.html.

59. David G. Littman, "International Bill of Human Rights," *The Myth of Islamic Tolerance,* 419.

60. Patrick Hennessy and Melissa Kite, "Poll Reveals 40p of Muslims Want Sharia Law in UK," *Daily Telegraph,* February 19, 2006.

61. Robert Spencer, *Onward Muslim Soldiers* (Washington, D.C.: Regnery Publishing Inc., 2003), 222.

62. Ibid., 222.

63. Ibid., 234.

64. David Littman, "Universal Human Rights and 'Human Rights in Islam,'" in *The Myth of Islamic Tolerance,* 322.

65. Ibid., 328.

66. Ibid., 325.

67. Kim Barker, "Editor's Jailing Tests Afghan Democracy," *Chicago Tribune,* November 26, 2005.

68. Kim Barker, "Afghan Man Faces Death After Leaving Islam for Christianity; Prosecutors, Judge, Family Insist Convert Should Die," *Chicago Tribune,* March 21, 2006.

69. "International Religious Freedom Report 2006," U.S. Department of State, http://www.state.gov/g/clrl/rls/irf/2006/71431.htm.

70. "Jews Barred in Saudi Tourist Drive," BBC News, February 27, 2004, http://news.bbc.co.uk/2/middle_east/3493448.stm.

71. "Saudi Jailed for Discussing Bible," Reuters, *Washington Times,* November 14, 2005.

72. U.S. Department of State, *Egypt: Country Reports of Human Rights Practices, 2004,* Bureau of Democracy, Human Rights, and Labor, February 28, 2005.

73. Spencer, *The Politically Correct Guide to Islam,* 69.

74. Aisha's age—betrothed to Mohammed at six, marriage consummated at nine—is mentioned twice in the authoritative hadith collection by Bukhari, http://www.usc.edu/dept/MSA/fundamentals/hadithsunnah/bukhari/058.sbt.html#005.0 58.234 and http://www.usc.edu/dept/MSA/fundamentals/hadithsunnah/bukhari/062.sbt.html#007.062.064.

75. Ya'kov Meron, "The Expulsion of the Jews from the Arab Countries: The Palestinians' Attitudes Toward It and Their Claims," *The Forgotten Millions—The Modern Jewish Exodus from Arab Lands,* Malka Shulewitz, ed. (London/New York: Continuum, 1999), 94.

76. UN Office for the Coordination of Humanitarian Affairs, "Jordan: Special Report on Honour Killings," April 18, 2005.

77. Ibn Warraq, *Why I Am Not a Muslim* (Amherst, NY: Prometheus Books, 1995), 9.

78. Daniel Pipes, *The Rushdie Affair* (New York: Carol Publishing, 1990), 176.

79. Littman, "Universal Human Rights," in *The Myth of Islamic Tolerance,* 308–309.

80. Pipes, *The Rushdie Affair,* 32.

81. Mervyn Hiskett, *Some to Mecca Turn to Pray: Islamic Values in the Modern World,* (London: Claridge Press, 1993), 240.

82. Pipes, *The Rushdie Affair,* 34.

83. "'Allah' Ice-Creams Banned," Steve Kennedy, *The Sun Online,* http://www.thesun.co.uk/article/0,,2-2005430136,,00.html, http://www.jihadwatch.org/dhimmiwatch/archives/008141.php.

84. Dalya Alberge, "Marlowe's Koran-Burning Hero Is Censored to Avoid Muslim Anger," *Times Online,* November 24, 2005, http://www.timesonline.co.uk/article/0,,2-1887902,00.html.

85. Robert Spencer, "Fox Kowtows to CAIR," *FrontPageMagazine.com,* January 19, 2005, http://www.frontpagemag.com/Articles/ReadArticle.asp?ID=16691.

86. Trevor Paddenburg, "No Ham for Christmas: Muslim Menu for WA Hospital," *Sunday Times Australia,* December 18, 2005.

87. Patrick Goodenough, "Muslim Leaders Want UN to Outlaw Discrimination," *CNSNews.com,* February 21, 2006.

88. Pipes, *The Rushdie Affair,* 34–35.

89. Pipes, *The Rushdie Affair,* ibid 35.

90. Littman, "Islamism Grows Stronger at the United Nations," in *The Myth of Islamic Tolerance,* 309.

91. "IHEU Responds to Accusation of Islamophobia by the OIC," http://www.iheu.org/uncampaign/iheuresponse, August 23, 2005.

92. UN Sub-Commission on the Promotion & Protection of Human Rights: 57th session, plenum, July 26, 2005. Transcript supplied by David G. Littman.

93. Littman, "Jihad and Martyrdom as Taught in Saudi Arabian and Egyptian Schools," http://www.iheu.org/node/1543.

94. Littman, "Islamism Grows Stronger at the United Nations," in *The Myth of Islamic Tolerance,* 313.

95. Littman, "Human Rights and Human Wrongs," in *The Myth of Islamic Tolerance,* 340.

96. Ahmed Ali, *Al-Qur'an: A Contemporary Translation* (Princeton, NJ: Princeton University Press, 1993), 106. Sura 5, verse 60.

97. Middle East Media Research Institute, http://memri.org/ Search results "apes, swine."

98. Andrew G. Bostom, "Apocalyptic Muslim Jew-Hatred," July 17, 2006, http://www.americanthinker.com/2006/07/apocalyptic_muslim_jewhatred.html.

99. Littman, "Dangerous Censorship of a UN Special Rapporteur," in *The Myth of Islamic Tolerance,* 341.

100. Littman, "Dangerous Censorship," in *The Myth of Islamic Tolerance,* 348.

101. Littman, "Islamism Grows Stronger at the UN," in *The Myth of Islamic Tolerance,* 313.

102. Bat Ye'or, *Eurabia,* 192.

103. Ibid.

104. Jovan Cvijic, *The Balkan Peninsula: Human Geography* (Paris: Librairie Armand Colin, 1918).

105. Tom Leonard, "Christians 'Are Easiest Target for TV Satire,' " *Daily Telegraph,* December 29, 2003.

106. Hannah Cleaver, "Race Report Told to Change Findings on Muslims," *Daily Telegraph*, November 27, 2003.

107. "Angry Muslims Want Minister Out," Agence France Presses, December 5, 2003.

108. "Paris, Oslo, Helsinki," *New York Sun* editorial, November 12, 2004.

109. Angela Doland, "France's Chief Rabbi Warns Jews that Wearing Skullcaps Could Make Them Targets," Associated Press, November 20, 2003.

110. " 'No Christian Symbols at Christmas': Red Cross Store Bans Religious Décor Fearing It Might Be Offensive," *WorldNetDaily,* November 18, 2003, http://www.worldnetdaily.com/news/article.asp?ARTICLE_ID=35670.

111. "Texas University Scraps 'Crusader' Mascot," *Jihad Watch,* April 27, 2004, http://www.jihadwatch.org/dhimmiwatch/archives/001733.php.

112. Nenad Stojanovic, "Lugano Puts Veil Over Christian Sites," *swissinfo.org,* February 27, 2005.

113. Bat Ye'or, *Eurabia,* 197.

114. Ibid.

9. MEN, WOMEN . . . OR CHILDREN?

1. Richard Goldstein, "Neo-Macho Man," *Nation,* March 24, 2003.

2. Peggy Noonan, "Welcome Back, Duke," *Wall Street Journal,* October 12, 2001.

3. Mary Foster, "New Orleans Police Chief: 60 Officers Fired," Associated Press, December 8, 2005.

4. Captain Roger Lee Crossland, USNR, "Why Are Victims Our Only War Heroes?" *Proceedings,* April 2004.

5. Ibid.

6. Ibid.

7. "A Super Bowl Omission," http://michellemalkin.com/archives/004475.htm, February 6, 2006.

8. Bat Ye'or, *Islam and Dhimmitude* (Madison, NJ: Farleigh Dickinson University Press, 2002), 330.

9. Crossland, "Why Are Victims Our Only War Heroes."

10. Joel Brinkley and Ian Fisher, "U.S. Says It Also Finds Cartoons of Muhammad Offensive," *New York Times,* February 4, 2006.

11. "Storm Grows Over Mohammad Cartoons," *CNN.com,* February 3, 2006.

12. John Plunkett, "BBC Defends Cartoon Coverage," *Guardian,* February 6, 2006.

13. Fleming Rose, "Why I Published Those Cartoons," *Washington Post,* February 19, 2006.

14. Byron York, "Clinton Has No Clothes," *National Review,* December 17, 2001.

15. Charles Krauthammer, "Curse of the Moderates," *Washington Post,* February 10, 2006.

16. Peggy Noonan, " 'It Is As It Was' Mel Gibson's 'The Passion' Gets a Thumbs-up from the Pope," *Wall Street Journal,* December 17, 2003.

17. Transcript of the interview available online: http://www.radioblogger.com/archives/january06.html#001282.

18. Daniel Pipes, "The Pope and the Koran," January 21, 2006, http://www.danielpipes.org/blog/574.

19. "When Even the Pope Has to Whisper," Spengler, *Asia Times Online,* January 10, 2006.

20. Rod Dreher, "Pope Says Islam Can't Reform," The Corner, *National Review Online,* January 9, 2006, http://corner.nationalreview.com/06_01_08_corner-archive.asp.

21. K. S. Lal, *Muslim Slave System in India* (New Delhi: Aditya Prakashan, 1994), 175.

22. Yusef Al-Qaradawi, "The Prophet Muhammad As a Jihad Model," Special Dispatch No. 246, Middle East Media Research Institute, July 24, 2001.

23. Andrew G. Bostom, "Hirsi Ali: The Empowered Apostate," http://www.americanthinker.com/2005/05/hirsi_ali_the_empowered_aposta.html.

24. Robert Spencer, "Preferring Fantasy to Reality," Jihad Watch, March 2, 2006, http://www.jihadwatch.org/archives/010459.php.

25. Robert Spencer, "Fallaci: Warrior in the Cause of Human Freedom," *FrontPageMagazine.com,* November 30, 2005.

26. Spencer, "Preferring Fantasy to Reality."

27. Michael Dobbs, "Probe Targets Cleric in London; Radical Preacher Draws Followers While Enjoying British Public Aid," *Washington Post,* October 28, 2001.

28. Kenneth Levin, *The Oslo Syndrome: Delusions of a People Under Siege* (Hanover, NH: Smith and Kraus, Inc., 2005), vii.

29. "Foreword," Jacques Ellul, in *The Decline of Eastern Christianity*, (Madison, NJ: Farleigh Dickinson University Press, 1996), 18.

30. Ibid.

31. "Preface," Jacques Ellul, in *The Dhimmi: Jews and Christians Under Islam*, (Madison, NJ: Farleigh Dickinson University Press, 1985), 25.

32. Ellul offers as an example the purely religious war that broke out between Hindus and Muslims in 1947, killing one million people and leading to the creation of the Islamic state of Pakistan—"Land of the Pure"—more than thirty years before the advent of Ayatollah Khomeini. Ellul continued: "Hardly a year has since passed without its marking some new stage in the religious revival of Islam (e.g., the resumption of the conversion of Black Africa to Islam, the return of alienated populations to religious practice, the obligation for Arab socialist regimes to proclaim that their states were 'Muslim' republics, etc.)." He added an important, often overlooked point: "The extremism of the Ayatollah Khomeini can be understood only in the light of this general tendency. It is not something exceptional and extraordinary, but its logical continuation."

33. Ellul, "Foreword," in *The Decline of Eastern Christianity*, 18.

34. Ellul, "Preface," *The Dhimmi*, 33.

35. See *The Legacy of Jihad* for a compilation of Muslim theological and juridical writings, eyewitness historical accounts, and essays by distinguished scholars on the history of jihad through the centuries.

36. President George W. Bush, "State of the Union Address," January 31, 2006.

37. "Radical Islamism in Europe," Interview with Irshad Manji, Steven Emerson, and Gilles Kepel, Aspen Instiutute Berlin, 2005, http://www.aspenberlin.org/special_feature.php?iGedminId=8.

38. Winston Churchill, *The River War,* Vol. II (London: Longmans, Green & Co., 1899), 248–250.

39. Ibn Warraq, "Democracy in a Cartoon," *Der Spiegel Online,* February 3, 2006.

EPILOGUE

1. "Publisher's statement," William F. Buckley, Jr., *National Review,* November 19, 1955, posted at *National Review Online,* January 29, 2004.

2. Interview with Gertrude Himmelfarb, *Religion & Liberty,* Acton Institute, July and August 1995, vol. 5, no. 4.

INDEX